NEW YORK STATE
HISTORICAL ASSOCIATION SERIES

DIXON RYAN FOX

EDITOR
—

NUMBER II

WAR OUT OF NIAGARA

BY

HOWARD SWIGGETT

A WALTER BUTLER RANGER

WAR
OUT OF NIAGRA

Walter Butler
and the
Tory Rangers

HOWARD SWIGGETT

The Scholar's Bookshelf

WAR OUT OF NIAGARA

First Published in 1933

This edition published 2005 by

The Scholar's Bookshelf

110 Melrich Road
Cranbury NJ USA 08512
www.scholarsbookshelf.com

ISBN: 0-945726-53-8
Library of Congress Control Number: 2005931235

Printed in the United States of America

TO THE ABIDING MEMORY OF
MY FATHER
CHARLES HOWARD SWIGGETT
MARCH TWENTY-FIRST NINETEEN TWENTY-NINE

PREFACE[1]

The defenders of an old régime which is destroyed have usually to wait long before history does them justice. Their conquerors write the accepted history books, and the world is always inclined to adopt what Lord Acton called the "edifying and popular maxim *Die Weltgeschichte ist das Weltgericht*," and believe that the success of a thing is a proof of its justice. In Richelieu's famous words "les grandes desseins et notables entreprises ne se vérifient jamais autrement que par le succès." In a civil war the loser is in a worse case, for the cause he opposed has become the cherished loyalty of a nation, and opposition to it is felt to carry a moral as well as an intellectual stigma. As a consequence he will be credited with many infamies. To take an instance from British history, the Whigs and Presbyterians came uppermost in Scotland in 1688, with the result that a great figure like Montrose was for the better part of two centuries encrusted with the mud of prejudice.

What I have written is especially true of a campaign fought in a wild country where legend takes the place of written records. History becomes for the victor partly a saga and partly a hagiology. No blemishes are credited to the one side and few virtues to the other. Tales circulate and grow in the telling, until it is hard to recover even the innocent from the fog of mythology. A good example is the reputation of Claver-

[1] By John Buchan, Member of Parliament for the Scottish Universities. It seemed to Mr. Swiggett and to the New York State Historical Association an attractive idea to invite Col. Buchan to write a preface for this book. Distinguished as an historian, as a writer of historical romance, many of them dealing with border warfare in Great Britain, and as the biographer of Montrose and Scott, he has a many-sided competence to test in terms of general human interest, of historical technique, and of literary values this story of young Walter Butler and the bitter war between Tory and Whig in the forests of New York. In so generously acceding to this request from overseas he has shown a much appreciated courtesy. — THE EDITOR.

house in Scotland. Covenanting legend made him a monster
of cruelty, and it is only within recent years that scholarship
has revealed a man with faults and frailties indeed, but in-
herently sane and merciful.

The work of correcting legend is very different from the
freakish pastime of making saints out of satyrs and satyrs out
of saints, by which certain easy reputations have been won. It
is the praiseworthy task of reducing popular imagination
to verifiable facts and so making history credible. This is the
attitude of modern American historians to the great tale of
the Revolution. The bias of the old school-books has been
vigorously corrected, so vigorously that, if I may say so with
all respect, it seems to have occasionally tipped too much to
the other side. To give reputed devils their due it is not necessary to be sceptical about the angels. But the instinct is wise
and honourable. The cause of the Revolution was a great
cause and deserved to win — at least that is my judgment —
and it does no violence to its greatness to admit that the other
side had a faith in which they passionately believed, and for
which they fought heroically. The famous conflict would lose
its significance if it were presented as a mere design in snow
and ink, with all the decencies assembled under a single banner.

No part of the story is more difficult than the frontier
fighting in Northern New York along the route to Canada by
the Mohawk valley. Its importance was great, for it represented the instinct of the Continental generals to push their
country to its natural frontiers, and in any case the district
was the left flank of their battle-front. But the campaign took
place in an intricate country, and the belligerents were frontiersmen who left few written records. It was rich soil for
the growth of legend. The half-feudal aristocracy of the
valley, the Johnsons and the Butlers, were bitterly hated by
the under-dog, the Dutch and German peasantry of the border, and the under-dog won. They enlisted the help of the
Indians of the Long House, and every Indian atrocity was
naturally credited to Tory policy. The use of savages as allies

was condemned by Edmund Burke in a classic speech, but it is
hard to see how it could have been avoided. By the Continental
Congress Indian interests were as directly threatened as those
of the British Crown. Again, to the squires of the Mohawk,
living the life they led, the Iroquois seemed as natural allies
as the swamps and forests. Indians had fought in every war
in America during the previous century, and to have kept them
neutral in this war was beyond the power of man. As a matter
of fact they were miserable fighters, and the British would
have been far better off without them, but the thing was pre-
destined. Some atrocities were bound to follow, not all on one
side, though the generals of both armies did their best to
restrain them.

Mr. Howard Swiggett has taken one figure from the campaigns and endeavoured to find out the truth about him.
Young Walter Butler of the Rangers has been one of the most
hotly vilified characters of popular Revolutionary history.
His common designation has been "the infamous Walter N.
Butler," a middle initial being added which seemed to heighten
his villainy. His fight at Cherry Valley has been painted as
black as the massacre of St. Bartholomew. A dark mysterious
portent of evil, he rides through popular romance and popular
history. There, at any rate, his figure is clear enough.

As a matter of fact we know little about him, less than
about any other contemporary figure of equal importance. We
know neither the date of his birth nor the place of his burial.
But what knowledge can be gleaned Mr. Swiggett has set
forth in this volume, soberly, conscientiously, with mathemat-
ical exactness, and he has exploded once and for all the
popular myth. Walter Butler appears as a human being with
a hard road to travel — a young lawyer, reasonably well-
educated, ambitious, devoted to friends and family; a loyalist
who believed whole-heartedly in his cause; a soldier, hardy,
audacious and far-sighted, with a touch of genius in his wild
speed; a humane man and a most gallant one. He is not portrayed in too dazzling colours; he was no saint, or profound

thinker, only a plain man who was true to what he regarded as his salt. Mr. Swiggett has disposed of most charges, and on the others his argument points to a suspension of judgment. "The typical, proud, restless, unhappy, luckless figure of romance," he calls him, "who threw away his life for a lost cause," and in defending Butler he brings back the whole story to sanity. The purpose of his book, he tells us, is "to prove something, but something which I cannot feel is at variance with the most scientific point of view: that our enemies in the Revolution, as in all wars, were fellow humans, but little different from the run of patriots, with much the same motives and hopes. They were not all murderers. We were not all Galahads."

Mr. Swiggett had brought to his task not only the methods of sound scholarship, but a judicial integrity. He has sought his data far and wide in the libraries and museums of two continents, and he has been fortunate enough to discover much that has hitherto been unpublished. The material thus laboriously gathered he has used with scrupulous fairness, never over-stating an argument or over-colouring a picture. His enthusiasm, too, and his historic sense, have enabled him to recapture the atmosphere of another age, and to give the book the unity of a romance. He tells us that his writing and studying "have all been done at the end of long and exacting business days." May one, who has attempted the same kind of thing under the same handicaps, respectfully congratulate him on a fine achievement?

JOHN BUCHAN

ELSFIELD MANOR
OXFORD, ENG.
January, 1933

CONTENTS

ILLUSTRATIONS

INTRODUCTION

In my childhood, which began intellectually with the Spanish War, I delighted in the American historical novels of the Revolution and Civil War of which there were so many.

Even before the Spanish War I was profoundly interested in American history. It was the topic of most of the family conversation that I remember, and I was early aware that, except Confederate soldiers, there had never been such evil men as Tories who perpetrated terrible atrocities against defenseless patriots throughout the Revolution. I had no idea that either Confederates or Tories were human beings. They were simply fiends incarnate.

Shortly after the beginning of the century I read *The Maid at Arms*, by Robert W. Chambers, and there encountered the villainous Walter Butler. I have been trying to find out all about him ever since. Three years ago I finally became convinced that there was no book about him and began the research of which the present study is the result. For almost thirty years I have been fascinated by the mystery of this young man to whom every horrible crime has been ascribed, whose birthday and burial place are both unknown. Why was he, the youngest of the lot, picked out beyond all the Loyalist leaders for the unpardonable sins of the Revolution? That I cannot answer because I have found a very different person.

I should like to say, not in apology but in possible encouragement to others, that the study for this book and its writing have all been done at the end of long and exacting business days. The task, however, has been play far more delightful than golf or bridge, and I have no complaint other than that manuscript rooms in libraries and learned societies close at five and are therefore not available to merchant students except for about three hours Saturday afternoons.

It was in the January dusk of one of these late Saturday afternoons, at the New York Public Library, that I realized that at one end of the dim table where I was working was the distinguished New York State Historian, Dr. A. C. Flick, a veteran authority on Loyalism, engaged on some search of appalling vastness, while opposite me sat Dr. Frederick Pottle, actually correcting proof of the Malahide Papers of James Boswell, with an actual *Journal* of the little man's in his left hand. It was good company for Walter Butler. Dr. Johnson was a great Loyalist. Though I felt more the merchant and less the student in the presence of such scholars I could not but reflect that not even Dickens himself had ever invented, or assembled at the same board, such a trio of names as Pottle, Flick, and Swiggett.

The main delight of historical investigation is of course that it is a kind of detective work. It is a constant adventure, even to the point that you become sure, during it, that you are being followed. You are required in Manuscript Rooms to give your subject on the public register with your name, and I must confess to such fear of other suspicious-looking men in the room that I frequently gave a wholly unrelated subject. What a cold chill runs down your spine when your appplication for some obscure "Life and Letters" comes back marked "in use." You look around the room and try to decide who there could possibly be "tailing" Walter Butler. You peer over people's shoulders to see their subjects. You try to catch the whispered conversation between the librarian and a particularly untrustworthy type of old lady; you try to bring about a situation where you will be able casually to remark to the attendant, "Ah, you will of course say nothing to anyone of my, er, perfunctory interest in Walter Butler. It is, er, simply a matter of family interest." The librarian assures you your guilty secret is safe and you feel that fine sense of privileged communication you have after talking to a pawn broker or a taxi driver. They never tell.

There are, of course, moments of sheer horror in a research. I was almost through one book when I came on an
apparent fact that would have meant rewriting the whole first
half of the book. In *Cardigan* Mr. Chambers has Walter
Butler go out to Fort Pitt to consult with Lord Dunmore
about Cresap's War. While reading Jacob's *Life of Captain
Cresap* in the Library one night, I came on a passage saying
that "Butler's canoe had been attacked forty miles below
Pittsburgh by three Cherokees on April 16" that year. I
turned rapidly back to see if it was my Butler. Sure enough
his initial was W. My whole story was ruined. I had treated
the incident as fiction — it was true; I simply did not know
my subject. A great wave of despair went over me. It was
half an hour before I finally checked the fact that the
W. Butler was "Mr. William Butler, a leading Pittsburgh
trader."

At the beginning of my study I wrote several deprecatory,
polite letters to people I thought might have some special
information. These people usually replied the next day with a
great flood of information, clues, and suggestions. In three
years I have received over four hundred letters full of help.
Everyone was so nice that I stopped being polite myself and
simply wrote demanding aid.

Two of the most thrilling discoveries were the dozen
Walter Butler letters in the British Museum in London, with
the one of a hundred years before from another Walter
Butler curiously misfiled among them; and word, in reply to
an inquiry, from the Wisconsin Historical Society at Madison,
that there were twenty-five volumes of unpublished, uncata-
logued Draper Manuscripts about Joseph Brant there, with
references to Walter Butler too numerous for them to give.

Lyman Copeland Draper died in 1891. In 1838, at the age
of twenty-three, he conceived the idea of writing a series of
biographies of trans-Allegheny pioneers. He devoted fifty
years to the collection of material for biographies that were

never written. His life was a heroic intellectual tragedy in that, as Mr. Thwaites has pointed out in his short life of Draper,

His design was to be encyclopaedic. Unfortunately for himself he had accumulated so vast a flood of material that at last it was beyond his control. As early as 1857 he had ten thousand foolscap pages of notes and five thousand pages more of original journals and letters. He suffered the ceaseless torment of suspended judgment, and pathetically said, when he was old, "I have wasted my life in puttering."

But his papers are a great storehouse of information for those who followed him; they are not history but the raw material from which history, in part at least, is made. Students of the period are enormously indebted to him.

The great thrill of all, however, was the finding of the original minutes of the court-martial of Walter Butler, as a spy, after his capture at the German Flats in August, 1777. His capture is referred to in most histories, but what he was tried for, and why, has never, so far as I know, been made entirely clear. Claus does say in one of his letters, in the London Documents, that he was taken out of uniform, but there is no other detail.

I had hoped to find the court-martial with the Gates Papers in the New York Historical Society, and did find a letter there from Benedict Arnold saying that he was sending it along. It was not there. The letter, however, was addressed to General Schuyler, whom Gates succeeded — almost on the day of the court-martial, and it seemed possible that the court-martial might be in the Schuyler Papers in the Manuscript Room of the Public Library. It was not there. Three original letters of Walter Butler's are listed in the Papers and marked missing, and it has seemed to me possible that one of the most sanctimonious and garrulous of the mid-nineteenth-century writers had helped himself.

The papers could not be found in Albany. In Washington they seemed to think it was with the Board of War Papers which, however, are not catalogued; a letter from a com-

mitteeman, Petry, who was a witness at the court-martial, to
Schuyler about the trial and the circumstances of the arrest
is listed in the Congressional Library but marked miss-
ing. The trail looked very hopeless. I applied to the War
Department and they courteously suggested the *Pictorial
Field-Book of the Revolution*! A number of other leads
proved useless. At this point a friend gave me Greene and
Morris's *Guide to the Principal Sources for Early American
History in the City of New York*. I read each page with great
care. On page 152 there is the following item: "Willett,
Marinus. Military papers, 1775-97, consisting of letters, re-
ceipts, muster rolls, military returns, Minutes of Court Martial. M. Willett (box) N. Y. P. L." I went immediately to
the Library, found the box, and there were the original
minutes, a photostat of which appears in this book. There is
probably a book in itself in the story of how they got there.

In writing this book I have endeavored to take no opinions
from any book, but to let the story of the Butlers come out
from the principal primary sources, which are: their own all
too few letters, and those of other Rangers; the Haldimand
Papers in the Canadian Archives and the Michigan Historical
Collections; the *Public Papers of George Clinton* (ten volumes published); the material supplied me from the Sir
Henry Clinton Papers in the Clements Library; the Draper
Manuscripts; and other subsidiary original documents, including of course the voluminous Schuyler Papers and the Gates
Papers.

I have been very glad that there is no other book solely
upon Walter Butler to which to refer, and I have used no
material from books where he is mentioned, without credit
to the writer in question.

This book is not meant to be pro-Loyalist or pro-Butler or
pro-anything. I have, however, tried to see the events of the
Revolution as they must have appeared to some of the Loyalists. It does seek to prove something, but something which
I cannot feel is at variance with the most scientific point of

view: that our enemies in the Revolution, as in all wars, were fellow humans, but little different from the run of patriots, with much the same motives and hopes. They were not all murderers. We were not all Galahads. The two love letters exchanged by Captain Tice of the Rangers and his wife, mentioned in this book, are surely as poignant and charming as any similar ones ever published. Even Sir John Johnson, that dubious character, faces problems common to all men when he says to John Collins, regarding possible flight from Johnson Hall, "I don't know," says he, "what to do." Does he not speak with the same weary bewilderment most of us feel daily?

Books have made us all too prone to think of history and wars as solely the march of vast events, the record of a time when men think and act either heroically or villainously. Such is not the case. At the very moment when men care least for their lives and are most ready to die recklessly and magnificently, others, in Meredith's words, "wax out of proportion, overblown, affected, pretentious, congregating in absurdities, planning shortsightedly, plotting dementedly." All men in history, heroes, cravens, and bullies, are caught in the "incredible imbroglio of comedy."

What of John Dougherty, straight out of a comedy of Terence, confined in the Morristown jail, in 1776, as a traitor to his country, who petitioned to be freed because "being in a certain house in York in liquor, a bowl being broke, the guard being come in accused us of being Tories, my company fled and I sent to gaol for that."

What of the reference to the earnest delegates to New York Provincial Legislature, in the *American Archives*, where the index reads:

Credentials, Delegates from New York City mislay theirs.
    Delegates from Albany fail to bring theirs.
    Delegates from Charlotte County fail to bring theirs.
    Tryon County, error in
    Delegates from Kings County present defective.

What of the distracted Schuyler letter to General Gates written at Saratoga at seven o'clock of an October morning:

In your letter of the 24th you mention the want of spades in such a manner as if there had been a neglect in procuring them. They are not to be had, all that the country afforded, all that I could get made have been sent you. [And then in an afterthought], Where is Colonel Lewis for who I have so long ago written to you?

Is it not the war-weary voice of Marc Antony saying "The man from Sicyon, is there such an one?"

But all do not wear comic masks. Old John Butler is a bereaved father like other men when his eldest son is killed.

As to Walter Butler, I have not sought to vindicate him. Obviously he is no scoundrel, and certainly no murderer of women and children as all the books have said. He is the typical, proud, restless, unhappy, luckless figure of romance, who throws away his life for a lost cause. He is described, it seems to me, in Clarendon's words about Lord Falkland, another luckless Loyalist:

He had a courage of the most cleere and keene temper, and soe farre from feare that he was not without appetite of danger, and therefore upon any occasyon of action he alwayes engaged his person in those troopes which he thought by the forwardnesse of the Commanders to be most like to be farthest engaged, and in all such encounters he had aboute him a strange cheerefulnesse and companionablenesse.

I should like to say something here of the spelling of Indian names. Our Revolutionary forefathers differed greatly as to the spelling of the most ordinary words, and it is therefore no wonder that the Indian names and place-names are variously spelled by them. I have quoted their spelling as given in their documents, but where I have used the name I have given what seemed the simplest and most reasonable spelling. As to Thayendanegea, although Schuyler and many others called him Brandt in their letters, his best-known autograph is plainly "Jos. Brant" and I have used that style unless quoting someone's spelling.

There will also be possible confusion as to the Butlers'
rank. John Butler is progressively major, lieutenant colonel,
and colonel. He was not in an "established regiment," and
became a lieutenant colonel (and hence was called colonel) in
'79, but is referred to constantly before that, in enemy and
patriot letters, as Colonel. Young Walter Butler sought a
majority from Haldimand, which he never received, because
of the many older men ahead of him. The American *communiqué* announcing his death called him a major, but his last
rank was definitely captain.

Now as to the scene of this book: it is mainly Northern
New York. The Mohawk River forms a rough right angle
with the Hudson at Albany. On the south bank of the Mohawk are the Schoharie hills. Tryon County was then that
vast area of northern New York bounded on the east by
an almost straight line running north from the Mohawk
River near Schenectady to Canada, thence down the St. Lawrence River to Oswego, east again to Fort Stanwix (now
Rome, New York), then south along the Stanwix Treaty line
to the northeastern tip of Pennsylvania and back to Schenectady. West of Tryon were the lands of the Six Nations, the
Long House. All Tryon was a forest. There were three ways
to invade it from Canada. Up Champlain and by "back
trails" from Ticonderoga: the route of Burgoyne and again of
Sir John Johnson in '80; or east from a base at Oswego to Lake
Oneida across the "great carrying-place" to the Mohawk
River: the route of St. Leger and of Walter Butler's last
raid. Or east from Fort Niagara to Genesee, down the Chemung River to Tioga and up the Susquehanna toward Cherry
Valley, which was the route of the Butlers to Wyoming and
Cherry Valley in '78 and of Sullivan-Clinton against them
in '79.

I had not supposed it true, until I wrote this book, that it
was actually impossible for an author to acknowledge all the
help he had received in the work, but I find now, as I try to do

t, that such is indeed the case. Many people have helped me to whom I am deeply grateful. I am indebted to Miss Suzanne Baron who not only did the work alone on the untouched Draper Manuscripts, but worked on all the problems of investigation and construction with patience, good humor, and skill in research.

It is difficult to speak adequately of the help Mr. Robert W. Chambers has given me. His unflagging interest alone would have been a great help, but with it has come suggestions, information, clues, hospitality, sympathy, and the vast lore of Tryon and Indian warfare which he, beyond anyone in America, possesses. He is not in agreement with many conclusions of the book as he thinks, in his own phrase, that in giving devils their due I have, in places, hustled the angels. But his kindness and encouragement have been beyond all measure. Dr. A. C. Flick, New York State Historian, has been most considerate and helpful.

My former neighbor, Nicholas Roosevelt, now American Minister to Hungary, has been at once critical and suggestive. I have a special debt to Miss Jane Clark, of the Clements Library, where the Sir Henry Clinton Papers are; for three years she has been digging out material from that vast storehouse for me. At the New York Historical Society I have had the utmost help and consideration, and Miss Dorothy Barck of that Library has responded to countless requests with the most unfailing cordiality. Mr. Lydenberg and Mr. Paltsits at the New York Public Library have both helped me with numerous suggestions, as has the staff of the Manuscript Room. But my greatest debt, if I may make a comparison, at the Public Library, is to Mr. Ivor Avellino of the American History Room who has helped me night after night with expert knowledge and even temper under endless questions. Dr. James F. Kenney, Director of Historical Research and Publicity in the Public Archives at Ottawa, has responded to countless requests with the greatest kindness and thoroughness. Miss Eilleen V. A. Sergeant, of London, very kindly did the work there in the British Museum and the Public Records Office for me.

I am very much indebted to Mr. Willis T. Hanson of Schenectady, and Mr. William Pierrepont White of Utica, for their opposing views as to the burial place of Walter Butler, and for the helpful detail in which they have expressed them to me. Also to Mr. Seymour Van Santvoord of Troy, for many suggestions and much encouragement.

Both Arthur Pound and Dr. Richard E. Day, have gone to great trouble to help me run down the story of the Butler-Lafayette friendship, and Mr. Brand Whitlock, in far-off Mentone, has courteously gone through his voluminous notes on Lafayette for the same purpose. None of these gentlemen knew me and all did it out of the kindness of their hearts. Dr. Rosenbach's office most generously permitted me to examine the British Headquarters Papers (later acquired by Mr. John D. Rockefeller, Jr.) shortly after their arrival in this country, and to use material from them, as hereafter noted. There are two men who know nothing of this book to whom I owe great thanks: Professor John Milton Berdan and Professor George Woodbine of the faculty of Yale University. Their teaching at New Haven in English Literature and History respectively is responsible for whatever merit the work may have.

My uncle, the Reverend Frederick R. Sanford, of the Class of Yale College, 1877, made the original suggestions as to the course of the research and has been continually helpful to me. My wife has not only listened to the pages as they were written but has somehow, with great adroitness, amidst the pressure of ordinary life, made possible the time without which the book could not have been done.

Colonel John Buchan, of Elsfield Manor, Oxford, England, has found time from responsibilities of the greatest importance at the University and House of Commons and Pilgrims Trust and from his own writing of history to write the foreword. My debt to him is very great. It is to Professor Dixon Ryan Fox, of Columbia University, that I owe the publication of this book. He is not only a scholar but a critic whose "suggestions" it is a delight to accept. As always to the enthusiasms and criticisms of my friend and classmate, Henry Tetlow, I owe a great deal.

WAR OUT OF NIAGARA

CHAPTER I

THE VALLEY OF THE MOHAWK, 1752-1769

On November 9, 1781, Lieutenant-Colonel Thomas Grosvenor from Headquarters at Continental Village, New York, issued a General Order to the army, with word [1] "that the enemy have been completely disappointed in their designs on the Northern Frontiers of this State." A British invasion, seven hundred strong, coming from the westward under Major Ross had been met and turned back by Marinus Willett and his militia at Johnstown on October 26. They had been pursued northward. There had been a second engagement on the thirtieth with the British regulars, Rangers, and Indians defeated and pursued into the wilderness, after a desperate last stand at West Canada Creek. The *communiqué* stated that "the number of the enemy killed is not known: Major Butler, who has frequently distressed these frontiers, is among the slain." On the day after the action the *New York Packet* published the great headlines that Cornwallis was taken at Yorktown on October 17, and it is said the news gratified the people of Northern New York less than word that Walter Butler was killed. On November 17 Beverly Robinson, the British Chief of Intelligence in New York, reported to Sir Henry Clinton that a spy "Timothy Clason left Albany about the first. We heard they had killed young Butler and were bringing his scalp down to Albany with great triumph and rejoycings." [2]

The standard historians have represented Butler as the archfiend of the Revolution. Lossing says "miscreants like Girty and Walter Butler of the Mohawk Valley present

---

[1] *New York Packet and American Advertiser*, Nov. 15, 1781.
[2] Sir Henry Clinton Papers, Clements Collection, Pkt. 122 (2).

no redeeming quality to plead for excuse."[3] Benton calls him "a man of enterprizing boldness, whose heart was a compound of ferocious hate, insatiable cruelty and unappeasable revenge."[4]

There is an absorbing mystery about his life and character. The date of his birth is unknown. There is a legend of his marriage to a daughter of Catharine Montour, and another with a daughter of Sir William Johnson. The bloody massacre at Cherry Valley is laid at his door. He has been called "a libertine, notorious even for those times." There is no physical description of him except in fiction. Letters about him in catalogues even of the Schuyler Papers, the Gates Papers, the Library of Congress, and many other papers, are mysteriously marked missing. Timothy Dwight, the President of Yale College, invented a great myth about him that got into every American history in the nineteenth century. Lafayette is said to have been his friend but there is no authority for it. Haldimand is said to have refused to receive him after Cherry Valley and this book contains an original letter from Haldimand approving of his conduct that November day. He appears plainly to have broken his parole as a prisoner but, with every horror of massacre and rapine laid at his door, for some reason that seems to have escaped notice. Brant, the Indian, is portrayed as a noble paladin, horrified at Butler's excesses. Yet Simms, the gossip of the Revolution, in *The Frontiersmen of New York*,[5] tiresome in the multiplicity of its detail, never places Walter Butler at the scene of any of the atrocities in the North. Thousands of men are mentioned by name but young Butler is mentioned only at Cherry Valley.

The histories have contented themselves with denouncing him as a bloody monster, but back of the histories in the primary material of the Revolution there is an amazing figure. A young man who could not have been over twenty-eight when

[3] B. J. Lossing, *Pictorial Field Book of the Revolution* (New York, 1860), Vol. I, p. 264.
[4] Nathaniel S. Benton, *History of Herkimer County* (Albany, 1856), p. 102.
[5] Jeptha R. Simms, *The Frontiersmen of New York* (Albany, 1882), 2 vols.

he was killed, to the rejoicing of all New York, a most daunt-less and enterprising leader, eager, ambitious, tireless, offering to cover Albany, Fort Pitt and Detroit for Haldimand, grasp-ing early in the war the grand strategy of the long North-western flank, impatient of older men, defending his every action at Cherry Valley, scorning to make war on women and children, while pointing out the treatment of his mother and sister held as hostages in Albany. He is condemned for his red allies and was himself killed and scalped by an Indian ally of the Continental army and the newspapers announcing his death say "The Oneida Indians behaved well in the action and deserve much credit." [6]

Letters from Washington, Schuyler, Gates, Pickering, Madison, Sullivan, Benedict Arnold, Lord Stirling, Governor Clinton, George Rogers Clark, Lord George Germaine, Sir Frederick Haldimand, Sir Guy Carleton, Sir Henry Clinton mention the name of this young subaltern. There are scarcely a dozen letters of his own to be found, and a dozen more are listed and missing.

There appears to be no record of the date or place of his birth. Cruikshank, the Canadian historian, gives the year as 1752 but cites no authority. If this is correct he was twenty-eight or nine when he was killed, and, until August, 1777, there is scarcely any light on the obscurity of his boyhood. But if we consider the extraordinarily proud and self-confident figure revealed by the Revolution, and forget Cherry Valley, until we can critically examine the record of it, we are able to reconstruct a great deal of his life from birth until May, 1768, when his name first appears in written records.

It is almost certain that he was born in 1752. He was the son of Colonel John Butler, who was born at New London in 1725, and his wife, Catharine Pollock. There is record of his mother's death at Niagara, May 29, 1793, aged fifty-eight. She was therefore seventeen years old in 1752, and it is unlikely that her marriage took place before she was sixteen.

[6] *New York Packet and American Advertiser,* Nov. 8, 1781.

Thomas Jones, the Loyalist historian, states that "Colonel Butler had an only son, a youth of spirit, sense and ability," [7] but Cruikshank states there were five children, four sons, and a daughter, of which records from Niagara Parish and Revolutionary letters seem to leave no doubt. There had been continuous fighting with the French in North America until 1749, and John Butler had been constantly at the Northern front with his father and brother. There was peace from 1749 till '55, almost the only peace in his stormy life, and he had come back to the Mohawk Valley to marry and settle down.

These Butlers had first appeared in this country in 1711, when Walter Butler, the elder, came out from Ireland with his regiment in the army sent for the reduction of Canada. He was one of "certain Sargeants who received the Queen's Commissions to be lieutenants of post in America, January, 1711." It was the name of a famous Irish family, dating from the Walter who in 1192 became "Butler of Ireland," and descended from Sir Piers Butler who became Earl of Ormonde in 1513. There is continuously a Walter in the Ormonde-Butler lineage, and it was a Walter Butler who assassinated the star-struck Wallenstein in the Thirty Years' War. Scott in his "Legend of Montrose," makes Dalgetty say, "I took service with Wallenstein in Walter Butler's Irish regiment." James Butler, Duke of Ormonde, a great Cavalier, commanded the expedition against Cadiz in 1702.

There has always been considerable confusion as to where the Butlers came from and as to whether they were related to the Continental officers, Zebulon, William, or Richard. Butler was in fact a common name in America even before 1700. Simon Kenton, it will be remembered, called himself Simon Butler for many years after a man of that name who befriended him in the Cumberland. Washington's father's first wife was a Butler. As early as 1692 the name of John Butler appears in the Journals of the New York Legislative Coun-

[7] Thomas Jones, *History of New York During The Revolution* (ed. E. F. De Lancey, N. Y. H. S., New York, 1879), Vol. II, p. 337.

cil.[8] In New London where old Walter Butler settled there were John Butlers in the records before 1690, and the author of the *History of New London* says, "John Butler's family [an elder Butler] cannot be given with certainty, but nothing appears to forbid the supposition that Lieutenant Walter Butler, a prominent inhabitant, about 1712 was his son."[9]

It seems probable that they were related because this otherwise unknown lieutenant, late a sergeant, married "Mary Dennison regarded as the richest heiress in the settlement." After her death, "old Walter," married Deborah Dennison and she became the mother of Colonel John Butler of the Rangers, father of young Walter Butler, and of "the young children" Deborah and William Johnson Butler who were held with their mother as hostages in Albany during most of the Revolution. Colonel Butler was later to found the parish church at Niagara, and it is interesting to note that in the year of his birth, his father, Lieutenant Butler, with eleven others subscribed £216 to build a church in New London.[10]

In the expansive eight volumes of the Sir William Johnson Papers, the first letter [11] is addressed to Walter Butler then with his command at Fort Hunter. This is "Young Walter Butler's" grandfather. It is an obscure missive dated at Albany, February 6, 1737, and is apparently a plea not to allow one Doctor Dishington to seduce a Miss Dick, under his roof, or to "huddle up a marriage," but to "send her back to her bloods." It would be delightful to know just what it is about. It is practically the only mention of a woman in such a connection in the documents of seventy years that make up this history, and it is curious that the grandfather of the man whom legend has the despoiler of women, should be appealed to for the protection of a lone female from the villainous

---

[8] With it are the family names of Van Schaick and Willett, the former, young Walter's law partner, and the latter, Colonel Willett, who sat as Judge Advocate in '77 when "young Butler" was condemned as a spy, and who was at Canada Creek when he met his death in '81. *Journals of the Legislative Council of New York*, 1743-1775 (Albany, 1861).

[9] Frances M. Caulkins, *History of New London* (New London, 1860), p. 342.

[10] *Ibid.*, p. 339.   [11] *Sir William Johnson Papers* (Albany), Vol. I, p. 1.

Dishington. On March 3 of that year the unknown author writes again to explain that he did not believe Butler was "accessory to the cursed plot of that vile man's."

To grasp the situation of these years before "young Butler's" birth it is necessary to consider first the gigantic figure of Sir William Johnson, who came into the Valley in 1738, and died in his great house in Johnstown as the Revolution was about to break. He was in every sense the extroverted man of action. In those thirty-five years there were in a sense two types of men in America: those who were fighting for land, furs, and empire, almost, it would seem, unaware of the brewing Revolution; and another type of seacoast merchant traders, philosophers, and lawyers, either awake to the evidences of the discontent or themselves actively stirring it up. In the first group were men like Sir William Johnson and Washington, in the second the Boston malcontents, the New York merchants and lawyers, and the civil servants of the Crown.

Sir William Johnson was Superintendent of Indian Affairs in North America. His influence among the Indians was paramount past the Ohio and almost to Florida. The Crown's commanders in chief needed his support. He acquired a vast estate in the Valley and with his clansmen, Guy Johnson and Claus, and his son, and his brother-in-law, Joseph Brant, and his scores of bastards, and his baronial hall, and his forts and highland regiments, and his vast knowledge of men and affairs at home and abroad, dominated the American scene beyond the royal governors or the army commanders. Blessed were those that had been his friends.

Pound [12] says "a rather grubby family these Butlers seem to have been with no social ambitions and less luck, but faithful to the Johnsons to the bitter end." One of the most common errors of this portion of American history is that because the Johnsons and Butlers were neighbors and Tories they were close friends. Rather does it appear that after Sir William's

[12] Arthur Pound, *Johnson of the Mohawks* (New York, 1930), p. 88.

leath they were never friendly and the proud young Butler
would have lost his mind at the thought of his being "faithful" to anyone but himself and possibly the King. But while
Sir William lived they were his adherents, neighbors, and
intimates.

In 1742 old Walter Butler built the house which is still
standing in Butlersbury. It is a frame house on a hill that
looks southwest toward the Mohawk River. When it was done
he sent to New London for his family, a Mr. Hempstead
making note of it in his diary:[13] "November 6, 1742, Mrs.
Butler, wife of Captain Walter Butler, and her children and
family is gone away by water to New York in order to go to
him in the Northern Counties, above Albany, where he hath
been several years captain of the Forts." There is little record
of just who lived there before the fifties when John Butler
was married. The year after it was built old Walter went back
to his post at Oswego and his son went along as interpreter.[14]

In various letters that year, 1744, to and from Sir William,
there is great evidence of the confidence reposed by the government in the Butlers, old Walter, and his two sons, at
the difficult outpost at Oswego. They were evidently steady,
reliable men, as which indeed, when the smoke of the Wyoming massacre had vanished, Colonel Butler seems universally
to have been regarded.

The duties of such an outpost were many. Above all, they
must have eyes and ears for French movements and for the
feeling among the western Indians; they must promote
the vital fur trade and keep the good will of the Indians
with presents and money as their judgment dictated. There
are many twenty-page accountings by Sir William Johnson
to the Crown of tens of thousands of pounds sterling spent by
him, or the Butlers, or Croghan, or Claus, for help to individual Indians in distress. The management of Indian affairs
before the Revolution, with the peril of their turning to the

[13] *History of New London*, p. 342.
[14] *Journals of the Legislative Council of New York*, 1743-1775, p. 850.

French in every-one's mind, was like that of a vast united
charities.

	£ s d
To Modelena, a Mohawk widow	0-16-0
Tuscarora Chief, a laced silver hat	2- 0-0
Oghquga Indian, to carry him	0-16-0
To coffin and burial of a Mohawk chief	1- 4-0
To a Mohawk to buy fodder for his horse	0- 8-0
To a fat cow for the Canojoharies	4- 0-0
To a Sachem who lost all his family	2- 0-0
To old Noah, a helpless Indian	0- 8-0

and so on to the astonishing total in thirteen months of
£17,072-2-10¼.[15]

Thomas Butler, uncle of young Butler, writes in September,
1744, to Sir Wiliam, "by way of Miss Mary Butler in the
Mohawk Country," for Indian supplies for the winter.[16] It
is a fascinating puzzle to think why the letter should not have
gone direct.

There is so much of human interest in the Johnson Papers
that one approaches the letters, after the peace of 1750, with
the hope that someone will mention John Butler's marriage.
But the "less luck" which Pound speaks of further clouds the
obscurity of these Butler lives. They stand out in the flames
of Wyoming and Cherry Valley and then, as on that last
day at West Canada Creek, a heavy mist falls across them.

That John Butler was still at Oswego in May '51,[17] we
know from a letter of his brother's to Sir William complaining of the bad state of trade there and saying that "John
desires his compliments to you." It seems unlikely that even
John Butler would have taken a new bride at once to Oswego
and would appear further to put ahead his marriage. Later
in the same month, though, Thomas and John Butler secured
a license [18] to purchase Lake Caniunda and four thousand
acres of land around it, and that may have signified the coming wedding.

[15] *Johnson Papers*, Vol. III, p. 180.   [16] *Ibid.*, Vol. I, p. 22.
[17] *Ibid.*, Vol. I, p. 338.   [18] *Ibid.*, Vol. I, 334.

There is a letter written November 13,[19] 1751, by one
Leonard Cozzens from Newport, where he is getting hounds
and horses for Sir William, in which he sends his "kind love
to Captain Butler and his family," and says to "tell Mrs.
Butler I shall not forget her daughter Nancy's stayes." This
must have been an elder Butler. Young Walter's sister was
not wearing stayes in '51, and his father was not yet a Captain. Yet it is such an intimate matter it would seem that if
John Butler had just been married, or were shortly to be, there
would be good wishes for him.

It would be fitting that the marriage or birth should have
been that year, when Gray's "Elegy in a Country Churchyard"
was written, with its association of the dying Wolfe at Quebec, and its paths of glory leading to the grave. It was a
romantic year. Bonnie Prince Charlie went to London incog-
nito. Miss Walkinshaw joined him in France, and another
mysterious figure of history, Pickle, the spy, wrote his first
letter to the English government. Aaron Burr, the elder, had
just married the daughter of Jonathan Edwards.

An English writer [20] speaks of the aristocracy of the Mohawk Valley as a strange precarious little world, embedded
in illimitable gloomy forests haunted by the Iroquois and their
ghosts and devils, and certainly it was into a grim scene
that Walter Butler was born. Life itself must have been enormously difficult, with roads half the year impassable, food and
clothing often difficult to secure, and the ceaseless hazard of
Indian attack beyond everything. The children who were
not rugged could not survive, unless Huntington's theory, that
charming children always survive because of the extra care
taken of them, is correct.

The childish play of Walter Butler and his brothers and
sisters, and of all the children of the valley, must have been
that of the Delectable Ballad of the Waller Lot. Red coats
and good Indians against the white-coat French and bad Indians. The first dread hearsay of childhood must have been

[19] *Ibid.*, 355.   [20] Douglas G. Browne, *Cornhill Magazine*, Nov., 1921.

of scalping, of the prisoner at the stake, and running the gauntlet. There were other children, no doubt, in Butlersbury and the illegitimate horde of Sir William from old Fort Johnson must have lent reality to their play with their own redskins.

The Butler home was fatherless a good deal of the time and yet a strong family attachment was evidently built up by the mother. When the French were defeated at Fort George in '55, Mrs. Butler was a girl of twenty, the mother of possibly three children. Twenty years later in the Revolution her safety and that of "the young children" was of constant concern to her husband and her son Walter, and her treatment in Albany when a hostage seems to have inflamed them both.

In May of '55 Sir William sent John Butler,[21] then "a Lieutenant over the Indians," with dispatches to Braddock, at Williamsburgh, leaving Mrs. Butler alone as we know that her brother-in-law, Thomas, was on duty at Oswego.[22] Walter's father was apparently steadily gaining favor in Sir William's eyes, as he sat with the deputy-agent, Daniel Claus, and Sir William himself, at the Great Council Fire [23] at Mt. Johnson in June of that year. It was the month and year of Nathan Hale's birth. When he took the dispatches to Braddock he very likely met Washington and perhaps learned of the fatal strategy on the Monongahela which he later so tellingly used in the savage fight at Oriskany in '77.

It was on July 22, '55, that word reached Shirley, the Governor, in Albany, that Braddock was killed. A courier went for Sir William [24] at eleven o'clock and possibly was sent on to Butlersbury. The news struck terror along the whole frontier, and the three-year-old Walter may well have then first heard how better it was to have the red savages for you than against you.

There is a letter [25] of '57 from his Uncle Thomas, which speaks of "Captain Montour's aunt who, with all her family,

21 *Johnson Papers*, Vol. I, p. 516.   22 *Ibid.*, Vol. I, p. 496.
23 *Ibid.*, Vol. I, p. 625.   24 *Ibid.*, Vol. I, p. 662.
25 *Ibid.*, II, 694.

are great enemies of the English." This is the witch, Catharine Montour, said to have been a bastard offspring of Frontenac, with whose daughter legend has married Walter Butler.

In '59, when Sir William led the expedition against Fort Niagara, Walter, a boy of seven, must have seen them start. His father was on the staff, and in at the surrender on the twenty-fifth of July. Not even the prophetess, Catharine Montour, could have foreseen that part of Niagara would some day be called Butlersbury after their Mohawk home,[26] that years later John Butler would be buried there in a church he himself built, and that the little boy in the Mohawk country to whom he went back with tales of the wars, would be killed in almost the last action of the Revolution and his mutilated body left to the beasts. But so it was ordered.

Sir William must have come riding back from Niagara in the autumn of '59 to a tremendous harvest home. He was still living at old Fort Johnson. Mrs. Butler may well have taken the children down the stony Butlersbury road to the River to see their father go by with his troops, the drums banging out "The Huron." There are few things in life, as so subtle a soul as Charles Francis Adams has admitted, equal to the thrill of riding into a town at the head of a conquering army. What a show it must have been, with the red-coat riders and the painted red warriors, for the Butler boy to see, and how devoted he must have felt to wars and arms. In the four years of his own fighting the only such homecoming could have been to Niagara, but there was usually too much hunger and privation there for such a reception as this.

It was their conviction that "the Valley was now forever safe because he [Sir William] had won, because he had conquered at last the ravagers of the Mohawk Vale. . . . Strange that among the next to come that way a-burning would be his own son," [27] and the little boy who may have been watching the march.

[26] Buffalo Historical Society, *Publications*, Vol. II, p. 405.
[27] Pound, *op. cit.*, p. 280.

John Butler perhaps fell out at the Butlersbury Road and
went up the mile on foot with his family, while the troops
went on to Fort Johnson. The road is there today, steep and
winding, with a brooding secrecy about it. The Butler house
is a quarter of a mile from it down another road, and again
down a lane. The aged Miss Wilson, who lived in it for ninety
years, died in 1930, but there are still Wilsons there, with
queer inaccurate stories of the house and the Butlers. But
there is no inaccuracy in their statement that "it's a good
house. It doesn't shake when the wind blows."

The conventional picture of it in Lossing is of the back,
and the shed is new since 1743. The real front is now back,
but it looks away across the river and the valley. Even with the
many more trees in the eighteenth century, the surrounding
hilltops must have been clearly visible, and war parties could
talk from them readily with smoke. There were not a great
many more trees in this locality even then, as a great tornado
from Pennsylvania came across the valleys in the sixties leaving a wide path of bare destruction.

The range of vision from the house, though, must have had
as much to do with its location as the long look up the valley.
An alert watcher could have seen war parties coming from
the west, miles away. And the hills themselves were wonderful for snowshoes and coasting. There are grim slits for
loopholes and a half-moon at the base of the door for witches
to escape, and a room which the Wilsons tell you is "where
they kept their prisoners," which, of course, means nothing
as they were never in residence during the Revolution.

Inside, the house is remarkably large and the rooms nobly
beamed. What the rooms were is still quite obvious, and the
evidence of the secret staircase in full sight. A drive and horse
block used to be in the overgrown garden. There are lilac
bushes and tall trees, and doubtless were more when Walter
Butler was a boy. The house was never pretentious like Guy
Park or Johnson Hall, but a fine sturdy home that has stood
190 years, and roomy enough inside for the children to gather

BUTLERSBURY

THE CHERRY VALLEY MONUMENT

around the fire with many elders to listen to the dark and
bloody tales of French and Indian campaigns.

There John Butler must have come after the Niagara
victory. A bloody decade was ending. Old Walter, his father,
was there to greet him by the fire. He had been many weary
miles and in great enterprises. It must have been good to take
off his belt and boots, and take young Walter on his knee and
sip a glass of wine with his father. Old Walter died that
winter.

Jeffrey Amherst came through Fort Johnson the next June,
and Sir William went north once more, leading six hundred
Mohawks. John Butler went with him again but when the
brief campaign was over there was really peace and on
November 8, 1760, Amherst wrote from Albany to Sir William "I must desire that Captains John Butler and Jelles
Fonda and Lieutenant William Haire . . . have other occupations; that you will thank them for their past services and
strike them off the lists." [28] Amherst was always "much
obliged" to the Americans and refused the King's offer of the
high command to put down the rebellion in '76. The next
letter is to Haldimand, then a colonel at Fort Ontario, later
Sir Frederick Haldimand, Commander in Chief in Canada
and the Butlers' commanding officer in the Revolution.

Then a sudden civilization sprang up in the Valley. Men's
minds turned to ease and luxury after the long wars. Sir
William Johnson began to think of a great house. He sent
for eight pictures, and Smollett in four volumes, and a case
for the same, and a two-volume history of Louisiana, and a
cheval glass, and silver and china and wines, and magazines,
and velvet waistcoats.[29]

The panoply of Indian affairs went on, with Fort Johnson
"the very heart and center of Indian life," and a thousand
Indians gathered there for a council fire.

The lovelorn Daniel Claus wrote from Montreal of the
beauty of the northern lights "like a red fire over the sky . . .

[28] *Johnson Papers*, Vol. III, p. 277.   [29] *Ibid.*, Vol. IV, p. 358.

as clear as moonlight." [30] In the spring the ponderous Claus, who later so greatly rejoiced in the "less luck" of the Butlers was stingingly rebuked by Sir William for proposing to marry Nancy Johnson. "Honor and gratitude," Sir William wrote him on May Day, 1761,[31] "should have prevented your carrying on any intrigue of the kind privately in my family." Claus and the Butlers were so unlike that, in view of this letter and the later ill feeling between them, John Butler may have tried to thwart the German emigrant's suit. But he married Nancy and Sir William left him a share of his great fortune.

On July 5 of that year Sir William went to the council fire at Detroit where the fierce Great Lake tribes were pouring in. He was accompanied as far as Niagara by his son, later Sir John, and while there is no mention of it, it is not unlikely that Walter Butler, then nine years old, persuaded his father to take him along. He was later a master woodsman and his training must have begun early. It was the first time Sir William had ridden north in the pomp of his superintendency in peace. The boys of the Valley must have been wild to see the scenes of the fighting, and to see the Falls. It is curious that another omission from the papers of seventy years should be the great falls of Niagara.

William Maclay [32] in his journal for February 1, 1790, said that the Falls had retreated some twenty feet in the thirty years since Sir William Johnson visited them, but Sir William makes no mention of them in his papers. Walter Butler, though, in the diary he kept as he skirted the north shore of Ontario in '79 does give them some attention.

But if Walter Butler was allowed to go as far as Niagara then it was to camp at West Canada Creek [33] the night of July 13, perhaps on the spot where, twenty years later, he was killed. And Sir William came back from Detroit and Niagara on October 30 of that year, twenty years to the day, before Walter Butler's death.

[30] *Johnson Papers*, Vol. III, p 348.   [31] *Ibid.*, Vol. III, p. 381.
[32] *Journal of Wm. Maclay* (New York, 1890), p. 190.
[33] A. Pound, *op. cit.*, 321-23.

Though there was peace there was evidently a fatherless Christmas at Butlersbury that year. John Butler had gone south for Sir William on a mission and General Amherst [34] wrote Sir William, on the last day of the year, that Lieutenant Butler "who arrived the morning from the Miamis spent a great deal too much money." These officers of the Indian Department were always spending too much on the Indians according to the Crown's officers. Sir William usually came stoutly to their defense to the effect that the competitive "French had lately been there" and that British prestige demanded money.

There must have been more good stories on New Year's Eve at the Butler house, and possibly presents from New York or Philadelphia, and Mrs. Butler perhaps reminding Lieutenant Butler that Walter would soon be ten, and she twenty-six, and there may have been talk of the houses the Johnsons were planning. In February, '62, John Butler was made a justice of the peace [35] of the County and sat in the Quarter Sessions in Johnstown but not in the courthouse, which was not built until 1772.

All that spring and summer men were working on the new Johnson house just west of Johnstown, [36] and Walter Butler must have ridden over many mornings to watch the workmen. It was done in the fall and Fort Johnson was left by Sir William to his son John and his mistress, Miss Putnam. Sir William's son and heir was born in 1742 of Catherine Weisenberg, a German girl whose contract service Sir William is said to have bought. He was therefore approximately ten years older than Walter Butler. The stories of their friendship seem utterly without authority. But it is possible, of course, that young Walter may have been thrilled by the dull young man of twenty, the heir of the great Sir William, living with a mistress in old Fort Johnson. In those loose times he may have perfectly understood their relationship, and the legends which link his name with young Johnson's, in a long

[34] *Johnson Papers*, Vol. III, p. 592.   [35] *Ibid.*, Vol. III, p. 624.
[36] *Ibid.*, Vol. IV, p. 40.

debauchery in the Valley, may be true. But the opposition of their characters, the absence of later evidence to that effect makes it doubtful. After all when one is ten, however precocious, a libertine of twenty is poor company when the country around you is full of soldiers and Indians and the glamour of wars and arms. There is certainly no evidence in support of their attachment.

There is a letter from Sir William, written the next winter [37] by the fire in Johnson Hall, telling of "three feet of snow and more falling daily" and the country alive "with their flying slideing machines," so that it is more reasonable to think of young Walter coasting down the Butlersbury road and out on the frozen river than of beginning his instruction in life with John Johnson.

On a June night of that year a runner came into Johnson Hall with word of the rising of Pontiac at Detroit; the neighbors and tenantry were mustered and Johnson Hall was fortified. The thought of the possibility of an actual Indian attack must have been fascinating to young men of ten or eleven. There were bullets to make, water supply to look to and a glamourous importance to everything. There was a great council of the Iroquois Confederacy at Johnson Hall on September 7; and, with his father acting as interpreter, young Walter must have watched from a window in the Hall, surrounded by Molly Brant and Johnson's bastards, as Sir William threw down the hatchet before them.

Every important event of his boyhood had to do with the importance of having the Indians on your side, and it is not strange that, brought up in an environment like that of scarce another boy in America, he should later have thought of them as natural allies.

There is a letter in '63 from Sir William to Peter Silvester, a lawyer in Albany, significant only in that it was in his office that Walter was later to study law. It was that year that Guy Johnson, Sir William's nephew, married his cousin, Mary

[37] *Johnson Papers*, Vol. IV, p. 40.

Johnson, and, for them Sir William built the beautiful house, Guy Park, larger and lovelier than Johnson Hall, on the north bank of the Mohawk River near Amsterdam.

It seems inevitable that John Butler's family must have pointed out that their house was much less pretentious than those of even the Johnson cadets, and that next to Sir William they were really the most important people in the Valley. They perhaps urged him to build by the river where they could go swimming from the garden as at Guy Park. But for some reason this level-headed, cautious man did nothing and they lived on unpretentiously at Butlersbury while the Johnsons filled their houses with books and Chippendale furniture and wines and linen. It is conceivable that Butler may have pointed out that the display of the Johnsons was fitting to such meretricious alliances as Sir William's with Molly Brant, and his son John's with Clare Putnam, and that respectable people went more slowly. Or he may have pointed out that his '64 taxes were £27-5-6,[38] the largest, next to Sir William's, in the county and quite enough for the present.

But, at any rate, John Butler went down to Schenectady [39] on December 13, and brought a lot of "flowered serge" for Christmas out of which Mrs. Butler may have made some clothes or upholstered some couch. He went down with Captain Montour, the nephew of Catharine Montour, and the uncle therefore, of that Lyn Montour with whom, as we have seen, legend has connected Walter Butler. It is of course possible that Montour may have brought his niece to Butlersbury to stay, while he went to Schenectady and Albany, and that Walter, aged twelve, may then have met her.

One of the purposes of Butler's trip was to get one John Constable to go up and prepare the children for inoculation. To inoculate young children for smallpox in 1764 seems to indicate an unusually enlightened point of view for the times. There is just the possibility that Montour brought his niece

[38] Jeptha R. Simms, *Schoharie County and Border Wars of New York*, (Albany, 1845), p. 150.   [39] *Johnson Papers*, Vol. IV, p. 616.

to Butlersbury for that purpose as it could not then be done everywhere and must be prepared for long in advance — but of course this is only supposition. It may be said, however, that the letters of this month were among those badly injured in the Albany fire in 1911 and that their existence might bear out the possibility.

Pontiac made his submission to Sir William at Oswego on July 13, 1765,[40] and, with his father going as interpreter, it seems unlikely that any thirteen-year-old boy, given the circumstances, could have been left out.

During this year [41] John Johnson went to London "to wear off the rusticity of a country education," and, whatever the effect on Clare Putnam, it must have deeply impressed the Valley and made young Walter wish he could go along. On October 1 John set out, and, on the same day, Sir William writes that "Croghan and Pondiac are daily expected," so seeing them had to compensate Walter for the denial of a trip to England. Incidentally General Gage writes Sir William on October 28, regarding John's tour of education: "You have done right in sending him where he will imbibe other sentiments than the miserable, confined and selfish notions People adopt on this side the Atlantick."

On January 26, 1767,[42] Sir William wrote his "dear child," aged twenty-five, in London, that his letter of the eighth of November "was brought yesterday by the two familys below with all their progeny." This evidently refers to the Guy Johnsons and the Butlers, who were just below, as the Clauses appear to have been then in Virginia. Sir William says, "We spent the night most agreeably thereupon. You would laugh to see Guy drive his skeletons with all his family in a sled." Guy Park was perhaps costing more than he had thought, as there is another reference this winter to Guy's skeleton horses. Sir William went to New London that spring "for the benefit of the sea air and to enjoy some relaxation from In-

[40] A. Pound, *op. cit.*, p. 415.   [41] *Frontiersmen of New York*, Vol. I, p. 266.
[42] *Johnson Papers*, Vol. V, p. 475.

dian affairs." The Butlers must have recommended their old home to him.

It is important to note that there was a Congress at Fort Stanwix [43] that fall to establish a boundary between the Indian hunting grounds and the white settlements. The treaty was the last of many efforts of the English government to delay the entire absorption of Indian lands by the migration of colonists and one of the last to appease the resentment of the Indians over crimes committed against them by frontiersmen. The relations of Indian and colonist, forming one of the most complex phases of American history, are not part of this book, but it is important to know that there is vast evidence of the avarice and unprovoked ruthlessness of colonists against the Indians.

On February 18, 1768, [44] John Butler, Esquire, was commissioned lieutenant colonel in a regiment of militia foot for a territory from the west bounds of Schenectady to Anthony's Nose. Guy Johnson was colonel and Jelles Fonda, major.

As we read this we realize that Walter was sixteen years old, an age when lads of good families were ordinarily made cornets or ensigns. On the preceding page we find the roster of the men of the regiment, their names, occupations, height, color of hair and eyes, and the possibility that a physical description of Walter Butler may be found arises. But the muster rolls described the men to prevent desertion. There is no description of the officers, but two pages on, under date of May, 1768, there is "a return of persons recommended to be captains and subalterns for the new formed regiments of militia foot in the western parts of the county of Albany." [45] Here is Harry Hare, later executed in the Revolution, and, among the ensigns: Peter Conyer; Barent Frederick; Evert van Epps; Peter Groot; Hendrick Vrooman, Jr.; Walter Butler; John Dagstedder, Jr; [46] John Cline, Jr; Corn. Ab. Van Al-

---

[43] *Johnson Papers*, Vol. VI, p. 9.
[44] *Third Annual Report of the New York State Historian*, p. 887.
[45] *Ibid.*, p. 890.
[46] This is evidently John Doxstader who died on the Ross Expedition a week before Walter Butler was killed in '81.

stine; James Ramsey, Jr. This is probably the earliest extant
record of Walter Butler's name. It is curious to think that he
was then sixteen and that his name, which was to be so cursed
in this valley of his childhood, should apparently never before
have been recorded.

The young subaltern must have had some experience, and
the trips to Niagara and Oswego seem more plausible as we
find him here half matured. With this entry his obscure childhood is over. The possibility of the Revolution now began
to occupy men's minds. In June of that year, the next month,
John Hancock's old sloop "Liberty," loaded with wine, came
into Boston and the collector of the port was thrown into a
cabin and the wine unloaded against his protest. There had
been outbursts in Boston and New York, but there is hardly
a mention of it in the documents of the thirty years since Sir
William came into the Valley. The letters and papers were
by and about brave and avaricious men devoting their lives,
with sacrificial unity of purpose, to development of the fur
trade, subjugation of the Indians, defeat of the French, and
acquisition of land, land, land.

A letter of William Johnson to Peter Warren dated May
10, 1739,[47] sums up most of the correspondence of the next
thirty years. "Severall others tell me that Captain Butler has
an Indian deed for it, which I asked one of the chief Indians
who tells me the same; people here are mad everry day pur-
chasing land and surveying." And Sir William not least among
them.

This is in the Valley. They have the four objectives named
above, and they also say in their letters constantly that the
selling of rum to Indians should be stopped. But that is
the end of their interests. Down in New York there was a difference. There they were passing laws day after day.[48]

An act to revive an Act entitled, an Act for mending and keeping in
repair the Post Road.

[47] *Johnson Papers*, Vol. I, p. 7.
[48] *Journal of the Legislative Council of New York*, 1743-1775, p. 31.

An act for declaring Shrubb liable to the same dutys as distilled liquors.

An act to prevent the killing of deer.

An act to encourage the destroying of wild cats.

An act to revise, digest and print the laws.

An act for the better regulation of juries.

An act to prevent swine overrunning the country.

The impression from the correspondence of the British officers is of conservative and honorable men seriously alarmed by the reckless expenditure on Indian affairs. There is almost no word of political trouble in the Valley documents. There was too much foreign malice just defeated. The grown men had been at the wars for twenty years and wanted peace and ease.

The winter was mild.[49] In '69 there was no frost in Johnstown till January 23. But a great cold was coming. That May Virginia announced that the sole right of levying taxes lay in her own legislature.

[49] *Johnson Papers*, Vol. VI, p. 610.

CHAPTER II

BUTLERSBURY, EVE OF THE REVOLUTION

It is at once the despair and the incentive of the historian of the Butlers that the documents in their case are so scattered and incomplete. There are no "Butler Papers." But the Butlers are constantly mentioned in other people's letters. They were never off stage, but their own lives and thoughts are hopelessly hidden, and particularly in the years from the Stanwix Treaty to the Revolution. This was the outward political aspect of the America of those years: Thomas Gage, the British commander in chief, was in New York till June, '73, and in Boston, after he came back from English leave in May, '74. There were of course Royal Governors in each of the Colonies but Gage, to an amazing degree, was the center of authority. Under him were the two imperial officers, the Superintendents for Indian Affairs, Sir William Johnson in the North, and John Stuart in the South.

School histories, directly or by implication, picture Gage as a stupid and arrogant blunderer, trying to crush the proud spirit of a mighty people. The fact is that, like most of the imperial officers, he was carrying on a terrific job of executive management, outside the coastal cities, in trying to organize the lands west of the Alleghenies. The agressive and dominant groups, such as the Grand Ohio Company, presented such enormous problems that he evidently underestimated what the city malcontents could do. The political organization of the Mississippi Basin, from the Gulf of Mexico to the headwaters of the Monongahela and the Allegheny in New York, was what he concentrated on, and the crash of firing before Boston Province House, that snowy March evening in 1770 was, as his correspondence with Hillsborough shows, "an unhappy quarrel"[1] of less importance than the troop movements in West Florida or Croghan's last report to Sir William Johnson on the Chickasaws.

In the Mohawk Valley a quiet prologue to the long five-act tragedy of the Revolution was playing. It was a sober undramatic time in which, though, most of the actors of the later tragedy came on the stage. The whole country, from Washington and Sir William Johnson down, was land-mad and money-mad. General Gage had urged Sir William to send his son to London where people were less selfish. The vast land speculation made lawyers of great importance. It was therefore natural that Walter Butler, the most brilliant young man in the Valley, should go into Albany to read law in the office of Peter Silvester.

Silvester had taken a Peter Van Schaack into his office in '66, and it is to the latter that two of Walter Butler's pre-Revolutionary letters are addressed. It is for his family that the island in the Mohawk is named. Here Gates had his general headquarters before Saratoga, and here word came that St. Leger had beseiged Stanwix. The Van Schaacks were a prominent family in the Valley, most of them patriots, although the pious Peter was a philosophic Tory who spent a long exile in London during the war. A long, tedious *Life of Peter Van Schaack* was published in 1842 and in it there are numerous letters written in the fifteen years after 1770. There must have been in many of them mention of the Butlers, whose attorney and intimate Van Schaack had been, but doubtless the biographer, even as late as 1842, thought it best to show no link to the "infamous Butlers." Van Schaack came back to Kinderhook, New York, after the peace and old Silvester wrote[2] him there in July, 1790, of the "discontents" and reminded him that "all sublunary things are mutable." People had begun to forget the events of twenty years before. A Tory Butler would soon come to Albany to marry the daughter of a patriot Commissioner for Detecting Conspiracies.

---

[1] *Correspondence of General Thomas Gage* (ed. C. E. Carter, New Haven, 1931), Vol. I.   [2] Original letter in the author's possession.

There is a letter in the Johnson Papers [3] that places Walter
Butler in Albany in October, 1770. Dr. Samuel Stringer writes
from Albany that he is so engaged in inoculation that he cannot leave but adds, "bills of exchange have advanced. Please
send draught by Mr. Walter Butler, the bearer." Peter
Silvester also sent a letter by him to Sir William reminding
him of his engagement to pay the debts and costs in a
suit of Daniel Phoenix and Samuel Broome against Hugh
Denniston."

Dr. Samuel Stringer, though, comes on again and again in
the later tragedy. He went north to Canada with Arnold's
expedition in May, 1776, as Director of Medical Service and
later earned Gates' ill will by going "preferment hunting to
Congress" while the troops were suffering inexpressible distress for want of medicines. There is a cross bearing on
the good doctor, in the Governor Clinton Papers for August,
1781, in his fine mysterious letter to the Governor then at
Poughkeepsie in which he says

I have certain intelligence that a large packet from Canada was
brought to this place yesterday to be forwarded to New York. If you
should be acquainted with the channel the Enemies expresses generally
take tis possible you may make such a disposition as to possess yourself
of these dispatches. They have had one narrow escape. As it rained hard
last night from evening I doubt whether they are yet out of town.

It is fascinating to wonder what the narrow escape was or
where Stringer got the information. Of course the Committee
for Detecting Conspiracies, with its sinister inquisitional name
and methods, was well served. Possibly there is no connection
between this letter and the 1770 one by which we place Walter
Butler in Albany. But Haldimand's dispatches for Sir Henry
Clinton went through the underground at Albany, usually by
a Ranger, and it is not impossible that the good Dr. Stringer
saw a face in the summer rain, as he went up the steep street
to his house, that he remembered seeing years before at
Butlersbury.

[3] *Johnson Papers*, Vol. VII, p. 937.

If nothing else, the incident illustrates how irregular was the line of adherence. Apparently till the nineteenth of April, 1775, two men could live alike, think alike, feel alike, and the next morning, and thereafter, be at each other's throats. These friendships and intimacies of the Valley were very strong. Everyone knew everyone else. When the war ruthlessly broke them off, both sides were far more bitter against their "unnatural" foes, their former friends and relatives, than against a hostile invader. Neither could understand the other's position, but ascribed it to a long obscured viciousness rather than to principle.

The year 1771 saw the Butler estate increased to five thousand acres through a patent for reduced officers and disbanded soldiers,[4] an extent which it roughly maintained until its attainder in '79. We know from the London record of John Butler's claim for compensation that at the beginning of the Revolution he had "an estate of 4202 acres part by Royal Grant . . . 25 horses, 60 black cattle, 60 sheep, 45 hogs." [5] The times seem to have been good and men well disposed to their brothers. There is a sense of prosperity and generosity in the letters.

Gilbert Tice, who was to be a captain in Butler's Rangers, had come to Johnstown and opened a tavern there. He was thereafter almost constantly on the stage, a man who knew the whole countryside, as an innkeeper should, a witness of Sir William's will, wounded in the first action in the North, and the intended recipient of some of the most tender and charming love letters of the time, written by his wife, and captured by Schuyler's troopers. In February, 1771, Sir William Johnson himself interceded for him with his creditors, writing an open letter [6] attesting his rights to land and asking an extension for him "as he is a beginner in these parts and it may prove his ruin without saving his creditors."

The conventional picture of the Johnsons and Butlers living

[4] *Third Annual Report of the New York State Historian*, p. 766.
[5] Loyalist Papers, N. Y. P. L., Vol. I, p. 639.
[6] *Johnson Papers*, Vol. VII, p. 1152.

an arrogant, dissipated life of oppression over a brave peasantry is of course not true. Even the self-engrossed Walter
Butler defends a man, imprisoned for debt, without hope of
reward, and his father shows himself a good neighbor. He
wrote [7] Sir William in 1771,

Just now Mr. Perkins gave me your favor whearin you desired me to
send you my opinion concerning Sammon's Road. I have no objections
to the peoples yousing the old road and if you will be so kind to tack
the trouble to give the Pathmaster such directions as you may think
proper you may be assured it will be agreeable to me as I have no desire
that people shold be obliged to youse a bad road when they can have a
good one.

This letter goes well with an incident at a Council Fire at
Johnson Hall in '75 when Butler understands that a portion
of a Sachem's speech is aimed at him. He replies that he had
not told the Indians to banish their minister for refusing
baptism but that he said he looked upon it as very uncharitable
to refuse baptism to children for the faults of parents, "and
that he still thought so." [8]

It is absurd to believe this judicious and decent man "to
have been not only arrogant and supercilious in a high degree
but barbarous, treacherous, revengeful, ferocious, merciless,
brutal, diabolically wicked and cruel; with the spirit of fiends
[committing] cruelties worthy of the dungeons of the
Inquisition." [9]

It was in '71 though that Sir William received the jovial
worldly letter from Thomas Moncrieffe, in New York, which
so profoundly affected many people in the Valley. The things
which might not have been, if the letter had not been written,
are legion. Moncrieffe wrote:

What is the reason (If I may be so bold, as the Yankee says) that
you don't send Sir Jn° here — the finest race of young women I ever
saw are at present in New York. I should be glad to see him disposed

[7] Original letter, Emmet Collection, N. Y. P. L. 4671.
[8] New York Colonial Documents, Vol. VII, p. 552.
[9] W. M. Reid, *The Mohawk Valley* (New York, 1901), p. 227.

of to one of these beauties. Polly Watts, Hannah Vanhorne, Betsey her sister, an angel, Sukey Vanhorn, if I was two and twenty I would not wish for more than her, and six thousand bottles of her father's old wine. I could mention a niece of mine, Jennett Smith, not extravagantly handsome, but she has the finest disposition in the world, and I believe one of the first fortunes in this country. Then there is Philippa De Lancey, for beauty unrivalled — Let him come and please himself.[10]

Now what are the facts? First, Sir John was not two-and-twenty, but in his thirtieth year, living at Fort Johnson, with Clare Putnam his mistress, and their two children. Certainly a great catch for New York's wealth and beauty! Of course the times were immoral. Men of fashion, says the New York State Historian in his Introduction to Governor Clinton's Papers, passed the day in debauchery. Women rivalled men in libertinism. When Burgoyne came down from the North in '77, "his army was attended by a train of loose women." The great Sir William was of notoriously loose morals, the father of dozens of half-breeds, acknowledged and unacknowledged, and possibly, though not certainly, of Joseph Brant himself.[11] The unctuous Campbell delicately explains one liaison that, "being a widower he received into his family an Indian maiden, a sister of the celebrated sachem, Joseph Thayendanegea, called the Brant." Such were the times and the customs, and in spite of them John Butler and Catherine Pollock, his wedded wife, lived together for forty years until her death.

But to get back to Moncrieffe's letter. There of course was a young man of twenty in the Valley whose good looks and manners would indeed have stirred these heiresses. He is ordinarily portrayed as pursuing in these years a startling career of seduction through the Valley in the company of his boon companion, Sir John, the story of which persisted in the lore of the Valley for eighty years after the Revolution.

[10] *Johnson Papers*, Vol. VII, p. 1144.
[11] So well informed a man as General Philip Schuyler definitely called Brant a natural son of Sir William Johnson in a letter to Washington of July 5, 1777.

Max Reid, who as late as 1906 wrote two books about the Mohawk with the total disregard of any material but gossip which characterized early nineteenth-century historians, speaks of two girls who lived at Fort Johnson about this time. He says that "their education and social standing deterred many young men from offering more than respectful homage. The advances of such men as Walter Butler and Sir John Johnson were early received with such dignity and coldness as to prevent any repetition of others than most respectful." [12] This is the general implication of the legend, that young Walter Butler and "his close friend the new Baronet" were an inseparable pair of dissipated rakes. The fact is that they were not then friends, and later became bitter enemies. It seems not unlikely that if there had been any great intimacy, Moncrieffe's letter would have led to young Butler's going with Sir John, and mention of it would have been made in the letters.

Walter Butler was actually very seriously at work in the law at Albany. His life must have been fuller than that of the ordinary law clerk or he could not have played the part he did in the Revolution. The days and nights were doubtless not without revels, and there must have been dancing, drinking, singing, and swimming at Guy Park, and Butlersbury, with the Montour and Brant girls there, but that was not the whole of life.

Walter Butler was to leave the Albany law office in '75 for six years campaigning as arduous and extensive as any ever recorded. The young man who crossed the eighteenth-century Adirondacks alone in early spring; who led a small band of woodsmen from the Mohawk to Niagara, to Detroit, to the Ohio; who quit the ballrooms of Montreal to go snowshoeing; who spoke the Indian dialects and French; who, on the rare occasions when he wrote a letter, expressed himself with the grave measured indignation of an older man; who never mentions, however much historians insist on the friendship, "his close friend, the new Baronet" (Sir John Johnson);

[12] W. M. Reid, *Story of Old Fort Johnson* (New York, 1906), pp. 138 and 210.

was certainly impairing neither his physical nor mental vigor
these years by drunkenness or debauchery.

There is another piece of negative evidence against its
truth. General Schuyler knew Butler well in these years. He
must have been at the Schuyler Mansion frequently, attentive
perhaps to Elizabeth, who later married Alexander Hamilton,
five years his junior. Schuyler was a most high-minded gentleman and it is unlikely that, if Butler had been a rake in Albany,
he would have written in '77 the kindly tolerant letter of
intercession to General Gates, to which later reference will
be made.

Moncrieffe's letter was successful. In June, 1773, Sir John
married the lovely Polly Watts in New York, and Clare Putnam, with his children, left old Fort Johnson to live in
Schenectady, where she stayed till 1809, when her girlhood
lover sent for her to come to Montreal, gave her $1,200 and
deeds for a house and lot in Schenectady.[13] The wounding of
Stephen Watts at Oriskany, the looting of Johnson Hall,
the tragic correspondence of the pregnant, homeless Lady
Johnson with General Schuyler, and a long chain of incidents
came out of this jovial letter.

No one knows whether Walter Butler was ever married.
In all the letters and documents examined there was only one
mention of a woman other than his mother and sister. Legend
has him the lover, or husband, of the daughter of the Montour witch of Catharinestown. Max Reid, previously referred
to, says: "Molly Brant had a predecessor in the affections of
Sir William in the grandaughter or grandniece of King
Hendrick. . . . There were two daughters, Charlotte and
Caroline. . . . Caroline is said to have married Walter Butler
who was killed at West Canada Creek in 1781." [14] The marriage licenses in New York State before 1800, which are
voluminous, do not mention it, and the only corroboration
came in the summer of 1930 when an old inhabitant of the
Valley, with blood from most of the Palatine strains in

13 *The Frontiersmen of New York*, Vol. I, p. 266.
14 *The Mohawk Valley*, p. 122.

his veins, said to the author, as though it had happened yesterday, "Walter Butler married one of the Johnson girls."

Sir William Johnson in his will provided handsomely for his children by Molly Brant, three of whom were Magdalene, Mary, and Susannah. Their inheritances, 3,000 acres to Magdalene Brant alone, were sequestered and their guardian, Joseph Chew, presented a memorial for compensation for them in London in 1795.[15] The supporting evidence is detailed and abundant but there is no mention of Walter Butler. This would seem to establish the fact that there was no marriage or connection between him and Magdalene Brant, since to have been able to add, "Your memorialist's husband, Captain Walter Butler, was killed in arms against the King's enemies October, 1781," would have further supported the plea. The fact is that Walter Butler was intently pursuing his studies in Albany during these years. The marriage, the career of seduction, are both posthumous myths. He took himself with the utmost seriousness during the war, and that was probably no new attitude with him. He must have felt a great mental superiority to the Johnson Dynasty at the Hall and it required no great pride for a man of education and means to feel himself above the uneducated Palatine peasantry around him. Simms describes those who were Butler's neighbors as follows:

Few dishes were seen upon the tables of the Schoharie people. It was no uncommon sight to see a family of eight or ten persons seated at a round table, each with a spoon, eating from a single dish of supaan. Every member had a cavity in the pudding filled with milk from which he or she was allowed freely to scoop. Each member was given a large slice of bread upon which they ate their meat and potatoes thrust into a dish to receive a coat of dope [gravy].[16]

Doubtless the young man who was to order port wine for his own use sent up to the front, and hair powder and pomatum for his Rangers, did hold himself much above these yokels.

15 Loyalist Papers, N. Y. P. L., Vol. XXI, p. 325.
16 Jeptha R. Simms, *Schoharie County and the Border Wars of New York* (Albany, 1845), p. 161.

In considering the intellectual and social gap between
the Tryon County gentry who were later to declare for the
King, and the average Palatine peasant who declared for
liberty, and was dragged into one of "the most craven
and wretched" [17] of all the worthless Revolutionary militia,
we are for the first time faced with the necessity of forgetting
the ancient grudges and our ancient reverence for everyone
living in the Revolution who was not a Tory. But to recognize
that the Butlers, before the Revolution, appear to have been
decent successful people, infinitely more "socially valuable,"
as the psychologists say, than the run of those who later opposed them, does not mean that the Revolution was an error
in judgment, or need not have occurred. But it did not have
to occur because "bad people" were oppressing "good
people."

The year 1773 was full of events. We see, in what appears
to have been the isolation of the Mohawk Valley busy with
its lands and deeds and marriages and gossip, John Butler
on the bench of the General Quarter Sessions, Sir William
finding time from writing Gage and Hillsborough to attend
the Masonic Lodge he loved so well. But it was also the year
when a mob from the docks of Boston threw £18,000 of tea
into the harbor waters, which amount was about equal to what
Sir William had spent in a year on presents for His Majesty's
Indian subjects.

In 1773, Alexander Hamilton, who was to be Washington's
aid-de-camp and marry Betty Schuyler, entered King's College,
New York, and Nathan Hale, the patriot spy, graduated
from Yale College in September.[18] The idea of revolution
touched King's College, and Yale, and Princeton, long before
it did the Mohawk. It is fascinating to consider whether
Washington might have had Walter Butler's restless energy,
his will to win, his military ardor, on his side, if Butler had
gone to Yale. The Colonial troops going north through Johns-

[17] Original letter of Marinus Willett, Emmet Collection, N. Y. P. L., 6327.
[18] H. P. Johnston, *Nathan Hale* (New Haven, 1914), p. 34.

town for the French and Indian Wars had been full of Yale
men. Jones, the Chief Justice of New York, and Samuel Sea-
bury, both Yale men, were Tories, but Phineas Lyman, Yale
1738, had been a major general at Crown Point in '65 and
must have known John Butler. Colonel David Wooster,
of the same class, was at Crown Point with Lieutenant Colonel Dyer, of the Class of 1740, and a dozen others.

But, the month that Hale was graduating, there was apparently some uneasiness among the older men in the Valley.
They seemed to have some doubt of the reliance to be placed
in the Palatine families, and Sir William decided it was wise,
"in order to secure the greatest obedience" from his tenants
to secure such as differed from the people near him in manners, language and religion. He turned his eyes to the highlands of Scotland, and secured as many colonists as he
desired, all of whom were of the Roman Catholic faith. By
chance another Johnson, Samuel, the lexicographer, was in the
Hebrides at the time, and watched the recruiting with "grave
disapproval." [19]

It was to some of these men that the worst of the later
atrocities are ascribed — with what justice it is hard to say.
Certainly it is unlikely that uncouth Highlanders, unable to
read or write, were gentle foes. Certainly their presence in the
Valley must have presented new and difficult problems. Few
of them went into Butler's Rangers, though the Loyalist corps
generally were full of them. After all to an American fifty
years old, like John Butler, they must have seemed as alien as
the Palatines.

With the coming of 1774 the blockade of the Port of Boston was on everyone's tongue, and the feeling against King,
country, neighbor, the next province, the Indians, rose like
flood tide. There was trouble at Fort Pitt and down the Ohio.
A treaty had been made in '68 with the Indians and the Stanwix line drawn, beyond which they were not to be encroached

[19] Sir .G. O. Trevelyan, *The American Revolution* (London, 1905), Vol. II,
p. 33.

ipon. On its face, it was an act of guardianship over the red
wards of the King, but it was attended by vast intrigue between the dominant groups of Virginia and New York, and
even Sir William Johnson has been suspected of an ulterior
financial motive in the Iroquois cessions. But men were pushing west, as though driven by the Boston blockade, from all
the frontiers, without regard to treaty, personal security,
hardship, or anything but the reckless glory of the pioneer.

It was still peaceful on the Mohawk. A cargo of plows and
oysters and lemons were delivered at Johnstown in April.[20]

But on the Ohio the family of an Indian chief, Logan, was
murdered at Fort Pitt by Greathouse, a white man. Michael
Cresap fought a bloody war after it, in which the issues were
hopelessly lost. War was in the air. Men wanted to fight
whatever the cause. The British blockade of Boston became
an excuse for killing Indians. Nicholas Cresswell, the Tory
diarist, dined on the last night of May with Colonel Harrison
in Virginia, and the company forgot the horses and tobacco,
the women in the lovely house, and talked of the starving
children in Boston.

Sir William desperately sick, called a great council on
July seventh to consider the outrages to his wards. For four
days he listened to savage eloquence and, on the eleventh of
July, replied that the crimes were the work of individuals
whom the King would punish.[21] He died that afternoon.
Simms [22] has a story of a mysterious package reaching him
from England with a political message, and hints that he
committed suicide. There is no need of this rumor: he was
tired out. John Butler was an executor of his will and among
the more limited trustees, but Sir John became commandant
of the militia; Guy Johnson, Superintendent of Indian Affairs;
Claus, his deputy; and Joseph Brant, his secretary.

In September an Indian congress was held at Johnson Hall

[20] Richard E. Day, *Calendar of Johnson MSS.* (Albany, 1909), p. 532.
[21] *Johnson of the Mohawks*, p. 455.
[22] *Schoharie County and the Border Wars*, p. 116.

before Guy Johnson,[23] and Walter Butler was one of twelve white men attending, his father as usual acting as interpreter. The Indians hoped "Mr. Butler may continue to interpret and act faithfully," [24] and Sir John Johnson replied, "Mr. Butler, who has long been employed in the Department, is continued by me." It was inconceivable to them, as they stood there, that the next council fire would be at Niagara, and that, in another year, they would be gone, their houses and lands sequestered. It was the first council which Walter Butler, now twenty-two, officially attended.

We see him, a few months later, in two letters, apparently the only pre-Revolutionary letters of his now in existence; they are both to Peter Van Schaack, at Albany, from Butlersbury. One of Sir William Johnson's favorite charities was said to be helping men in debtors' prisons and, in the first of these letters, we find Walter Butler anxious to help "a very ignorant man," Wimple, without expectation of reward. Toward the close of the letter there is an outburst of the Butler pride, where, after denying the charge of being "abrupt to Mr. De Lancey," he bids Van Schaack to "remember full well he did not use me with common decency."

There is much evidence in the war letters that he was over quick to resent any hint of superiority or discourtesy from anyone. This is the first example of it. Much of the evidence to this effect is in the letters of others. There is no explanation of it. It is possible that after Sir William's death the Johnsons, who later constantly intrigued against them, treated his father and him less well than Sir William had. The conservative John Butler may have paid no attention to it, while the restless and brilliant Walter raged that the German emigrant, Claus, should precede him. The letter follows:[25]

Butlersbury, Jan. 9, 1775
DEAR SIR: I enclose you a State of a Case Between the Albany Corporation and one Ephraim Wimple, which Wimple Requests you

[23] *New York Colonial Documents*, Vol. VIII, p. 499.   [24] *Ibid.*, p. 500.
[25] Original letter in possession of Mr. Robert W. Chambers.

will please to examine it and give your Opinion what you think he had best do, in the Present case, or whether it is out of his power to have any relief in Law or Equity. If you think he has any then please immediately to do the necessary and he will send you a Warrant of Atty to act for him — he is a very ignorant man. Sir William Johnson in his life time promised him to be at the expense of the suit as he looked upon it to be a very unjust thing in the Corporation, they having persuaded old Wimple to take said lease from them.

They had no title to the lands (except a deed in trust) better than those of Wimple for which they have paid no consideration and which is much doubted whether it will cover these lands. He desires me to send you a Guinea as a fee which I enclose. Hendrick Wimple a very Poor man who has nothing at all, nor likely to get anything, is in Goal in this County for debt. He upwards of fifty is in upon execution. The judgment to ground which was attained through Mr. John Hanson of Albany, in whose hands the suit was, applied to Wimple for the payment. On Wimple telling him it was out of his power so to do he then told him if he would give a Penal Bill for the money he should never be troubled therefore as long as he yearly paid the interest. Upon this Wimple asked my father what he had best do, who advised Wimple to sign the same on the Hansens affirmed promise, the bond being made payable in a few months. The time was no sooner expired but Mr. Hansen, contrary to his promise, conferred judgment thereon against Wimple and issued a Cer. Ser. on which he was taken and imprisoned. I enclose you a petition of his to the House of Assembly praying Relief. If you will be so kind and deliver the same, and endeavor to have him discharged, his brother will with thanks pay you for whatever you do for him.

His debts are too great for his brother to pay, as he has a large family whom he would injure were he to do it — he has given notice of his intention to apply to the House by advertisement in Rivington's paper — Yours of the 2 of December last I only received three days ago. I am much surprised Mr. De Lancy should say I was abrupt when I applied to him to compare Titles as to the lands claimed by the Warran family. I wish he had pointed out to you in what particular I was so as I can't on the maturest reflections Charge myself of being abrupt to Mr. De Lancy in any particular. But remember full well he did not use me with common decency. I have some time ago sent you the Deed from Miln to my Grandfather for said lands which you will find no Declaration of Trust. I should like much to see the Deed Mr. De Lancy says he has from my Grandfather for said land which, if a deed from him, I can't find any way to account for, as he always laid claim to those lands and looked upon himself as greatly ill used by Miln. It must relate to some other matter — I sometime ago wrote you fully on this Head.

You sometime ago wrote me a New Commission of the plan was issued for this County. It has not as yet made its appearance. We can't account for the reason of its not coming up. Various are People's Reasons for accounting therefore. I can't recollect that I have neglected answering anything you have inquired from me. If I should please advise.

I am, with wishing Mrs. Van Schaick and you a Happy New Year, and that you may live to see many is the real desire of, Sir, your Friend,   and Humble Serv[t],

WALTER BUTLER

Peter Van Schaick, Esq[r]

Mention has been made of the strict attention Butler gave to business in these years. There is no question that the Butlers, father and son, quite aside from holding royal commissions in the Indian superintendencies under the Johnsons, were people of increasing position and respect in the Valley.

We find in the Loyalist Papers, assembled in London long after the Revolution that John Butler "says early in 1775 he was written to by Mr. Duane, a member of Congress, to take part with them which he refused." [26] If Duane had persuaded him into the patriot councils, how different the history of Tryon would have been. They were busy and exciting days for James Duane.

Some manoeuvers of Governour Tryon convinced Congress that he was perfectly acquainted with their proceedings. . . . At length doubt arose in the breast of Mr. James Duane that his valet, who had formerly lived with Governour Tryon, had at night when he went to bed taken his minutes out of his pocket which he copied and sent to his late master.

So reads a letter "to a gentleman in London." [27] It is easy to

[26] *Loyalist Papers, N. Y. P. L.*, Vol. XLIII, p. 650.
[27] *American Archives*, 4th Ser., Vol. V, March 2, 1776.

forget that purloined letters, cloaked men meeting in secret, whispers, scandal, blackmail, murder, all the trappings of melodrama actually occur through history often with more effect on it than the great battles. There is a letter dated at Butlersbury, January 14, 1775, which under its professional manner may have to do with other matters.[28] It is addressed to Christopher P. Yates and signed by Walter Butler. A copy of it goes to Bryan Lafferty, who was Surrogate of the County:

As we in conjunction with our Brother Practitioner, Bryan Lafferty, have for these four months past frequently talked of having a meeting whereat to fix an ordinance of fees among ourselves whereby we would be governed and also to enter into several other regulations tending to the advantage of the Resident Practitioners of this County which as yet has never taken place — and as a thing of this kind if done with due consideration and then strictly adhered to will tend much to the advantage and greatly to the credit of the said Practitioners makes me ardently wish for the same.

If agreeable to you and Time and place suiting, I could wish it might be at Veeder's, Innholder, near Cognewage on Monday the twenty-third day of January Instant by Eleven in the morning, Dinner on the table by two in the afternoon.

The letter may be no more than an ambitious attempt at a bar association started by one of the youngest members. Probably though he planned to talk in the inn of Congress and conspiracies against the King's justice under cover of this legal meeting. Certainly the thought was in the minds of the Northern gentry for, on March 16, 1775, the Grand Jury of Magistrates at Johnstown issued a very high-minded manifesto[29] signed, among others, by John and Walter Butler; all the Johnson Dynasty; Bryan Lafferty; John Fonda; the mysterious Jelles Fonda himself; Peter Ten Broeck, later imprisoned with Walter Butler; Henry Hare, later an officer of the Rangers and executed in '79 by the Patriots; Joseph Chew, guardian of Sir William's half-breeds; and Rudolph

28 Original letter, Chicago Historical Society.
29 *American Archives*, 4th Ser., Vol. II, p. 151.

Shoemaker at whose house Walter Butler was taken in '77.

> Whereas the supervisors of the several districts in the County of Tryon with the entire approbation of some of the most respectable persons in that County for character and propriety did so early as June last by letters to the government of New York Committee decline entry into the unhappy dispute between Great Britain and its Colonies . . . they did therefore resolve to bear faith and true allegiance to their lawful sovereign, King George III, and that in the true and plain sense of the words as they are or ought to be commonly understood without the prevarication which has so often accompanied the same expressions from his warmest opponents. And as these have been the sentiments of the most respectable persons in this County from the beginning, his Majesty's faithful Grand Jurors *will in any extremity exert themselves in the support of government as men who whilst they have a true sense of generous liberty are equally sensible of the just claim He has to their warmest loyalty.*

Certainly this is a direct statement of high seriousness, and a great mass of patriot pronouncements sound irresponsible and common beside it.

Meanwhile Van Schaack had apparently failed to reply to the earlier letter and there is another letter [30] to him still as full of land matters as his grandfather's had been thirty years before. There is no mention of revolt:

> I have just been applied to by a man to know what Messrs. Cruger and Holland would take for a certain lot of land in the Suchundage Patent, whereon Peter Witmore sometime ago lived — he says he will give 20 shillings for every acre and more if they will accept at that he will pay the cash on executing the deeds.
>
> My father is very uneasy at not hearing from you and Mr. Duane about the award between him and Wullard Hanson, he fears you have let it slip — be so kind and write on this and the several other matters I sometime ago wrote you on.
>
> In the suit of Garrison and Cupernal Garrison tells me Cupernal is dead.
>
> I am with respects to Mrs. Van Schaack,
>
> your well wisher WALTER BUTLER

[30] Original letter, Emmet Collection, N. Y. P. L., 4645.

It will be noted that these letters are signed, as are they all, Walter Butler. The Walter N. Butler of the histories is an invention of the 1840's.

The above letters were written in January, 1775. Lexington was in April, and in May the Butlers were fled to Canada, and Mrs. Butler and the young children taken to Albany as hostages, never to live again at Butlersbury. Ninety days and the uneasiness over the award between Wullard Hansen and John Butler mattered little. And Peter Van Schaack was gone to Europe, a refugee. Mr. Duane had other business with Butler than awards.

The last letter [31] from Butlersbury is to Major Fonda, dated May 17, 1775. It is signed John Butler but appears to be in Walter's writing. It reads:

Please send me two Gallons of new rum per bearer and you will obliged
Your sincerely
JOHN BUTLER

It was fitting that it should be the last letter. Messages for supplies had been going to the Fondas for thirty years. "Please send me half a gallon of wine as the Docktor has ordered wine for the child." They had been out to the wars against the French together, and Jelles Fonda had kept his misspelt, fascinating Journal of their camp fires and war dances.

Their long friendship was over with this delivery, though the Tryon Committee would say "Major Fonda . . . very little trusted" and his patriotism would be questioned; he would be quoted by spies as saying

he was not such a fool as the other Tories, Tenn Broock and others he had more wit as them, if they stood at home, they would be in the possession of their goods if the Country would loose or gain the Point. He said he would come up too, when Butler should come down, maybe, he would go through the woods to them, maybe he would go along the river and go into the fort and stand by the Colonell [Butler].[32]

[31] Draper Collection, 20F, Brant MSS, p. 1.
[32] *Papers of George Clinton*, Vol. II, p. 282.

Tales of his secretly favoring the Loyalists, of his spreading defeatism, of his secret contact with Butler would persist, while from him would come a stream of military intelligence as to Loyalist and Indian movements and rendezvous.

Five years later, with Sir John Johnson laying waste the Valley, John Fonda would escape [33] from the Loyalist camp and bring word to Fort Hunter that the enemy, at five o'clock, was six miles from Johnstown. Escaping with him would be Abram Veeder, to whose tavern in Caughnawaga young Butler summoned the barristers of Tryon for dinner, January, '75. Wimple, whose brother Walter Butler defended for debt in '75, would command at Fort Hunter and sign the report with Fonda's and Veeder's news. The report is addressed to Colonel Van Schaack, Continental Commander in Schenectady. He is the brother of Butler's law partner.

So do the characters throng back on the stage after this last order for rum goes to Jelles Fonda.

Later that May night, just five years afterward, expresses bring in more word of Sir John's savage onslaught at Tripes Hill. Word comes that old Douw Fonda, the father of Colonel Butler's friend, is murdered by the Tories, and with him a Mr. Hanson, the one between whom and John Butler, Mr. Duane and Peter Van Schaack were to make an award, and the Indians knock in the head of a cask of rum to celebrate the killing. Militia four hundred and fifty strong under Colonel Wimple, brother of the pauper client, go out to meet the enemy. So much does the Valley change.

[33] *Ibid.,* Vol. V, p. 742.

CHAPTER III

THE LOYALIST ISSUES

To understand the part played by the Butlers of Butlersbury in the Revolution we must understand the general facts
regarding the use of Indians and something of the relations
between Whigs and Tories. This chapter will consider these
points and endeavor to state in simple form the complex
causes of the War as a general problem without definite relation to the Butlers. Perhaps it should further be said that,
after the evidence is presented as clearly and impartially as
possible, the whole question of the War will still be obscure,
the motives and conduct of the run of men will still be incomprehensible.

It seems fair to state the American historical position
regarding the use of Indians in the Revolution as follows:
the British enlisted red savages as their allies, loosed them on
the frontiers, and encouraged their atrocities by imitation
and by a horrible commerce in scalps of men, women, and
children. The Americans scorned the use of such allies but
treated them kindly and sought their neutrality.

This statement of the American Indian policy has two
implications: first, that, given the facts, the Continental Congress could reasonably expect Indian neutrality; second, that
Indian assistance was neither considered nor desired.

From the astonished condemnation of Burgoyne's Army
with its hundreds of Indians, it would be natural to suppose
that they were employed as the result of a sudden decision in
London, similar to the decision to use poison gas in the World
War. The fact was that they had been attached to one side
or the other in every war fought in America during the previous century. Enormous sums had been spent by the Crown
and the Provincial assemblies for fifty years to ensure their

alliance against the French. The Colonial regiments from New England and the other colonies had always fought in alliance with them not only without protest but with strife among themselves as to who should have the Indians with them. When Lord Stirling, later one of Washington's division commanders, was secretary to Governor Shirley in 1755,[1] he went on a mission to the Iroquois Castles along the Mohawk with rum and presents to bid against Johnson for the war parties to join Shirley in the march on Crown Point.

Roosevelt says [2]

It was idle for them [the British] to prate about having bidden the savages be merciful. The sin consisted in having let them loose on the borders; once they were let loose it was impossible to control them. . . . Making all allowance for the strait in which the British found themselves, and admitting that much can be said against their accusers . . . the fact must ever rest a dark stain on their national history.

The conclusion of this statement is plainly that their use was novel, and not contemplated by the Americans. Such was certainly not the case. It is a fact that the Indians, partially in desperation at unprovoked outrages against them, behaved worse and worse until the British high command, disgusted further at their military worthlessness, and alarmed at Burke's unctuous noncombatant eloquence in London became more and more apologetic about them. But in a sense the British had no other choice than to use them. It was absurd to suppose a great war could be fought across the lands of a savage and warlike race and that race be neutral. It further appears that the American high command realized this, but that the British with greater financial resources and with the machinery of Indian Superintendencies in their hands, were able to secure their alliance first.

The personnel of the Indian Superintendencies were not aliens whose own women and children were snug and warm

[1] *Johnson of the Mohawks*, 187.
[2] *Winning of the West* (New York, 1894), Vol. II, p. 4.

n London. They were living on the exposed frontiers of
Tryon, Susquehanna, and the Ohio. These men had vivid
memories of the French wars of the fifties, when Johnson and
Shirley with difficulty prevented the Indians from knocking
Dieskau, the French General himself, and his staff, on the
head. There was to be war across these same lands. They
did not suddenly conceive a new idea of "loosing savage
hordes" on innocent homesteads. Without the controlling
unity of the white men and the Superintendencies these savage
hordes would loose themselves. It was a question of *whose*
homestead.

No one was in a better position than the Continental Congress to realize that "liberty," "no taxation without represen-
tation," "the rights of man," "death to King George" notwithstanding, a gang of reckless, ambitious, and enormously
capable men were pushing west, hungry for Indian lands,
eager for a general Indian war in which they might exterminate the Indians and own their rich lands in western New
York, Pennsylvania, Ohio, and Kentucky. These American
frontiersmen formed parties for the purpose of killing Indians, whether on a winter's hunt, or bound to a friendly
council. Cresap's war was a small beginning of it.

In May, 1776, Congress passed a resolution that it was
highly expedient to engage Indians in the service of the colonies. On April 27, a few days before, John Adams wrote to
Gates, "I think we need not be so delicate as to refuse the
assistance of Indians provided we cannot keep them neutral.
I should not hesitate a moment in this case." The next year
Schuyler, as American Superintendent, won three hundred
Oneidas and Tuscaroras to the American cause. In 1776 New
Hampshire offered £70 for each scalp of a hostile male In-
dian, £37-10-0 for each scalp of a woman or of a child twelve
years of age. Congress granted Washington full power to use
Indians as auxiliaries.[3] Governor Clinton of the State of New
York wrote to one Hoornbeck:

[3] *Journals of the Continental Congress* (new ed., Vol. IV, p. 395).

Tell the Indians that if their young men are fond of fighting and choose to be in war that they can come and join us who are their brethren, born in the same country against our common enemies and we will pay them as we do our own young men.[4]

Lafayette invited "300 of their young warriors to come down to Albany and join him." [5]

Scalping and buying scalps was no novelty in 1776. Pound [6] points out that

Johnson sent out scalping parties, checked in scalps on their return and paid for them at the rate established by the thrifty New York assembly which insisted on this proof that the Indians had really been at work in their interest.

The royal Governor, Clinton,[7] bade him "send out as many parties of the Indians to take prisoners, likewise scalps . . . for each scalp . . . [they] shall receive the award allowed by the General Assembly." Johnson had to complain at the slowness of the Assembly in supplying funds for the business.[8] But slow or not in paying, the American legislators were not new to the traffic they so abhorred in their enemies.

In the Gates Papers [9] there is a letter to him which says "the affair of scalping as relating to Indians is delicate but your knowledge of their disposition will conduct you into such measures as will not deprive them of their trophies of warlike achievement." It is a routine report [10] to Governor Clinton which reads "Captain Long of the Riflemen fired at and shot Smith through the head. General Stark received his scalp last night." When Walter Butler was killed they brought his scalp a hundred miles to Albany. The American riflemen scalped in frontier fighting as a matter of course and of reprisal. It was a natural act. But it was the traffic in scalps that caused the greatest bitterness. The British contention was that by buying scalps they were in effect restraining the Indians

---

[4] *Papers of George Clinton*, Vol. II, p. 274.
[5] *Ibid.*, Vol. III, p. 118.   [6] *Johnson of the Mohawks*, p. 243.
[7] *Johnson Papers*, Vol. I, p. 93.   [8] *Ibid.*, Vol. I, p. 60.
[9] Gates Papers, N. Y. H. S., letter from Tim Edwards, Sept. 22, 1777.
[10] *Papers of George Clinton*, Vol. III, p. 616.

from atrocities because they paid a higher bounty on living prisoners. The subject provides a whole field of major inquiry in itself, but the conclusion is that scalping was customary on the frontiers, that both sides bought scalps, and had been doing so in all previous wars, and finally that a measure of prevention did lie in the higher bounty on prisoners. All this of course applies to the frontiers and not to the major armies.

If this is true the extraordinary bitterness toward British "hair buyers," not only in America but in Europe, is still not explained. Ryerson [11] says

the history of the Indians and Tories was written by their adversaries and it was considered a master stroke of policy to exaggerate the alleged misdeeds. . . . When facts could not be sufficiently seasoned to stimulate recruits for the army and appropriations from the people for its support, fiction, pure and simple, was resorted to, and Dr. Franklin himself did not think it unworthy of his antecedents, age and position to employ this method to bring disrepute upon the Tories, the Indians, and the British government itself.

Franklin understood propaganda long before the word was known. His famous fabrication of the scalp story is still part of the mental background of many intelligent people. Franklin wrote a letter with the trick of accurate, specific, plausible, and voluminous detail, purporting to come from a New England militia captain. The letter, describing the capture of some military booty, says in part,

The possession of this booty at first gave us pleasure but we were struck with horror to find among the packages 8 large ones containing scalps of our unhappy folks taken in the last 3 years by the Seneca Indians and sent by them as a present to Colonel Haldimand, Governor of Canada, in order to be transmitted by him to England. The packages contained 954 salted scalps of men, women and children. Each scalp was elaborately marked with symbols indicating the age and sex of the person, where they were killed, and how.

This fiction got to Europe and back into our school books and there must be fleeting memories of it in many minds today.

[11] Egerton Ryerson, *Loyalists of America* (Toronto, 1880), p. 115.

What is the conclusion regarding the use of Indians? It is not that the British were innocent of war crimes, or that sanction was never given to the killing of women and children by the Indians. Certainly no record has been found of punishment for these atrocities. The Indians, and their methods of warfare, however, were employed on both sides of the frontier, and to employ them was practically inevitable. The histories of the frontier have been largely American. In them it is naturally supposed that everyone living in this country had the moral obligation of declaring for independence. To harry and kill those who did not declare was, therefore, a moral right. Hence we hear little of atrocities by our own armies.

Lord George Germaine, whatever his faults, was undoubtedly sincere in writing to Sir Henry Clinton [12] of "the success of Colonel Butler in relieving and protecting His Majesty's faithful subjects on the back settlements in Pennsylvania." The exact apportioning of crime and guilt on the frontiers is impossible. "All had sinned and come short of the glory of God." Sir Henry Clinton himself thinks it best "only to lament the causes which induced so much misery and destruction to the human race." [13]

But the irony of it all is that the Indians as fighters were worthless and the British high command were early sick of them. Time and again, as we shall see, their fighting qualities proved lower than the most worthless militia. Ross particularly condemns them in his report on the action in which Walter Butler was killed. The problem of feeding them was terrific. They poured into the northwestern posts from Oswego to beyond Detroit, cold and hungry, and the £17,000 spent on them by Sir William Johnson in thirteen months was to be quintupled in a few months, and all for naught. They brought disgrace on the British arms and confusion to the management of the war. The late William Bolitho accurately summed up their fighting worth as follows: "With the same

[12] Sir Henry Clinton Papers, Clements Collection, Oct. 24, 1778, No. 15.
[13] Clements Collection MSS, 2 vols. "An Historical Detail of Seven Years Campaigns," Vol. I, pp 125-26.

arms, without choice of position, a band of members of the three fighting stocks, English, German and French, could out-fight, outkill, outscalp any so-called race of fighting savages in the world." [14]

Unfortunately, though, they had been first in the theatres of the war and they would not withdraw. The Butlers have been condemned for having Indian allies. There is much evidence that they would agree that they should never have employed them; and American and British opinion, at the close of the Revolution, and today, is fairly unified in regard to Indians.

The relations between Whigs and Tories are more tangled, and have given rise to more bitterness than the Indian question.

If we should try to state the historical American position regarding Tories in the simplified form that we used for the Indian we should probably say: the Tory opposition to the Revolution was composed of men of alien outlook, swayed by the lowest considerations of self-interest and toadyism, notoriously cruel and treacherous, unable and unwilling to fight unless against a far weaker foe. Our traditional attitude toward Loyalists is exactly what Royce describes in his *Philosophy of Loyalty*:

War songs call the individual enemy evil names just because he possesses the very personal qualities that, in our own loyal fellow countrymen, we most admire. No refuge could save the hireling and slave. Our enemy, as you see, is a slave because he serves his cause so obediently. Yet just such service we call, in our own country's heroes, the worthiest devotion.

Those who take that position see the Revolution as a struggle between an arrogant king and a brave oppressed people of republican ideals. The Beards say [15] "In the light of the authentic records which tell of the interminable clashes between

14 Review of Elizabeth Madox Roberts' *The Great Meadow, New York World*, Feb. 12, 1929.
15 Charles and Mary R. Beard, *The Rise of American Civilization* (New York, 1927), Vol. I, p. 201.

province and metropolis, the concept of the American Revolution as a quarrel caused by a stubborn king and obsequious ministers shrinks into a trifling joke."

To the student of frontier documents this is particularly true. A great army of restless and powerful men were not so much fighting against a king as for a continent which they intended to control. The Virginia Commissioners at Fort Pitt summed up the American frontier intention when they told the western tribesmen: "We are not afraid these people will conquer us. They can't fight in our Country, and you know we can; we fear not them, nor any Power on Earth." [16]

Trevelyan draws a strained parallel between the American leaders and "those Puritan country gentlemen who, in the summer of 1642, travelled down from Westminster to raise and organize the armed power of their respective counties in opposition to the Crown." [17] This business was far different, and the only parallel was in the fierceness of that persecution of neighbor by neighbor which characterizes all civil wars.

The corollary of this concept of Tories mentioned above is that a proud, brave American people sprang to arms "between sunrise and sunset" to fight an alien invader, and that a great war was carried on by them with sacrificial and equal devotion, astounding unity, and determination. They fought this war, we understand, with what Woodrow Wilson called "proud punctilio." As Rupert Hughes points out, "we have only to quote Washington's own opinions of his fellow-countrymen to see that these qualities were not universal."

There was not a homogeneous population throughout the Thirteen Colonies when war broke out. Economic and social conditions varied enormously. On the far frontiers men wanted the Ohio and Cumberland valleys and the West; on the seaboard there was an aristocracy of culture, of learned men, of officers and hereditary wealth,[18] who opposed the Revolu-

---

[16] James A. James, *George Rogers Clark* (Chicago, 1928), p. 38.
[17] *The American Revolution*, Vol. I, p. 412.
[18] C. H. Van Tyne, *The Loyalists in the American Revolution*, 2d ed. (New York, 1929), p. 5.

tionary party, and looked on its committees as we should regard workmen's soviets today. Van Tyne very properly stresses the point that this Tory party was never "formed." It was there, satisfied in the main with the *status quo*, concerned with the preservation of its culture from the excesses of Whig mobs.

New York was the most essentially Tory of all the colonies. There was greater wealth in New York, and a greater contrast between rich and poor. It was the last state to agree to the Declaration of Independence. It furnished 23,500 Loyalist troops during the war,[19] and 17,700 to the Continental armies.[20] The Loyalists were in the right, if we are to believe in majority rule. But the function of these figures is not to settle the merits of the case, but to show that it was more "natural" there to declare for the King.

The fact that Washington and a group of Virginia gentlemen declared for war has made it appear that all right-minded gentlemen should have done so at once. There was a larger percentage of aristocrats in the Whig party in Virginia than any other state, and it is no reflection on them to realize that Virginia gentlemen were the largest stockholders in the Ohio Company, and that the frontier policy originated in Virginia. These Virginia gentlemen were the partners and bankers of Clark and Boone, and the rest of the hard-bitten, glorious gang that pushed west.

Not so in New York or Tryon where the Johnsons and Butlers had no mountain range to block the long valley westward, where their own lands were widening. British Canada, too, ran along their right hand.

Even in Virginia, however, not all good men declared for Congress. William Byrd, of Westover, and the Reverend John Camm, president of William and Mary, never declared for independence; and, as Van Tyne [21] points out: "it must not

[19] *Encyclopaedia Britannica*, Vol. XVII-XVIII, p. 78.
[20] Maj. Gen. Emory Upton, U. S. A., *The Military Policy of the United States*, 4th imp. (Washington, 1917), p. 59.
[21] *War of Independence* (Boston, 1929), pp. 31, 33.

be forgotten that John Jay, John Dickinson and Robert Morris, wavered in their decision, and only narrowly missed turning to the Loyalist cause." Sabine's list of refugees, banished as Loyalists, often reads "like the beadrolls of the finest and oldest Colonial families."

Over one hundred thousand of respectable and conservative Americans were either banished, or persecuted to death, during the war. It is impossible to believe that the majority of these people fit our description of the Tory. Economic considerations may have swayed the Johnsons and Butlers against the Continental Congress, as it did the Virginia gentlemen for it, but, in both cases, they must have assumed the hardships of a long and terrible war from motives arising from their inner consciences.

Howe says very fairly that:[22] "Sir John Johnson was unquestionably a Loyalist from principle, else he would scarcely have hazarded, as he did, and ultimately lost, domains larger and fairer than probably ever belonged to a single proprietor in America, William Penn only excepted." But Benton [23] is amazed "at the infatuated conduct of the Johnson family. . . . They must, on the outbreak of the struggle, have concluded that all their princely estates were lost to them." Yet he goes on to admit that they did "not embrace the cautious policy of having someone or more of their number nominal adherents to the patriotic cause to protect their possessions, which was adopted by others."

When it is realized that the Butlers and John Johnson were as American as Washington, that they were urged to come into high places in the Continental Councils, that they lost everything, and Walter Butler his life in the war, that they chose the hardships of a wide frontier when they would have been welcomed to the pleasant brothel of Sir William Howe's headquarters, it is impossible to believe they did not act from principle, however wrong the principle now appears. Cruik-

---

[22] J. W. Barber and H. Howe, *Historical Collections of the State of New York* (New York, 1842), p. 273.
[23] Benton, *History of Herkimer County*, p. 122.

shank [24] observes that "it may be said that these were hard, fierce and revengeful men, but it should be remembered that they lived in a stormy time in a hard, fierce and revengeful world."

Trevelyan, who thought the Revolution arose from a difference in political theory between liberals and conservatives, is particularly condemnatory of the northern Loyalists. They were a "noxious type," [25] he says, and poor fighting stuff unless backed by the British regulars, whom he regards so highly. As American Army letters will indicate, even when accusing the Loyalist forces of atrocities, Trevelyan is alone in his estimate of their fighting qualities. He and other writers condemn them for the use of Indian disguises. Certainly the idea of the blue-eyed Indian was not a chivalrous business, but Clark's men in Indiana followed it as a matter of course. [26] And Washington, as Trevelyan [27] grudgingly admits, wrote Daniel Morgan to dress one or two of his companies "in the Indian style and let them make the attack with yelling and screaming as the Indians do."

The strength of Loyalist feeling in New York was so great that the persecution there was probably the most severe. In New York City, before the British conquered it, tarring and feathering of Tories was the favorite vice. One man was hoisted on a landlord's sign and exposed with a dead catamount. Another was put in the pound and had herrings thrown in to eat. And then grown men took charge of the matter and these boyish pranks were forgotten for a deadly round-up. Loyalist lands were appropriated to the amount of four million dollars, a vast sum for those days. The people were harried north and south toward the British lines. It was the most tragic and irreconcilable conflict of the Revolution. In the North they made for Niagara with untold hardships.

Women and children of Loyalists were taken as hostages,

[24] Ernest A. Cruikshank, *The Story of Butler's Rangers* (Lundy's Lane, 1893), Intro.   [25] *The American Revolution*, Vol. IV, p. 140.
[26] *George Rogers Clark*, p. 210.
[27] *The American Revolution*, Vol. IV, p. 62.

Mrs. Butler and the young children among them. The Council of Safety for the State of New York, on August 30, 1777,
"*Resolved* . . . that the said commissioners be empowered to
remove the wives and children of such disaffected Persons
as aforesaid from their habitations to such place or places as
they shall conceive best for the security of the State," but the
policy was then two years old.

In the Clinton papers there is a typical letter dated October 23, 1776, from Colonel William Allison.[28] It says:

A report is circulating hear that 3 Tories is sentenced to be hanged at
your camp, which, if true, will, I believe, strike a panick on some of our
sniveling Tories here. Had 96 confined in the gallery of the church
in this town last night . . . 75 of which is going into New England in
the morning.

This letter would be hard reading if it were a captured British
document. The minutes [29] of the Committee for Detecting
Conspiracies, which resolves to summon Peter Van Schaack
before it, orders "George Drawyer leaving all other business,
do forthwith make and send to this Committee 6 pairs of
manacles and handcuffs."

Stark writes to the hapless Alden, later killed at Cherry
Valley, on August 15, 1778:[30] "If your scouts should be fortunate enough to fall in with any more of these painted
scoundrels I think it would not be worth their while to trouble
themselves to send them to me; your wisdom and that of your
scouts may direct you in that matter." This is good military
law but there were "painted" patriots also with Clark and
Morgan. The tragedy of this war behind the lines lies not so
much in the sorrow and killing as in the age-old conviction
that the enemy is born with natural depravity. Our foe snivels
and murders, we mourn and fight for the right.

In the Clinton Papers covering 1778 there is case after
case of Tories in danger of life and liberty, refusing to take

[28] *Papers of George Clinton*, Vol. I, p. 390.
[29] *American Archives*, 5th Ser., Vol. III, p. 1547.
[30] *Papers of George Clinton*, Vol. V, p. 414.

the oath. Captain Long reports the interrogation of a name-less civilian Tory before an American officer:[31]

> I asked him if he assisted the King's men, he said he did. I asked him in what way he assisted them, he said in letting them have a cow. I asked him if he did it willingly, he said he did. I then asked him if there was all he had assisted them in, he said he had no more. I further asked him if he was willing to assist them again in anything he was able. He answered he had assisted his King in whatever he was able to do and was willing.

This unknown man was, not inappropriately, called a Loy-alist. The opportunities to save himself by a little compromise during the questioning are in every answer. The temptation must have been great. He was shot when he had finished.

Through these state papers there is a long tale of human woe. Tory women,[32] Peggy McIntire, Nelly Cameron, Nelly Grant, Florey McDonald, Jane Dickson, Nancy Grant, Jane McGregor, Gressa Frazier, Nancy McMillan, none of whom can write, "unable to seport our families among a people who looks on us as their enemies, seek passport to Caunaday."

Simms reports [33] as an ordinary matter: "at some period of the Revolution, lead being very scarce the vault [of Sir William Johnson beneath the Episcopal Church in Johnstown] was opened and the leaden coffin taken by the patriots and moulded into bullets. The coffin containing the body having become somewhat broken." Had this been a Tory action there would have been horrified protests to the Governor as there was from Ben Shanks and John Renhope after a visit from the New York Militia:[34]

> They desire me to inform you that when an officer from Colonel Butler's first came on this River he found both Whigs and Tories but made no difference: they left every family that had any cow of their own, one or two according to their stock and family, without distinction; but you [Continental] Rangers has stript severall familys and not left them a cow; they have stript the women and children of all their blankets

31 *Ibid.*, Vol. IV, p. 105.   32 *Ibid.*, Vol. V, p. 843.
33 *Schoharie County and Border Wars*, p. 122.
34 *Papers of George Clinton*, Vol. II, p. 644.

and bed clothes and a great many more of their cloathes; their knocking women down and many more acts unbecoming men.

There seems no reason to doubt the conduct of the militia, when even the Continental Line got so out of hand that Colonel Varick on October 28, 1777, after Saratoga, wrote to Gates:[35]

The scandalous depredations committed on the property of General Schuyler, as well as the insufferable destruction by the troops under Major Dearborn of his fences, oblige Mrs. Schuyler to make an application to you for a remedy. She requests that you will issue your order for preventing the shameful boarding and tarring to pieces of board fences in the vicinity of her house, and that the troops may be farther removed to prevent their robbing her of her poultry, garden stuff, etc.

A general order [36] was issued to the army before Saratoga relevant to

the shocking complaints made by many of the inhabitants of the infamous plunder and depredations committed by the troops of the Continental Army. To multiply the calamities of our unfortunate county men by the very soldiers who were paid to protect them . . . reflects dishonor upon our arms.

With the Continental Line so accused by its own commander there is little reason to doubt the savage persecution of the Tories, men, women and children.

They were persecuted particularly by committees of noncombatants and such patriots as those whose letters to Schuyler [37] are summarized:

Letter from Robert Gorden, August 4, 1775, wishes to know whether the civil law is to be without force at this place, the military having prevented the arrest of one indebted to him for £2-5-6.

Henry Glen, July 1, 1777, Schenectady, is at a loss what to do in regard to Duane's barn, the carpenters asking the unreasonable wages of 16/ per day. Needs the barn. Wishes orders.

Edward Fleming, January 6, 1777, wishes to resign his commission on account of urgent personal business.

[35] Original letter, Gates Papers, N. Y. H. S.
[36] Orderly Book of the American Army, Aug. 21-Dec. 31, 1777, N. Y. H. S.
[37] Calendar of Schuyler Papers, N. Y. P. L.

William Gilliland, November 3, 1776, Desires a pass for himself and
ervant to go to and return from Ticonderoga to seek work.

We may summarize the Tory problem about as follows:
Half the Tory refugees were from New York, which state
gave more men to the Royal armies than to the Continental;
these New Yorkers were largely people of culture and position
and, among the lower classes of them, there is evidence of a
sincere and simple loyalty to the King; there was an organized
and natural persecution of Tory men, women and children,
and a confiscation of their lands by the Whigs whose own conduct in, and attachment to the war, is not that of Washington
and the high-minded leaders who held the Revolution together.

There has been no attempt here to balance a Whig atrocity
against a Tory one. In the history of the Butlers which follows, the facts and the conclusions from them will be presented
as impartially as possible. As in the Indian problem, however,
not all virtue was on one side, nor all "snivelling" treachery
on the other. Nathan Hale and Hamilton and Trumbull and
Humphreys, of Washington's Staff, would have been far more
at home with Walter Butler, as the war broke out, than with
Allison, whose letter we have read, or Sullivan, Putnam,
Greene, or the Edward Fleming who wanted to give up his
commission because of urgent personal business.

The secondary sources of the Revolution in New York,
which are examined at the end of this book, are full of Tory
atrocities, and it has long been the custom to suppose that
every fighting Tory was a monster, and every noncombatant
one, a depraved conspirator. Such was not the case. The ideas
determining a man's loyalty to either cause were in the main,
moral ideas deeply held in their inner consciences. Simms has a
story [38] of an American militiaman meeting his Tory brother
at Wyoming and offering to become his servant if his life is
spared, only to have his fiendish brother kill him. It is an absurd story but, if it were true, it would contrast badly with
the moral courage of the unknown farmer, questioned by Cap-

[38] *Schoharie County and the Border Wars*, p. 282.

tain Long, and shot for his simple loyalty. Lossing, in his 1812 Field Book, adds a particularly revolting sexual cannibalism to the habits of Butler's Rangers, evidently feeling his Revolution Field Book had not convinced. It is an ancient story used from time's beginning to the World War.

But the impression of Tory and Whig, as the primary letters and documents of the Revolution are examined, is of human beings, woeful and worried, beset by terror and death, yet unable to escape the little daily things of life pressing on war, past and present. The conclusion is close to that of the English soldier in the World War watching the bleeding German prisoners coming back:

> But when I saw. . . .
> How from tired eyes looked spirits broken down
> How each sad face showed the pale flag of defeat
> And doubt, despair and disillusionment
> . . . I knew that we had suffered each as other.

CHAPTER IV

FIRST BATTLE ACTIONS, 1776

Although the Walter Butler of romance will be dealt with in a later chapter, it seems wise to quote here the first and only physical description of him which we possess, except the similar one in Robert Chambers' five Revolutionary novels. It is from the late Harold Frederic's novel *In The Valley* which appeared in the early nineties of the last century. It is unlikely that Frederic had any written authority now in existence which has not been consulted for the present book. To a man writing in 1890, however, there were living links to the Revolution hard to realize forty years later. Men were then living who, when fifteen, could have talked of the Revolution with grandfathers born in the year of Walter Butler's birth. If, as is the case, the Revolution is a living interest today to the old families of the Mohawk, there were vital legends about everywhere then with which Frederic must have been familiar. He may have talked to Lossing, or Simms, and they both had talked to veterans said to have been in the Canada Creek action. Lyman C. Draper spent sixty years assembling material for a life of Joseph Brant and, in his scrapbook,[1] he tells of the papers of a Mr. Dudley Burwell "who spent a great deal of time overhauling the state records about the Johnsons, the Brants and the Butlers" only to leave his papers to his executor with instructions that they be burned. This was a common, if inexplicable practice of many investigators of the last century, but Frederic may have had access to material of this kind which is no longer in existence.

He says of Walter Butler:

He was about my own age and oh! such a handsome youth with features cut as in a cameo, and a pale, brown smooth skin, and large eyes

[1] Draper MSS 18F, p. 2.

that look upon me still sometimes in dreams with ineffable melancholy. He was somewhat beneath my stature but formed with perfect delicacy. . . . Walter Butler was most perfectly built — a living picture of grace. He dressed too with remarkable taste, contriving always to appear the gentleman, yet not out of place in the wilderness. He wore his own black hair carelessly tied or flowing, and with no thought of powder.

There was certainly something about this young man, other than the cruelty ascribed to him, which made him mentioned in so many places and it may well have been in part his personal beauty. In the Canadian Archives there is a profile miniature of his father, Colonel John Butler, and it is a not unpleasant face, with deepset eyes, and intelligent forehead, and a humorous mouth. Bryant wrote [2] to Lyman Draper in June, 1889, that he had visited William Kirby

a descendant of the fighting Tories of the Revolution [who] is inclined to look at us a little askant, undecided whether it be safe to admit us to his confidence, and inclined to regard us as hereditary enemies. By the way he has a strong portrait of Col. John Butler, the miniatures of Sir John Johnson, Guy Johnson, Col. Clause, Butler, the father and son. . . .

This portrait of Colonel Butler is evidently the one referred to above. There is none of Walter Butler in the Archives and it is likely that Bryant was misinformed about it.

The Butlers had been snowbound on the Mohawk waiting to hear of land awards. Spring came. The redcoats went out to Lexington on the nineteenth of April. The Butlers probably heard of it about the twenty-fifth, possibly the twenty-third, the same day New York City did. By the time they heard the news the British were shut up in Boston by 20,000 Minute Men. On the twenty-ninth Benedict Arnold arrived at Cambridge with his New Haven company, asked to be allowed to seize the Champlain forts in New York State: he was made a colonel, left on his raid, met Ethan Allen bent on the same goal, joined the Green Mountain boys and was in at the taking of Ticonderoga on May 10.

[2] Draper MSS 13F, p. 135.

We have no record of the scene at Butlersbury when the express came in. Riders had climbed the hill from the river to that house, even then, for almost forty years, bringing alarms of war. They may have come in the early morning with mist from the drowned lands heavy over the fields, and sleepy slaves groping to the first drawing of water, or at night with Walter Butler ceasing the singing he is said to have loved so well as the hoof beats came steadily down the lane. From the hint of Duane's urging, many men must have come to Butlersbury those last weeks asking John Butler to declare for Congress or join the Committee of Safety with the Valley Dutch "Joseph Borst, Joseph Becker, Peter Becher, Peter Vrooman, Peter Zieke, Peter Swart, William Zimmer, William Dietz, and Nicholas Sternberg." [3]

A fortnight later a provincial congress met at New York and the first two regiments of militia were authorized. The Valley was in turmoil, the Palatine Dutch seeing a chance, at last, to strike back at the warrior gentry that had lorded it over them, however benign the control, for so many years.

There is provokingly little recorded of these weeks before the action at Bunker Hill. The Johnsons and Butlers were drilling and the great "underground" chain of communication with Canada was being welded. In scraps of evidence here and there, though, the story is told, as when in vivid alarm in May, the Tryon Committee protests [4] "Colonel Johnson's conduct in raising fortifications around his house, and stopping and searching travellers upon the King's Highway and stopping our communications with Albany." The Albany highroad ran along the river directly between Fort Johnson and Guy Park. What hurly-burly in the sweet May nights with the Scottish Loyalist patrols challenging riders, tramps, and market men, their claymores ringing out as they prodded the flour bags from Jelles Fonda's mills to see if there were powder or rifles hidden in them!

But, on the evening of June 16, Colonel Prescott moved out

[3] *Schoharie County and Border Wars of New York*, p. 208.
[4] *American Archives*, 4th Ser., Vol. IV, p. 665.

of Cambridge, Massachussetts, fortified Breed's Hill, and the
next afternoon at three o'clock, under the terrific heat of a
cloudless summer day in Boston, received the British attack.
Immediately after word of the superb American resistance [5] at
Breed's Hill reached the Valley, the Butlers, Guy Johnson, and
Brant went north to Oswego. They waited a long time at
Stanwix and tried to get Sir John Johnson to join them. He
was in a most human dilemma; Lady Johnson was expecting
a child and Sir John for once appears, from the evidence, capable of human feelings. John Collins, a farmer, testified before
the authorities June, 1776:[6]

He met Sir John going to his barn. Sir John informed him that he
had received a letter from Guy Johnson, Coll. Claus and Mr. Butler,
inviting him to come up to Stanwix and to go on with them. I don't
know, says he, what to do, it would kill my Lady in her circumstances
to go in an open boat and there is no road by land to go with a
carriage.

Gage had written Johnson in late May, before the battle, advising this action. When his letter was received, Gage had
almost disappeared from history.

On the seventeenth of July they reached Oswego, but four
days earlier there was a letter [7] from Christopher Yates to the
Committee of Schenectady with the first mention of Walter
Butler in the Revolution dated at Canajoharry, July 13, 1775.
The letter begins:

GENTLEMEN: Mr. Ebenezer Cox informed this Board that Mr.
Peter S. Degert told this informant that he was informed by a person
who we have reason to think has it from good authority that Coll.
Johnson was ready with eight or nine hundred Indians to make an
invasion of this County, that the same Indians were to be under the

---

[5] It is interesting that in so recent a book as Robert Grave's *Goodbye to All
That*, the very nonmilitarist author, in proudly listing the battle honors of
his regiment, the Royal Welsh Fusiliers, speaks of The Boyne, Malplaquet,
Minden, and adds "the surrender at Yorktown in the American War of
Independence was the regiment's single disaster, but even that was not a disgrace. Its conduct in the hard fighting at Lexington . . . and in its suicidal
advance up Bunker's Hill had earned it them," p. 107.
[6] Schuyler Papers, N. Y. P. L.
[7] Tryon County Minute Book, p. 150.

command of Joseph Brandt and Walter Butler, and that they were to fall on the inhabitants below the Little Falls in order to divide the people in two parts and were to march yesterday or the day before. . . .

Here is the first of the long American evidence against Walter Butler. The report in its slow but nervous style is characteristic of letters of its kind, where military intelligence trickles in through rumor and from anonymous men miles away. The fear of surprise is in them all. It is almost impossible today to realize how foremost in military policy then was the element of surprise. Men smoking in the evening after supper looked up in astonishment to see an enemy come out of the trees at the edge of the clearing and fire at them. Everywhere were trees through which Indian and frontiersmen moved to murder with the ease and silence of light.

The letter goes on,

Capt. Jacob Klock informed this Board that this morning about an hour before Day three Indians of Fort Hunter came to his house from Oswego on their way home; that he was informed by a free negro man a servant of him that they each had a Bag of Powder on their horses that they stayed about an hour and then went off in great haste.

The terror of war is coming closer in this vivid reporting, the Indian horsemen in the dim dawn outside the house, talking to the free negro. The letter goes on to the scarcity of ammunition, the throwing out of scouting parties, the concern for the harvest, the plea that word be sent by express to Schuyler and the Provincial Congress, and the last word that "Deygert was obliged to promise not to disclose the person's name, who informed him of the above, but be assured that the Person is well acquainted with the Indians and therefore if found it is in great danger."

There was no massacre and a few days later Guy Johnson held a great council at Oswego with 1,450 Indians, including sachems from the Hurons at Detroit.

It should not be forgotten that, although there was a rebellion in the Colonies, Guy Johnson had a responsibility for the Indians and that Butler was his deputy. There was not a sudden rebellion and a decision by these men to put it down with Indians. They were far too capable and experienced not to have realized, even then, the military worthlessness of Indians except in special situations. There was a rebellion to which they were hostile, the seriousness of which was suddenly apparent after the slaughter of the British on the seventeenth of June, at Breed's Hill; the Indians were under their superintendency; they could not be allowed to go over to the rebels; the northern and western ones would have to be controlled if the economically vital fur trade was to go on. There is impressive hostile evidence later in this chapter that neither of the Butlers planned to "loose red savages on the valley." There was never any denial on their part that they planned to use Indians, as they had always been used, against armed enemies.

At the Council Indian delegates were chosen to go with Guy Johnson to Montreal and in August he and the Butlers set out "in a sloop and several batteaux." [8] There fifty Indians under the command of Captain Gilbert Tice, who had been one of the four witnesses of Sir William Johnson's will and the first innkeeper in Johnstown, with Walter Butler and Sir William Johnson's half-breed, Peter, as lieutenants, went out as scouts, made contact with a body of Americans advancing on Montreal on September 20 and "drove them back with heavy loss."[9] Tice was slightly wounded in the action and wrote his wife on September 22 a simple, genuine letter that should be remembered when all Ranger officers are thought of as villains. It is interesting also to see how brief he thinks the war will be, like the school-teacher who thought it would be "a few weeks."

I can't tel when I shall be hom; dou the best you can for your safty and eas. Let no one ride or youes   nor   to hors till I come home. I am your loving husband til Death. I beg you will content yourself like a woman of Sperit.[10]

Mrs. Tice wrote back one of the most charming letters of its kind ever written:

   [8] W. H. Siebert, *The Loyalists and Six Nation Indians in the Niagara Peninsula* (Ottawa, 1915), p. 80.   [9] *The Story of Butler's Rangers*, p. 22.

I am now in good health and no rebel shall ever have the pleasure of knowing by my outward behaviour my inward concern. May the all powerful cover the head of my deariest in the day of Battle and send you soon home victorious to longing arms so wishes, so prayeth, my dear, your ever loving wife. I send you herewith a pair of mittens as they are the first I ever knitted I hope and know you excuse me.[10]

Evidently both letters were captured as they are in the Schuyler papers. A patrol may have come to the inn as Mrs. Tice was finishing her letter. Perhaps just as she had received her husband's.

A week later Ethan Allen appeared suddenly before Montreal with 140 men after an amazing march. Crawford went out to meet him and engaged him while Walter Butler with thirty Indians and Rangers went around his flank and beat him off. These were soldierly actions and well fought on both sides. The success of both actions, in neither of which he participated, apparently led Guy Johnson to seek permission to lead a very large band against northern New York. He was refused and, with Claus, his brother-in-law, applied for leave of absence to go to England. The matter is not clear but it decidedly appears that Johnson and Claus, who were now to begin their intrigue against the Butlers, father and son, shared with Joseph Brant an idea of war repugnant both to Guy Carleton and to the Butlers, and that Carleton had far more trust in John Butler than in them. Butler believed in putting down the rebellion. Like a true Loyalist, in Royce's philosophical definition, both Butlers showed "a willing and practical and thoroughgoing devotion of a person to a cause," which the noncombatant Claus and Johnson never attempted. Cruikshank calls the latters' application for leave "very like a desertion at their post at a most trying and critical time." They were a dull and selfish pair given to writing letters.

When they were gone Carleton sent John Butler to Niagara, thereafter to be his headquarters. He was instructed by Carleton to retain the Indians in an attitude of absolute neutrality. The bitterly hostile Claus letter to Knox at the War Office

[10] Original letters, Schuyler Papers, N. Y. P. L.

in London, which is later to be quoted, leaves no doubt either that these were his instructions or that he faithfully carried them out. To do so he called council after council at the great falls, speaking in the Indian tongue with its long, beautiful circumlocutions, as he had so long for Sir William. He spent a great sum on presents for them, and, as we shall see, ended by refusing powder to Brant. In his journal James Deane, Schuyler's agent, reports that Colonel Butler, in the Council Fire at Niagara, advised his brethren the Six Nations to observe a perfect neutrality in the present quarrel and to mind nothing but peace." [11]

Back in Tryon County the net was beginning to close about the disaffected. Mrs. Butler and Lady Johnson were shortly to be taken as hostages; houses were searched, roads guarded, and the Committees of Safety began their sinister but necessary work of detecting disaffection. On Friday, the twenty-fourth of November, 1775, we read of a meeting of the Tryon County Committee at the house of Gose Van Alystyne. [12] Simms, in commenting on this meeting, says that the arrests reported followed a rumor that "Colonel Butler was returning in a bateau to the Valley." [13] Far to the north, that same night, Montgomery received Arnold's letter and set out to join him in the wintry siege of Quebec. [14] It is not improbable that the drama of these meetings in the candle-lit cabins of Tryon, with their sense of danger and importance, were a compensation in the drab lives of these Dutch farmers. The regalia and ritual of Masonry had been popular in the county perhaps for the same reason. The rooms were small. They must have been jammed that November night with coughing men wet with mud and rain, their woolen clothes steaming. The lack of waterproof clothing must have been one of the worst hardships of the time.

By a guard kept in King's Land District [the minutes say], Cap't

[11] *American Archives*, 4th Ser., Vol. VI, 1499.
[12] Tryon County Minute Book of the Comm. of Safety, p. 99.
[13] *Frontiersmen of New York*, Vol. I, p. 522.
[14] F. V. Greene, *The Revolutionary War* (New York, 1911), p. 25.

George Herkimer took prisoners from suspicious persons as enemies acting against us in the Province of Canada and having been now in their return to our county, viz:

James Cameron — Scotchman
John Freil — of Kingsborough
John Pichen — of Johnstown
George Crawford —▸ of Butlersbury

James Cameron was examined under oath and said that he, coming lately from Scotland, he agreed with one Robinson to wait on him in his home journey at 3/ per day although he had an offer of Colonel Butler to go with him at 4/ per day, but he really always disliked the company and engagement of Colonel Johnson and his party. . . . George Crawford, one of the prisoners above mentioned, upon examination, declareth under oath that Colonel Butler decided him to come to Colonel Guy Johnson who wanted to employ him in some business which interest would be more valuable than his schooling salary. And upon reply that he would not like to lose his school said Butler answered him that as his school year was now expired he might accept all such service by Col. Guy, being only for a few weeks, and then he might return to engage himself to school again for another year. He should consider the difference of pay. The Deponent then went to Colonel Guy Johnson and engaged himself to Assist him in holding a Congress with the Indians at John Thompson's.

In this case, as in so many, the impression is of ordinary men either acting in what they believe to be the right way, or of adopting a course of action from the most ordinary motives, rather than from the blood-lust all men's enemies are supposed to have. It is interesting to note how, as in all wars, it is believed it will soon be over and Crawford back in his school. There were eight years of it to come.

All this year Sir John Johnson continued to live at Johnson Hall, drilling his Highlanders and his tenantry for the King. Both the Butlers doubtless came and went to confer with him. The Mohawk River was the thoroughfare west from Albany. Questioned by the Committee of Safety as to his activities, Sir John replied that "before he would sign any association or would lift up his hand against his King he would suffer his head to be cut off." [15] In January, 1776, the Continental Congress, upon advice that munitions were pouring into Johnson Hall, ordered General Schuyler to move up to Johnstown and come to plain terms with Sir John.

On January 13 Schuyler wrote in his high-minded way, "If Lady Johnson is at Johnson Hall I wish she would retire (and therefore enclose a passport) as I shall march my troops to that place without delay.[16] On the seventeenth they met, presumably at Guy Park, and terms were arranged which involved Sir John's giving his parole to hold himself at the orders of Congress, and not to abet its enemies. Whatever the rights in the case he fled from Johnson Hall in May with a broken parole, Colonel Dayton occupying Johnson Hall, and the courageous Lady Johnson, then pregnant, was sent to Albany. It was probably then that Mrs. Butler and the young children were also taken in, and Mrs. Sheehan, her sister-in-law, of whose divorce we read, with them. The Committee of Safety observed that as long as their wives and children were in their hands neither Johnson nor Butler would dare to act against them.[17]

Nothing in the war inflamed the Butlers so much as this action. It is claimed they were well treated, and certainly General Schuyler was scrupulous in his kindness to enemy women and children. But it was not good war — this taking of hostages. It is what we hate our enemies for, and it occurred at a time when the Albany Committee of Safety was sending "snivelling Tories" to the Connecticut mines, and writing Schuyler, "There is but one room fitted up for the Tory jail. We have determined to fit up another room. The expense will, we suppose, be between 5 and 10 pounds. There we will confine McAlpin, Swords, Monroe and three others." [18] One room, six people!

John Butler was meanwhile at Niagara, organizing the western superintendencies where anarchy threatened if the

[15] *Frontiersmen of New York*, Vol. I, p. 521.   [16] *Ibid.*, Vol. I, p. 563.
[17] *Story of Butler's Rangers*, p. 31.   [18] Schuyler Papers, N. Y. P. L.

King's authority was abrogated. He wrote [19] Alexander Mc-
Kee, Deputy Agent of Indian Affairs at Fort Pitt, regularly,
and, on February 29, 1776, desiring him "to meet me here at
this place." He indicates that his runners were not getting
through to Fort Pitt and asks to be informed "of anything
worth notice that you may know respecting the proceedings
of the rebels your way." Everything was quiet at Niagara
except the news of the American reduction of Montreal. There
is a postcript: "I have much more to say to you than the com-
pass of this paper will admit of but must defer it on account
of the precariousness of the times." It was well he said no
more because the letter was captured and "a true copy made"
by the Continental Lieutenant, Richard Butler, and read to
Congress, April 22.

James Deane reported [20] to Schuyler, March 10, with that
amazing accuracy of all his intelligence, that Butler was still
working for Indian neutrality, but that the Senecas were
alarmed by Sir John Johnson's confinement:

Several expresses have passed this place from Sir John Johnson to Niagara
since the capitulation of Johnstown . . . the Mohawks are frequently
passing and re-passing without any other apparent business than that of
carriers to and from Niagara. . . . One of the Quigoga chiefs has just
now been here and informs that about a hundred Senecas have lately
met Mr. Butler at Niagara.

The same day the missionary, Mr. Kirkland, reported [21]
that "the late Sir William's son, William, was at the Central
Council House . . . sent by Colonel Butler." The Mohawks
were said to boast, "if there should be a passage only two feet
Sir John would beat his way through." Indeed he did in the
spring.

But all this movement at Niagara did not necessarily mean
war plans. The Indians were a voracious lot and they had been
on a dole from the Superintendencies for years. The Continental Zebulon Butler reported to Roger Sherman that year,

[19] *American Archives*, 4th Ser., Vol. V, p. 818.
[20] *Ibid.*, p. 770.   [21] *Ibid.*, p. 773.

"The Indians when they come here expect presents . . . they come to me and I have frequently given them but find the burthen too great." [22] There is abundant evidence that they thronged to Niagara, and to all the British Posts, for gifts, shelter, food, seed, money, and drink, far more than to satisfy their warlike natures. In fact Deane met some Mohawks coming back from Niagara the next week and "in one of the drunken frolicks they threatened to take [his] life." The Senecas at a Council, March 29th, accused the Oneidas of dickering with Schuyler to take Colonel Butler prisoner and it was alleged that Schuyler offered them two hundred and fifty dollars for his scalp or person. [23] Guy Johnson heard of it in New York, on August 9, and wrote Lord George Germaine the story, reducing the reward, however, to one hundred dollars. [24] It is interesting to note that Schuyler reported the altercation directly to Washington, for Washington himself made about the same proposal to the Onondagas taken in Van Schaack's Spring Raid in '79, before the Sullivan-Clinton Expedition.

Everyone wrote straight to Washington whenever opportunity offered, Dr. Samuel Stringer writing [25] him May 10 that a hospital for the Canadian Expedition would require "at least 4 seniors, 12 mates, 1 matron, 1 or 2 clerks, 1 or 2 stewards." Everyone in the army wanted to be sure the Commander in Chief knew about him. Even Lady Johnson wrote him direct after the looting at Johnson Hall that because of "threats from General Schuyler too indelicate and cruel . . . [I] would prefer my captivity under your Excellency's protection." [26]

On St. Patrick's Day the British evacuated Boston, and Washington rode in with the Continental Army. The bayonets and sabers of that army began to dwindle as men's enlistments were up, and in New York the militia began to go its slipshod, undisciplined, uncombative way, going home when it rained, and to the rear at the first firing. But they seemed to have had

[22] *American Archives*, 5th Ser., Vol. II, Oct. 1, 1776.
[23] *Ibid.*, 4th Ser., Vol. V, March 21, 1776.   [24] *Ibid.*, 5th Ser., Vol. I, p. 866.
[25] *Ibid.*, 4th Ser., Vol. VI, p. 417.   [26] *Ibid.*, 4th Ser., Vol. V, p. 930.

a good time doing it. John Dusler made an affidavit in February, 1833, of his Revolutionary service in order to obtain the benefit of an Act of Congress.[27] He was a private in the militia regiment of Col. Cox and testifies that the regiment paraded several times on the ice of the Mohawk River and that in May the Company was called out to go to Tripes Hill where

Guy Johnson and Col. Claus, who lived down by Tripes Hill, were coming Up the Mohak with flour, rum and other liquors, Brandy, gin, and it was said the flour barrels had kegs of powder inside. . . . Capt. Copeman was the man who inspected the boats. They marched up to Fort Stanwix and found the boats there. They found no powder but some excellent liquor and they remained there three or four days and then marched home.

It was apparently a pleasant campaign. This soldier missed the sack of Johnson Hall that was to come and it must have been a lifelong regret.

On May 22, 1776, Samuel Kirkland, a missionary among the Oneidas, wrote a letter to Schuyler that was captured.[28] It tells of the council called at Niagara by John Butler after the Six Nations had all resolved to maintain peace both with Congress and the King, to which Butler replied, "I am surprised to find you talk of maintaining peace with the Americans" and went tempestuously on till they declared for the King.

A week before, on May fifteenth, the fort at the Cedars, on the north shore of the St. Lawrence at Three Rivers, had surrendered to a party of the 8th Regiment, in which Walter Butler was present as an ensign,[29] supported by Brant's Indians. It was an advanced post of great value, halfway from Montreal to Quebec, and when it fell the American threat to Montreal was relieved. Its loss secured the "uppoer posts." Cruikshank[30] says that the Colonel "felt not unreasonably that no small share of the credit was due to him as the organizer."

---

[27] Draper Collections, 3F, p. 34, Wisconsin Historical Society.
[28] *New York Colonial Documents*, Vol. VIII, p. 688.
[29] *Wisconsin Historical Collections* (Madison, 1908), p. 356.
[30] *Story of Butler's Rangers*, p. 39.

Brant was in the action and, as usual, when he was present, there was some killing of prisoners by his Indians. It is one of the mysteries of American history that this savage, who long after the war murdered his own son, and whose influence over his followers was never sufficient, if indeed it was ever exercised in that direction, to restrain them from atrocities, should be represented as a noble foe, almost, one historian says, "a saint compared to Walter Butler."

Though the Rangers were not yet mustered at the Cedars, many of them fought there, and though Trevelyan mistakenly says they could not fight except against women and children, they executed a well-planned action with complete success and great damage to the American cause. The American officers at the Cedars conducted themselves so badly that Washington wrote Schuyler in a just fury to punish them, adding that the defeat was "occasioned entirely by their base and cowardly behaviour."

The progress of the war in Tryon County was somewhat delayed by the investigation of the looting that took place when Johnson Hall was taken. The rank and file helped themselves to whatever they wanted, and Major General Schuyler, with the court-martial of the commanders at the Cedars on his hands, and reports of militia wanting to go home pouring in, while Howe and his fleets and 32,000 men were disembarking on Staten Island watched by Washington with barely 8,000 officers and men, was outraged. Strict orders had been issued not to "destroy or take away the most trifling part of his property except arms." It turned out that Colonel Dayton's officers were the thieves and not the men. Captain Ross wrote the General [31] that he had taken

those things contrary to the orders of Colonel Dayton, and as soon as we can possibly collect them together we pledge all the honor we have left, nay, all we hold dear and valuable in life, that we will strictly return them to the most trivial article . . . let our fate be what it may.

Colonel Anthony White wrote him the next day [32] "I send you

[31] Original letter, Schuyler Papers, N. Y. P. L.
[32] Original letter, Schuyler Papers, N. Y. P. L.

a list of the things I took, as also a list of the officers I frequently saw there, and have reason to believe many of them
took things from the Hall but, at the same time, do assure you
upon my word of honor that I never saw any of them take the
least things of value. Captain Potter took a blanket coat which
he said he had my leave to take. I believe he had. . . ."

On August 10 there were two letters,[33] as apparently the
General was not satisfied. Captain Ross and Patterson wrote
jointly as follows:

We undoubtedly should have given you a list of the things retained in
our narrative had we known exactly what they were. Our not being
able to mention every particular article induced us to omit it. . . .

Articles *retained* [34] by Captain Ross:
  2 coats, one of them a Green Regimental faced with red.
  2 jackets, cloth
  2 or 3 pairs of breeches
  1 large China bowl
  A number of fiddle strings
  8 or 9 books
  A large injecting syringe
  An old Map of North America
Articles *retained* by Captain Patterson:
  3 or 4 books
  3 Notebooks
  Jacket and breeches
  1 blanket
  A few hooks and lines
  A large seal
Articles known to be *retained* by Lt. Mott:
  A few green handled knives and forks
  A blanket
Articles known to be *retained* by Lt. McMichael:
  8 shirts
  2 pairs of breeches
  1 Jacket

---

[33] Original letter, Schuyler Papers, N. Y. P. L.
[34] Author's italics.

Some silver lace

A few green handled knives and forks

Articles known to be *retained* by Ensign Clark:

2 Jackets

2 pairs of breeches

4 or 5 books

Articles known to be *retained* by Captain Potter:

Blanket coat

Articles known to be *retained* by Lt. Cox:

A pen knife

These Sir (we call God to Witness) are all the articles we know to have been *retained*. There possibly may be some trifling articles in our possession which we cannot call to mind. If there should be we solemnly repeat we will deliver them up.

We are (etc)

JOHN ROSS
THOS. PATTERSON.

We have just recollected some other things that were to our knowledge *retained*: a gold medal by Volunteer Thinny, and some gold ear rings by Doctor Dunham.

Chacun a son gout! The domesticated Ross and the piscatorial Patterson are not common soldiers but officers, and, by their own assurance, gentlemen. The hard-bitten crew at Niagara never wrote letters like these.

Colonel Anthony White wrote the other letter of the tenth, and it tells how he went around looking for "papers of consequence," and broke down doors and saw "a number of Roman Catholic Things" and "Indian things of very little value," which he took, and "some of the letters." At least Colonel White did not merely "retain" them.

But the patriots were active in Albany that same night [35] by raiding the house of Richard Cartwright where they found Abraham C. Cuyler (formerly mayor of Albany), Stephen De Lancey, and Richard Cartwright, and accused them of being "with a number of the lower sort of people, carousing and singing *God Save the King* . . . and committed them to the

---

[35] *American Archives*, 5th Ser., Vol. I, p. 890.

Tory jail," and subsequently, Cuyler and De Lancey to the grim Connecticut prison. Cartwright was later an officer of the Rangers, and Butler's military secretary. The raided house was sequestered in '79 and he applied for compensation in London after the war, to the amount of £859.12.0.[36] A gloomy government allowed £265 to pay for the carousing and singing "with the lower sort of people."

The incident ends when "M. Johnson" [Lady Johnson], writes [37] Schuyler on September 13, at Albany, at about the time Howe was landing at the foot of Thirty-fourth Street after his victory on Long Island

I was much surprised when Mr. Glen informed me that the Committee was averse to my returning home as I did not look upon myself as to be in their power: I was compelled to leave my house by your order and by your order have been detained in this city. I can't imagine that my staying here can be of service to anyone and I am certain it has been greatly prejudicial to myself as the destruction of the Hall never would have happened had I been allowed to remain there.

We have no account of the looting at Butlersbury. It must have been much the same, and it is a wonder that the grey timbers of the house were not fired, so splendid a beacon it would have made in the night across Tryon.

This same week Colonel Dayton, who commanded at the looting of Johnson Hall, but appears to have disapproved of it, received a letter written at six in the morning, September 4, by Thomas Spencer, the American's Indian spy. Spencer apparently maintained a chain of counterespionage north and west from the Mohawk among his fellow Oneidas. He writes:[38]

News from Onondaga informs that there is 700 Indians and Whites at Swagatche that will be at Oswego this day and that there is partys out for destroying the Inhabitants along the River and they desire them to be on their guards, they are to come first to Stony Arabia and go down and there is particular Parties designed for to take Major Fundy

---

[36] *Loyalist Papers*, Vol. XXX, p. 227, N. Y. P. L.
[37] *Calendar of Schuyler Papers*, N. Y. P. L.
[38] Original letter, Congressional Library.

and Col. Herkimer, the Indians here desire that word may be sent with all speed down to the places exposed. The number unknown — they make fine roads where they pass in the woods. . . . I am guarded by my neighbors at present, though I expect I shall not be able to stay here long here on account of private villains in the neighboring towns, though I shall be advised by the Indians who have undertaken to protect me.

Your H'ble Servant,

THOMAS SPENCER

N. B. The party designed for Oswego are commanded by Walter Butler. I am at a loss whether they are yet arrived at Oswego or not — Great numbers will soon arrive,   700 at Oswego.

It is another of those thrilling military intelligence letters of a war when all information must be written or spoken, and where there were "private villains in the neighboring towns" to intercept it.

Colonel Dayton moved out to reconstruct Fort Stanwix, and develop the other forts up the Valley. Autumn and rains and mud would soon begin and they must be ready. Ethan Allen was taken on the twenty-fifth of September, near Montreal, and sent in irons to England, Claus, Guy Johnson, and Brant going on the same ship. On November 12, two years before Cherry Valley was to arouse all the North, Montreal surrendered, and the next day, Arnold all but took Quebec from Wolfe's approach. The Continental Army was beginning to show the stuff it was made of, while the militia behaved as it always did. Ten Broeck wrote Schuyler [39] from Fort Edward: "I think it my duty to inform you of the shameful conduct of the militia. There is not a battalion but what some have gone off. I could only get them to engage to work three days." This complaint of the utter unreliability of everyone but the Continentals, repeated by all the American high command, never came out of Niagara. For better or worse they, at that post, had their hearts in it, though Schuyler's scouts reported to him, November 18, that John Butler was at Niagara with hardly two hundred regulars in great fear of attack.[40]

---

[39] Original letter, *Schuyler Papers*, N. Y. P. L.
[40] *American Archives*, 5th Ser., Vol. III, p. 755.

On Christmas Day the ragged Continental regiments, re-treating across the Jerseys, turned and, superbly led, attacked Trenton and took a thousand men. The day Montgomery had taken Montreal, the main Continental Army had lost Fort Washington on the Hudson. The reckless audacity of the Trenton and Princeton actions seemed to compensate for Long Island, White Plains, and Fort Washington, but, except to make them evacuate New Jersey, it seemed to have little effect on Howe and his staff.

To the British Headquarters Staff the war problem was the defeat or dispersal of Washington's Army. Accustomed to the dynastic wars of Europe, it appears to have been inconceivable to them that there was more than this "contemptible little army" — mighty as it was. They were quite unaware that they were being opposed by a most remarkable body of leaders who, as Brooks Adams says, "though doubtless in a numerical minority, taking the country as a whole, by sheer weight of ability and energy, achieved their purpose." Furthermore they were headed by the greatest man of the eighteenth century.

A great part of Washington's military ability lay in what Brooks Adams called his balance of mind. He thought in terms of grand strategy, and he was in a sense a westerner. He realized that his first objective was to pin down Howe's army. But while he was achieving that he was thinking of peace after the war — and of the West: he must turn in the long north-western flank, the "upper posts" out to Detroit. There is evidence that the Butlers, being as American as Washington, had two ideas in common with him. They were out to win the war and to turn in, from their own side, the line that went west to the angle of the Mississippi. The restless energy dis-played by the Butlers in the next three years is scarcely ap-proached on the American side. They never seemed to give up the idea of winning. John Butler knew Washington of old. He knew and respected, as we shall see, the stuff of the Continental Army. The Johnson dynasty, with its intrigue and letters, is like the cabal that whispered and scribbled from Lancaster and Easton against the men at the American front.

Without comparing Washington's greatness to John Butler's dogged resoluteness, it is a fact that, to both of them, the defeat of the enemy's main army was but an incident in the long question of who was to run this continent.

The Butlers were near Niagara as the year closed. The anonymous letter [41] to "a gentleman in London" grimly confirms it: "The following is the winter quarters of the Army. . . . Sir Jo. Johnson's regiment at La Chine, La Point Clare, and St. Cum; the Eighth Regiment [Walter Butler's] in the back posts of Canada." *The back posts of Canada*, how bleak the very words! Here is a brief letter [42] from Walter Butler at Fort Erie dated November 16:

SIR: In compliance with an order from Capt. Potts I have sent you a corporal and Party with a batteau to expedite you in your journey.

I have the Honor to be, Sir, Your very

Humble Servant, WALTER BUTLER
E. King's Regiment

To MR. LANGLAND [43]

It is addressed on the back in Walter Butler's hand to Mr. Langland, On His Majesty's Service, and there is a multiplication in the same writing of

$$
\begin{array}{r}
28 \\
2\frac{1}{2} \\
\hline
14 \\
56 \\
\hline
70
\end{array}
$$

There are so few of Walter Butler's letters [44] in existence that unusual interest attaches to each of them. Why did he want to know just then what 28 times $2\frac{1}{2}$ equalled? It was very likely a computation of rations to be drawn for his company.

[41] *American Archives*, 5th Ser., Vol. III, p. 1029.
[42] Original letter, Wisconsin Historical Society Library.
[43] This is possibly the agent, Langland, mentioned by Parkman in the *Conspiracy of Pontiac* in the assault on Michili Mackinac in '63.
[44] None signed Walter N. Butler, the name the historians gave him. *The History of the Settlement of Upper Canada* (Toronto, 1869), by William Canniff, a much-quoted writer, even calls him "Colonel Walter N. Butler" (p. 80).

CHAPTER V

SPY AND PRISONER, 1777

As the year 1777 opened Washington was lying in winter quarters at Morristown, threatening Howe's flank if he quitted New York for Philadelphia or the North. His own communications were open to Philadelphia and the South via Trenton and to the North and New England through Peekskill where Putnam commanded. Howe was on the island of Manhattan with a great army reduced to salt provisions from England.[1]

The British High Command had plans "to finish the war in one year." The traitor Charles Lee was their prisoner and advisor. Burgoyne in London proposed that Howe come north to Albany, that another expedition under Barry St. Leger come east from Oswego, and that he himself go from Canada up the lakes, as Champlain had with his Algonquins one hundred and seventy years before, and that they all meet in Albany. The war arrows were aimed at the heart of Tryon. "The fall of Albany," as Lossing says, "was of dreadful consequence to America. It was the terminal of the road west, the head of navigation on the Hudson, the way to New England, and a great warehouse for supplies." Trevelyan sums up the Burgoyne strategy as follows: "they would converge upon the Americans in front, flank and rear, so as to dissever the New England states from the rest of the insurgent colonies," [2] and this severance of New England is given in most histories as the prime object of the campaign.

It is interesting to note, however, that Van Tyne,[3] who has had access to primary papers [4] not available, as yet, to others,

---

[1] *The Revolutionary War*, p. 75.

[2] *The American Revolution*, Vol. IV, p. 71.

[3] *War of Independence*, 370.

[4] The Germaine Papers, the Sir Henry Clinton Papers, and the British Headquarters Papers in the Clements Collection.

states flatly that "in all the available correspondence as to the aim of the campaign not a sentence makes any such proposal. Its purpose was to reinforce Howe." This view, incidentally, is closest to Ramsay's old eighteenth-century history which says "to effect a free communication between New York and Canada" was the principal object. Burgoyne left London March 26, and the amazing disunity in the British command which followed, led to his surrender in October at Saratoga. No one knows who was to blame for the debacle. Bad communications probably as much as anything.

The Butlers were to go with St. Leger, Carleton having so ordered on June tenth.[5] With St. Leger's advance the Butlers came back to the Valley for the first time, unless secretly, since their flight after Bunker Hill in '75. The story is that their last public appearance in Tryon in '75 had been the spring day when the Liberty Pole was set up in Caughnawaga, and patriotic speeches were being made; they had ridden up with the Johnsons and Claus, armed to the teeth like hill-lairds out of *Scottish Chiefs*, and broken up the meeting with their riding whips. The story is doubtless true enough as they were then in great power in the land.

Now it was very different. Butlersbury was abandoned, and Mrs. Butler and the young children were held as hostages at Canajoharie, where Isaac Paris commanded. The Butlers visited her, if at all, by stealth. There is reason to believe this silent Mrs. John Butler kept in close touch with her husband and son during these months, as Schuyler wrote to Honikol Herkimer, July 4, from Albany: "Yet permitting Mr. Stewart and Mrs. Butler to reside [in Canajoharie] is putting these people in a way to do more mischief than they could have where they were." [6]

Mr. Stewart was the Episcopal clergyman who was a missionary to the Indians of the Mohawk. He was constantly under suspicion in '76 and finally arrested. Colonel Dayton

---

[5] Haldimand Papers, B. 54, Canadian Archives, Ottawa.
[6] Schuyler Trial Revolutionary Papers, Vol. I, p. 135, N. Y. H. S.

had him on the carpet then demanding to know if he had any
intelligence from Sir John. Old Stewart replied,

If he had, not all the Col. Daytons and Committees in Tryon County
should force him to reveal it let the consequence be what it would, as
he had an inviolable affection for Sir John and would give him and his
family all the assistance that lay in his power.[7]

There is no record of these midnight visits to Mrs. Butler,
but they must have been like the mysterious ones reported, in
so many of which there is a crippled or disfigured man.

It was one of these visitors whose testimony [8] to the Council of Safety gave the first warning of St. Leger's coming. The
informant said

that he came to James Jones' house and a man with a blind left eye
was sitting in the house; that he had on a speckled under Jackoat,
Brown Surtout coat, Blue Wooling stockings and strings in his shoes;
that he asked Jones where that fellow came from; that Jones told him
he did not know him; that then he, Jones, and the one-eyed man set
out together in company; as they were going along he asked the one-
eyed man what his name was, but the man would not tell him, but told
him he came from the Mohake River thro Albany; that the one-eyed
man had a bundle of letters with him; that the one-eyed man was
about five feet ten inches high; that said man told him he heard
the Regulars were across the Lake, and that the Indians were to come
down; that one Butler was the head of them; that they all stopt at a
mill at night . . . and in the morning one Jacobus Seeny with a thick
man came to them but went away again . . . that they stayed that night
in the woods and in the morning set out till they came to a house where
Rose called the men in to take down their names, that they all gave
their names but him and James Jones; that then, he, Jones and the
one-eyed man went out and sat under an apple tree.

This is the mysterious incoherence of so many witnesses
questioned by courts or officers at the time. It probably sprang
from the dreadful and ceaseless uncertainty everyone felt as
to the allegiance of every stranger he met. There was prob-

[7] Original Testimony, Schuyler Papers (Military Information), N. Y. P. L.
[8] *Papers of George Clinton*, Vol. I, p. 795.

ably little comprehension among the peasantry, such as this
witness, of the causes of the war, and no national or even
provincial feeling. The way of life as the narrator had known
it had disappeared; men were roaming the countryside; one-
eyed men with "bundles of letters;" the men whom he had
known as justices of the peace were reported leading Indians.
No wonder he and James Jones and the one-eyed man went
out and sat under an apple tree to think it over.

The American western outpost in the Valley was old Fort
Stanwix built in 1758 near the present city of Rome. Gansevoort had moved out to the fort with the Third New York in
the spring, where he was later to be joined by that other cock-
of-the-north, Marinus Willett, as his second in command.
On June 25 word came that Burgoyne was at Crown Point in
great power. What Trevelyan calls the great *posse comitatus*
was mustering to meet him. It was characteristic of Washington's grasp of affairs that on June 1, as he moved out to
his chess match with Howe at Middlebrook, New Jersey,
with full knowledge of Burgoyne's rapid advance in the North,
he remembered the grand strategy and sent General Hand,
one of his best brigadiers, to take command at Fort Pitt,
heartening the frontier with the presence and authority of a
Continental officer. Burgoyne was coming steadily on, word
reaching Albany, July 7, that Ticonderoga and Mount Independence were in his possession. He wrote [9] Germaine vividly
of the swift advance: "I am informed that the Ottawas and
the other remote nations, who are within two days march of
joining me . . . are under the directions . . . of one Langlade,
the very man who projected and executed, with these very
nations, the defeat of General Braddock." This Langlade or
Langland must have been he of Michilimackinac and of Fort
Erie to whom Walter Butler wrote. On July 11 Burgoyne
wrote [10] again: "I have certain intelligence that all the country
round Fort Stanwix is in alarm; but I imagine it proceeds
from the appearance of some savages detached by Colonel

[9] *A State of the Expedition from Canada by Lieut-General Burgoyne*, (London, 1780), p. xxxviii.   [10] *Ibid.*, p. xxxix.

Butler, not apprehending St. Leger can be got quite so forward." He was a little confused by the campaign anyway as he speaks of Sir *William* Johnson [11] as St. Leger's second in command.

To the west the long Butler-Willett duel opened July 28 when Willett wrote Frederick Elmone at the German Flats:[12]

SIR: We have received accounts which may be relied on that Sir John Johnson has sent orders to Colonel Butler to send a number of Indians to cut off the communications between this place and the German Flats who are to set out from Oswego in five days from this, perhaps sooner, and that Sir John is to follow them as fast as possible with 1000 troops consisting of regular tories and vagabone Canadians with all the Indians they can muster. I hope this will not discourage you but that your people will rise up unanimously to chistise these miscreants and depend upon it we will not fail to do our part.

I am, Sir, etc.,

MARINUS WILLETT

German Flats is down the river southeast from Stanwix. The move was good war, and Willett's knowledge good intelligence, the facts being exactly as reported, unless Cruikshank is right in the minor detail that Butler's orders were from Carleton and that "Sir John Johnson volunteered to accompany him at the head of his light company." Word went down the river to Fort Dayton, now Herkimer, N. Y., where, under General Herkimer, the Tryon militia was mustering. The terrible fratricidal war was on; Herkimer's own brother, brother-in-law, and nephew were serving as officers with the invading Indians.

There was great apprehension in Tryon among the militia and, at Stanwix, even the Third New York began to get out of hand. They were not there to dig ditches. It was useless to fortify a place that would soon be evacuated to Burgoyne. Willett is said to have confounded them by announcing that Burgoyne's destruction was prophesied in the Bible, and thereupon read from the second chapter of Joel, the twentieth verse: "But I will remove far off from you the Northern

[11] *Ibid.*, p. 221.   [12] Draper Collection, 3F, p. 162.

Army, and will drive him into a land barren and desolate, with his face towards the East and his hinder parts toward the utmost sea." [13]

It is a question as to what was in the minds of the Butlers as they came up to the siege at Stanwix and realized that shortly they would be at grips with old tenants, old neighbors, old friends. It is likely that they came back more or less as Charlie's Jacobites did in the '45, intent that the King and they should enjoy their own again. They knew by that time of the stuff of the Continentals, and that such men as Schuyler and Gansevoort matched the Butlers in blood, property, and ambitions, but they could have had little idea that the Palatines would fight, as they were shortly to do in the corduroy road at Oriskany, and certainly did not grasp the vast moral power animating the high-minded minority of the Continental command. Their agents, and possibly they themselves, were in touch with numbers of Loyalist sympathizers in the Valley, and again, as in the '45, they probably expected there would be a great flocking to the King's Standard. Of all the invasions they were to make, this was the only one where, win or lose, the necessity of a terrible retreat did not face them. This time they unquestionably expected to come riding down the steep streets of Albany to the Hudson, Walter Butler looking straight over his horse's head past the girls he had known in his student days with Van Schaack.

On August 2 Governor Clinton wrote [14] grimly to General Herkimer that "it cannot be expected that the Continental Army can be scattered on the frontiers of any particular state but must be so posted as to oppose the main body of the enemy," and directed him to send five hundred men to the "most suitable passes in your county." At Schenectady, on the fourth, Colonel Van Schaick wrote Governor Clinton, "I have with me Lt. Col. Brock with near 100 men and boys — none of the militia can be prevailed to march with me." Even Lossing admits that the mass of people in the Valley were a

[13] Draper Collection, 3F, p. 159.
[14] *Papers of George Clinton*, Vol. II, p. 164.

craven lot, word of the invasion "seemed to paralyze them with alarm." [15]

On the third St. Leger had arrived before Stanwix with his main force, embracing the flower of the Tryon gentry, Walter Butler and Stephen Watts among them. St. Leger's bombast before the fort is well known. It could hardly have impressed the Tory Americans more than it did the derisive defenders.

The next day word reached St. Leger that Herkimer was coming up the river to relieve Stanwix and he sent off his Indians and his Loyalists to ambush them near Oriskany. The Butlers were in this bloody action but Sir John, characteristically, remained at Headquarters with St. Leger. The surprise in place and timing was like that one long ago when Braddock was killed at the head of the Coldstream Guards. The details of it may have been learned by Butler from Washington.

The Oriskany action was of enormous consequence in the Revolution. The great slaughter among the Seneca Indians there is said to have provoked their worst excesses in the years that followed. It was the first check to the Burgoyne-St. Leger successes, and thereafter every Loyalist invasion ended in rout or retreat. The fighting was of great ferocity and the Palatines held their own.

It is said that General Herkimer's regimental commanders, Cox, Paris, Visscher, and Bellinger, taunted him so with being both a traitor and a coward that he marched to Oriskany against his judgment, and even allowed himself to be overruled as to advance and flank guards.

The militia which he commanded was undoubtedly unruly, and hard to command, but they knew that Indians and Rangers were ahead of them, and it is hard to understand how they could have walked into the ravine, where they were ambushed, utterly without reconnaissance. Only a few months before half of them, under Herkimer, had marched to Unadilla to "converse with his brother, Captain Brant," and his five hundred warriors; (Cox had been there too and, in reply to Brant's

[15] *Pictorial Field-Book*, Vol. I, p. 241.

question as to whether he was Klock's son-in-law, had called him a "black son of a bitch") ; the most ignorant peasant knew that an ambush in the woods was the way to fight; they must all have heard of Braddock's defeat, and the butchery at Bloody Bridge, near Detroit, in '63 when Pontiac and his Ottawas caught Dalzell's Regulars in a "wild and rough hollow." But come on they would, whosesoever the fault, without skirmishers, patrols, or point, through the hot summer dawn.

What a column that must have been! Halts unorganized, men drinking water when they wanted to; bad marching discipline, some officers joking with their men who called them by their first names; some, good soldiers, bawling at them to close up, catch the step and cover in file; the wagons sticking in the ruts and mud.

So they came to the ravine where John Butler and his Rangers and Indians "lay silent as snakes, for now they could hear the distinct tramp of the approaching column." There must have been terrific excitement there under the silence, Walter Butler, Watts, Ten Broeck, and the other young officers, moving along the lines, cautioning men not to speak nor fire until the command was given.

No one of course knows just what happened. Evidently Herkimer had come down the ravine, across the bridge, and was going up the western bank; and the wagons were evidently on the bridge itself. Visscher's regiment jammed together in the rear, cursing at the mules and waggoners, and yelling "way to the right." It was still early morning, six o'clock. There was probably a long piercing shriek from a Ranger whistle, a war-whoop, a blaze of firing in a great circle around the whole column.

The officers went down in the first burst of fire like clay birds in a riflerange — Herkimer; Cox, his great roaring voice choked; Thomas Spencer, the Oneida, who lived in Cherry Valley; Eisenlord; Klepsattle; and a dozen others. Herkimer, propped against a tree, bleeding slowly to death, is said to have lit his pipe and organized the defense. Visscher's regiment ran at the first whistle, but the Canajoharie men somehow held together in the murderous hand-to-hand fighting. There was to have been a sortie from the fort timed to Herkimer's advance. It came later after there had been a lull in the fighting during a terrific thunderstorm, like the one in the wheat at Chateau Thierry. Willett came out of Stanwix, attacked Johnson and his Greens, and drove them across the river, the Indians in full rout. A great booty was taken.

The fighting at Oriskany was resumed after the rain. John Butler heard the firing back at the fort and guessed what was happening. He conceived the idea of having the Greens turn their coats to appear like Americans coming up with relief. Young Stephen Watts led them up almost to Herkimer's ring before the Palatines recognized them and fell on them with new fury; the tide turned; young Watts, Sir John's brother-in-law, was knocked over. The Indians, after appalling losses, fled in confusion, and the Loyalists fell back under pressure to their lines around Fort Stanwix. Herkimer, mortally wounded, his field officers killed, or taken prisoners, was unable to follow up, and fell back toward the river eastward, probably with less than four hundred men on their feet.

The issue of the battle was not immediately clear, for two days later Captain Deygert, a militia officer at Canajoharie, reported [16] to Schuyler that "the militia are entirely cut to pieces; the General is killed with most of the field officers . . . send assistance or this Quarter must of course fall into the enemies' hands." The letter was written in such great trepidation that it is dated May 6. Even on the twelfth Deygert was uncertain of what had happened except that Stanwix was desperately holding out, "Major Watts of the enemy is killed Joseph Brandt, William Johnson [Jr.]." [17]

A few more men, a little better discipline, better soldiering, would have had vast results. The whole Five Nations probably did not muster more than 1,800 warriors. If St. Leger's whole army could have been killed or taken, the horrors of Tryon would never have happened, but the Palatine peasants

[16] *Papers of George Clinton*, Vol. II, p. 191.   [17] *Ibid.*, p. 204.

had behaved beyond anyone's expectations, and St. Leger never was east of the narrow bridge where so many of them died.

Colonel Bellinger and Major Frey, of Herkimer's militia, were taken prisoners and, according to the benevolent Lossing, "were forced to write a letter to Colonel Gansevoort which contained many misrepresentations and a recommendation to cease resistance." Of course no officer worthy of the name could be "forced" to do such a thing. John Butler was sent with the letter and a flag to the fort. He had probably been there many times before. Old Jelles Fonda tells in his Journal [18] of how John Butler and he spent a June night there in 1750. Gansevoort said he would only talk to St. Leger. The next day Butler went back with a flag and two officers.

Willett tells in his manuscript [19] of how the officers with the flag were blindfolded and led into the Commandant's dining-room "where a table was spread with crackers, cheese, and wine. The windows being shut the room was lighted with candles. After passing around a glass of wine with a few commonplace compliments" (they were mostly old friends and neighbors except Ancrom, a British Regular, who made a truculent speech in St. Leger's manner). What could the talk have been of as they sipped their wine? Of the great rain at Oriskany, the difficulties of the journey, the heat? Was Stephen Watts a prisoner, from one side? Was it true that Brant was killed, from the other? For a moment or so there must have been that uncanny absence of belligerency that can exist when soldiers talk under a flag of truce. The amenities, though, were forgotten with Ancrom's speech. The garrison said it would hold out. It will be noted that it was Butler who commanded the attack on Herkimer, while Sir John Johnson was losing his coat; Butler who took two flags to the fort; and Butler whose word was pledged for the safety of the garrison.

On that night St. Leger sent a written demand for the surrender of the fort, to which Gansevoort replied in his grand letter:

[18] Draper Collection, Brant Miscellanies, IG, p. 150.
[19] Willett MSS, N. Y. P. L.

In answer to your letter of this day's date, I have only to say that it is my determined resolution, with the forces under my command, to defend this fort at every hazard, to the last extremity, in behalf of the United American States who have placed me here to defend it against all their enemies.

That night Willett himself, with one companion, slipped through St. Leger's lines to seek aid from Schuyler, then at Stillwater facing Burgoyne. When they were past the pickets they could not get oriented and Willett tells simply of how they waited the summer dawn. "We accordingly placed ourselves against a large tree, stood perfectly quiet for several hours until by the appearance of the morning star we were enabled to direct our course." [20] They reached Schuyler, and Benedict Arnold left the next night with eight hundred men for the second relief of Stanwix. He had Livingston's First New York and some of Learned's Massachusetts line.

Schuyler was still at the head of the Northern Command and, in addition to giving Arnold marching orders, explained to him that "the inhabitants of Tryon county are chiefly Germans, especially those at German Flats. I think it would serve a good purpose to extol the action under General Herkimer, to praise their bravery, and give assurances that you wish to be joined by men who have so bravely defended themselves."[21] There was still, and till the end, a vast uncomprehension in the Valley of the great issue of the war. Defeatism was always in the air. Everything must be done to keep up the allegiance and morale.

The British, then, were besieging Stanwix at the head of the Mohawk, as Arnold left Stillwater and moved south to the river to march along it and raise the siege. There was an old town called German Flats on the Mohawk River about half-way from Stanwix to Stillwater. It was well within the American zone. About two miles from there, down the river, lived Rudolph Shoemaker, a signer of the Loyalist manifesto of '75, whose house, Simms says, "was a sort of neutral ground during

20 Willett MSS, N. Y. P. L.
21 Schuyler's Trial, Rev. Papers, Vol. II, p. 188, N. Y. H. S. *Collections*, 1879.

the war as Provincial scouts and those of the enemy were alike there hospitably entertained with food and a draught of buttermilk," [22] It was evidently a rendezvous a good deal like the King of Prussia Tavern near Valley Forge, but otherwise a rude and filthy place, though Shoemaker had been one of the King's justices of the peace.

We have seen that the command at Oriskany had gone to John Butler as well as the unsuccessful negotiations for the surrender of the fort. Walter Butler evidently came out of the Oriskany action unwounded and, it appears, immediately volunteered for one of the most hazardous exploits of the war. On Sunday or Monday, August 10 or 11, he started down the river to German Flats, with about fifteen men, carrying St. Leger's proclamation and an exhortation from Johnson and John Butler to the countryside to declare for the King. He placed his enemies between himself and his main body, apparently expecting to live on the country and recruit his force within the American zone. He apparently counted on his own ability and that of his men to cut their way through any number of Palatine militia. It was one of the bravest and most audacious enterprises of the war. It is true he carried a flag, evidently a flag of truce, but it can only be supposed that he carried it as an extra evidence of his unconcern with his enemies' capacities. Flag or no flag, no one but a madman would suppose that your enemy would let you come in his zone, raise recruits, and take them out. For cool effrontery surely it has seldom been equalled. Of course, except at the Stanwix and Hunter clearings, the forests were everywhere, and once in the woods the little party was lost to sight. But the militia even had eyes to serve it, Deane the Oneida and his spies among them.

Walter Butler reached Shoemaker's evidently on Tuesday or Wednesday, the twelfth or thirteenth, made known his purpose, and called in the neighborhood that night to address them on their duty to their King and on their next day's activities.

We can picture the scene at Shoemaker's one sultry August

[22] *Frontiersmen of New York*, Vol. II, p. 87.

midnight, the room full of sweating Palatines glancing fear-
fully at Walter Butler's grim Senecas, and his own Loyalists
just out of the Oriskany action. It must have been ghastly hot
in the crowded room with the doors and windows closed,
Shoemaker prowling nervously around, glad to be considered
a Loyalist at the moment, but not having quite bargained for
such a meeting. Butler was there to get recruits. While he was
addressing the crowd the house was surrounded by some of
Colonel Weston's troops who had been informed of his presence; he was taken by surprise and made a prisoner. Simms
calls "the act of coming there a very impudent and bold one."

Word that young Butler was taken reached General
Schuyler near Stillwater on Saturday, the sixteenth, and he
immediately wrote a three-page letter about it to Washington.
Schuyler's letter [23] begins:

"DEAR SIR: Last evening I received a letter from Mr. Petry, Chairman
of a Committee in Tryon County, inclosing a letter from Sir John
Johnson and others to the inhabitants of Tryon County, and one from
two militia officers, taken prisoners by the enemy in the action with
General Herkimer; copies whereof I do myself the honor to inclose.
These were taken from Butler. . . . From the contents of these papers
and Butler's declaration that his business lay with individuals and that
he did not inquire for any officer either civil or military I could not
consider him as a Flag and have therefore ordered General Arnold
to send him and the party with him prisoners of war to Albany. I hope
this step will meet your Excellency's approbation, etc. etc.

Walter Butler was then an ensign in the 8th, or King's
Regiment. When the Continental Army captured an ensign
the major general commanding did not always write a personal
letter to the commander in chief about it, even if the ensign
was taken on a special mission. But this was "young Walter
Butler" and everyone seemed to like to write about him,
though he was quite unknown then. Cherry Valley was still
fifteen months away. Schuyler was apparently sure Washington
would know who Butler was, as he made no indentification.
When he was killed, in 1781, Lord Stirling wrote a six-page

[23] Original letter, Library of Congress.

letter about it to Washington, in Yorktown. This would all have seemed quite natural to Walter Butler, whose ideas of of his own importance were well established, and there is evidently some reason, which history has not revealed, why many people of prominence shared his idea.

Schuyler's letter begins with mention of a letter from Mr. Petry, whom he identifies as "Chairman of a Committee in Tryon County." He had evidently been on the Tryon County Committee for at least two years,[24] for in the Resolution of July, 1775, we read that Petry, a member of the Committee, testified that being at Johnstown in search of a runaway servant, Sheriff White stopped him in the street and told him he must go to jail. Somehow the civilian Petry tracking a runaway servant is not an appealing figure. It would be splendid to have his letter,[25] which doubtless contained the story of how he heard of Walter Butler's being at Shoemakers', of how he got Colonel Weston to send soldiers, and how he did it all for the cause.

Arnold reached the German Flats on the twenty-first and that day they court-martialed Walter Butler. Colonel Willett sat as judge advocate.

Walter Butler, an Ensign in the King's or 8th Regiment, in the service of the King of England with whom these States are at war was brought Prisoner before the court and charged with being a trayter and Spy, in that under the pretense of being a Flagg from the enemy he was found endeavoring to sudduse a number of the inhabitants of this state from their alegiance to the United States of America.

To which charge the prisoner upon being challenged pleads Not Guilty.[26]

William Petry was the first witness. He said he had "heard a few days ago that the prisoner was at one Mr. Shoemaker's as a flagg. That he enquired whether the prisoner had sent to any of the Committee but did not understood he had.". . .

<hr />

[24] *Frontiersmen of New York*, Vol. I, p. 513.
[25] This letter is catalogued as being in the Library of Congress but is one of the many there, and elsewhere, about Butler which are reported "not found."
[26] Original Minutes of Court Martial, Willett Papers, N. Y. P. L.

The Evidence being finished & the Prisoner & Spestators withdrawn, the Court proceed to form ~~Judgment~~

The Court upon due consideration of the whole matter before them, is of Opinion that Walter Butler the said prisoner is Guilty of being a spy. and adjudge him to suffer the pain and penalty of Death —

Joseph Schuyler charged with deserting from the armey of the American states and going over to the Enemy, was brought Prisoner before the board, who upon being Challenged pleads. Guilty —

The Court adjudge that the said Joseph Schuyler receive 100 Lashes upon his bare back & that he be confined dureing the General's plea =sure — And then the Court Adjorned untill farther orders - -

The aforesaid ~~above~~ proceedings being signed by the President was carried off to the General for his acceptance —

State of New York German Flats Augst 20th 1777

M. Willett Judge Advocate —

Turn over both Sheets

WALTER BUTLER CONDEMNED TO DEATH

That at Shoemaker's he found Capt. Tygert, chairman of the Tryon County Committee, who had reported all lost at Oriskany, with papers found on Walter Butler, including the proclamation of Barry St. Leger, letters from Claus, John Butler, and Johnson, as well as letters from Frey and Bellinger, the captured American officers, all urging the population to lay down its arms.

This was the issue of the trial: if Walter Butler was a flag, it was his duty to go to a commanding officer in the American Army and state his business. The prosecutor alleged that he had no business other than to "sudduse the inhabitants" and that hence the flag was without validity.

From the various evidence presented it is apparent that Butler stayed several days at Shoemaker's "arguing with the inhabitants and endeavoring to persuade them to lay down their arms," while Petry came to listen, also a Captain Tygert, a Captain Whiley, a Doctor Thomas, a Lieutenant Welsh, and a Colonel Brooks, who finally "not without a considerable deal of difficulty took him and his party." The whole neighborhood was driven into confusion by this astonishing young man who was urging them to lay down their arms while the officers of their own army came up to ask him what his business was.

The testimony at the trial is confusing. It appears that, when at Shoemaker's, they warned Butler about the law, although he was a lawyer, and he said, "he was ignorant of these laws"; when they spoke of the Constitution, he said, "he despised all there constitution"; when they "recommended him to apply to Colonel Weston, the officer commanding at Fort Dayton," he answered them that his business was "with the inhabitance and that he knew no Colonel Weston nor Fort Dayton." He stated he knew "no commanding officer nor any magistrate or other person in authority except Mr. Shoemaker who was a justice of the peace." From the Loyalist point of view the only law in the land was the King's Justice, in this case Shoemaker, and to him, with plausible logic, he has gone. He does not go to the patriot authorities, civilian or military, because legally there are no such people. It is rather good bravado, annoying as it must have been to the Court.

Tygert "questioned the prisoner about a man of his party going about to sudduce the inhabitants from their allegiance, but the prisoner denied knowing anything about it."

Shoemaker, when questioned, replied very carefully, with the gallows before him, that Butler came in with the flag and he simply invited the people to listen to him. Shoemaker himself was not arrested, though he was unquestionably an accessory. Probably there were reasons of local politics for it. He may have known many things that Petry and Tygert would not have cared to have aired in any court. There must have been some such reason for his immunity, for the next year, when Caldwell of the Rangers reported the burning of the German Flats to John Butler, he said that of course "Shoemaker's house was left." [27]

It was hardly the sort of a mission on which an officer would be ordered to go. The hazards were beyond the call of military duty, and it is likely that, like Nathan Hale, Walter Butler had volunteered. The strain of those days at Shoemaker's must have been terrific. He was just out of that horrible action at Oriskany, undoubtedly shocked and haggard. He must appear unconcerned with the militia officers, assured with the inhabitants, and extremely confident with his own men. There is no indication of what he considered a successful end for his mission, nor any mention of when he expected to leave. Shoemaker probably wanted to be rid of him and "his armed men." Here as always there is no way of telling whether men like Butler and Shoemaker actually expected to have the country lay down its arms or to have the specious logic of their testimony accepted. In the trial he typifies with extraordinary perfection the whole Loyalist point of view. It is like Pitcairn that April day at Lexington saying, "Disperse ye rebels."

He had chosen to go into this most perilous position with great bravery. He seems very much alone at the trial, and while the court was gone to form judgment, he must have

[27] Haldimand Papers, Michigan Historical Collections, Vol. XIX, p. 354.

begun to realize that the verdict would be guilty with "the pain and penalty of death" to follow. Yet it could hardly have failed to astonish him to be condemned as a traitor in the land where he was born and his father before him, where his father and his friends were the chief magistrates, because he was urging men to cease their rebellion against the lawful King. It was absurd to him to hear they were fighting for liberty. He and his associates had had every liberty.

The verdict came in guilty and the penalty death by hanging. Arnold approved the sentence and asked Willett to notify the prisoner. Willett went to his tent and told him. In his manuscript he says nothing of how Butler took the news, but, if he had broken down at all, Willett would probably have mentioned it. The anguish of Nathan Hale's last hours (he had been executed eleven months before to the day), and of John André's, who was to be hung in October of '80, must also have been Walter Butler's. The air had been heavy in the Valley all that August, so heavy that Herkimer had said he could not hear the Stanwix signal guns before Oriskany. The vanity of all human wishes must have come over Walter Butler in that breathless summer night: the vanity of loyalty to a distant king: the vanity of his youth and strength which had led St. Leger and the Johnson Dynasty, and his own father, to use him in this great hazard now to end in a disgraceful death, while a deserter, Joseph Schuyler, was condemned to a hundred lashes.

The night Butler was waiting to die other things were happening. The Dutchess County militia were refusing to go to the front. Willett was wishing "Oh! that the militia of the State of New York might do something to immortalize their names with those of New Jersey and New England," [28] and getting Clinton to rush a letter to Mrs. Willett "who has received no letters from me in some time." Arent Wimple, for whom Butler had interceded in Albany, was petitioning Schuyler to be released from gaol where he was imprisoned for debt as his creditors had gone over to the enemy; and a mys-

[28] Original letter, Draper Collection, 3F, p. 162.

terious "man with a lame hand lodged that night in the barn
of Hendrick Feere." When they asked for his pass he said "he
was to show his lame hand but he was on his way to Sir John
Johnson."

What Walter Butler did, what last letters he wrote, we
have no way of knowing because a very astonishing thing happened the next day, which was set for the execution. His
sentence was commuted. Willett has little to say about it, except that, as he was preparing for the execution, General
Arnold called him in and told him that a dispatch rider had
come in with advice that "General Gates had taken command
of the Northern Department and arrived at Van Schaick's
Island."

Word got around Arnold's camp that Walter Butler was
to be hung. The officers of the First New York swarmed into
the headquarters tent to protest. Feeling ran high among those
who had been at school with him. Yet such is the habitual
force of discipline, it is unlikely any but the most magnetic
and charming personality could have aroused feeling enough
to secure a reprieve.

After Butler's death, in 1781, Lord Stirling jeered to Governor Clinton that his commission showed he was only an
ensign, not the major he claimed to be. Willett says, "his
liberation gave me this opportunity of being present at his
death (in 1781) and the very commission which he produced
at his Tryal was found in his pocket after his Death is now
in my possession." The question of this commission is part
of the Walter Butler mystery. The fact that Willett was an
old, old man, with death close to him, when he wrote this,
suggests that this may not have been the commission found
in Walter Butler's pocket "after his death" fifty years before.
On the other hand we know he was commissioned captain in
the Rangers by Sir Guy Carleton toward the end of the year
1777; and the fact that this original commission is in the New
York Public Library in the Myers Collection, in physical
proximity to the Willett papers, justifies an equally reasonable
presumption that this was the commission taken from his

body. Quite possibly Lord Stirling simply wanted to make a better story of Butler's fall by lowering his rank from captain to ensign. Yet the circumstantial evidence of the physical existence, in an American collection, of Walter Butler's captain's commission is strongly against, not only Lord Stirling's but also Willett's, veracity. Certain it is that the assembling of circumstantial evidence, scores of years after the event, has time and again upset the sworn testimony of eyewitnesses and made liars of honorable men.

Benedict Arnold,[29] apparently unwilling as yet to recognize Gates as the army commander, wrote that day to Schuyler, as follows:

DEAR GENERAL: Your favor of the 16th instant I received, as I have had no opportunity of sending Butler down, and the evidence against him were here I ordered a general court martial to sit on him. Their sentence is endorsed, which is not yet executed. He remains at this place for the present.

B. ARNOLD

The next day St. Leger's Indians, alarmed and discouraged by their losses and rumors of Arnold's great numbers, began to desert, and he raised the siege and retreated toward Oswego, Lernoult, one of the half dozen men,[30] who so long governed the "upper posts," covering the retreat. Trevelyan says that: "The Royal Greens were very poor hands at fighting with grown men and not in the least inclined for an armed collision with Benedict Arnold." Surely Colonel Isaac Paris, Colonel Cox, and General Herkimer, killed at Oriskany, must turn in their Tryon graves at learning their foes "were very poor hands at fighting." The Bennington action had already been lost by the British and, with St. Leger gone, troops poured in to beleaguer Burgoyne.

But there were two other results from the Oriskany-Stanwix Campaign: the military worthlessness of Indians was established, if it was not already known; secondly, the Indians, embittered by their losses, were out for an easy vengeance.

[29] Original letter, Gates Papers, Box 7, N. Y. H. S.
[30] Haldimand, De Peyster, Mathews, John Butler, McKee, Lernoult.

There were not countless hordes of Indians in New York
State. A war party of 200 braves was a large one. They lost
over 100 of their best at Oriskany. The Six Nations possibly
had, all told, two thousand warriors. New York raised, as we
have seen, about 23,000 Loyalist troops and 17,000 Continental. The Indian armed strength was one in twenty to
the white.

The Butlers and other officers at Oriskany had not had
regular white commands but had been distributed among the
Indians to steady them, a military usage of the French.[31] It
apparently became evident then to John Butler that he must
raise a fighting corps of white men, as that fall in Niagara he
mustered the Rangers "by beat of drum."

Walter Butler was taken down to the Albany jail late in
August. Cruikshank,[32] who is not much given to citing source
or authority, says that "Walter and two other officers were
confined at Albany, heavily ironed, and otherwise cruelly
treated." He adds that "four hundred women and children belonging to the families of the principal loyalist refugees were
seized and confined at Albany as hostages for the safety of
the frontiers." What Cruikshank says of the four hundred
women and children is very likely true. There is a letter from
Pierre Van Cortlandt to General Gates [33] dated August 30:
"You will perceive by the enclosed that this council are desirous of securing the families and effects of those who during
the present invasion or that of last Fall have gone over to
the enemy."

The New York historians of the mid-nineteenth century,
who supplied practically all local material for general historians, usually state that Walter Butler brooded so on the
treatment he received in prison, that Cherry Valley was vengeance for it. There seems to be no authority for this. He was
anxious not to be executed as a spy. So were Nathan Hale
and John André. He was anxious to get out of the Albany
jail, and so would anyone have been. He was enraged that his

[31] Orderly Book of Sir John Johnson, CIV.
[32] *Story of Butler's Rangers*, pp. 39, 42.   [33] Gates Papers, N. Y. H. S.

mother and the young children were held as hostages in Albany. This was not unnatural. He says in a letter to Governor Clinton after his escape "I did not receive common justice at your hands." It is quite possible. Gillilance, the jailer, wrote to Schuyler: "Some of the prisoners being insolent it was thought necessary to bind them . . . if they escape to Canada they will certainly stimulate the enemy there to injure if not destroy us all here." The binding of the prisoners which Gillilance speaks of was probably but a small part of the cruelty. Conditions must have been very bad in '77 for Governor Clinton to write [34] in October, '78: "I am informed, however, and have reason to believe, that our State prisoners are not now treated with the same degree of rigor which they formerly experienced and, as it is not my desire to increase the distresses of individuals by close and rigorous confinement, I have to request mild confinement."

The times were rough, danger was in the air. Many of the people on both sides were illiterate and their action was largely motivated by the suspiciousness and cruelty of the illiterate. It is always easier to believe Tory stories of their illtreatment after reading the complaints of Americans against the depredations of their own army.

Gates, in a general order [35] to the Army from his headquarters, in September, '77, would one day accuse the enemy of the "mangling of blooming virgins and of inoffensive youth" and the next express his astonishment

at the shocking complaints made by many of the inhabitants of the infamous plunder and depredations committed by the troops of the Continental Army. To multiply the calamities of our unfortunate countrymen who have been driven from their own peaceful dwellings by a savage enemy, by the very soldiers who were paid to protect them and whose duty, humanity and principle it should have inflamed to treat with tenderness and compassion than to plunder and rob them of the little they have left reflects dishonor upon our arms. The first person convicted of marauding must expect to suffer death.

[34] *Papers of George Clinton*, Vol. IV, p. 206.
[35] Orderly Book of the American Army, Aug. 21-Dec. 31, 1777, N. Y. H. S.

There must have been tremendous excitement all through this area at the time. St. Leger was in rout, Baum beaten, and things were plainly blowing up for a great victory over Burgoyne — possibly his surrender. But campaigning is not all actual conflict, and it is interesting to note some of the little things that the army commander must think of as part of beating Burgoyne. On the twenty-eighth of August, Albany was put out of bounds for the army. It had "become a place of public rendezvous with the officers," [36] and the morale of the army was threatened by drink and women there.[37]

On September 2, Willett wrote Gates [38] "Towasguate, an Onondaga Chief, sends these strings of wampum as a testimoney of his complying with General Arnold's direction in endeavoring to get the prisoners from Butler." We find no explanation of this letter but it seems likely that the army was anxious to get back Bellinger and Frey who were "forced" to advise Gansevoort to surrender and to give Walter Butler a letter advising the people to lay down their arms. Butler apparently felt in honor bound to keep them much as Sir Henry Clinton kept Arnold. The Tryon County Minute Book states that they were sent to Montreal and supplied "through the kindness of Colonel John Butler with some necessary things and a little money."

On September 4, Walter Butler addressed Gates [39] personally in a letter from the Albany Gaol as follows:

SIR: My situation I need not mention, but my case being particular; and, in my opinion, hard — Your granting me a hearing will tender me that justice which I have the greatest reason to expect from you. I

[36] Orderly Book of the American Army, Aug. 21-Dec. 31, 1777, N. Y. H. S.

[37] Those who contrasted the quiet of the popular English play of the World War, *Journey's End*, with the uproar of the American contemporary, *What Price Glory* will be interested to know that noise in our army is traditional. There is a reflection of a perfect *What Price Glory* scene in Gates' General Order in the same Orderly Book: "Pickets and advance guards of the army complain that there is such a noise and disturbance and games from 8 until 11 at night that there is no possibility of hearing, or of being alarmed by the approach of any of the enemy during that period."

[38] Original letter, Gates Papers, Box VII, N. Y. H. S.

[39] Original letter, *ibid.*

should have asked it when at the camp, but the thought of a possibility of a public refusal prevented me.

The above will be esteemed as a favor done, Sir,

Your most obedient servant,

WALTER BUTLER, En:

8th or the Kings Reg't.

It is evident from this that, even after the reprieve, the Judge Advocate was puzzled as to what law of war applied to recruiting under a flag of truce. Butler had evidently been taken before Gates and the Butler pride kept him from asking to be spared the degredation of the Albany jail. Apparently Gates made no answer to the letter, although the captured English officers in Burgoyne's Army were well treated.

While Butler stayed in jail Haldimand was writing Lord Germaine on September 13:

Major [John] Butler's Rangers and the Indians have been constantly employed since the beginning of the campaign and have effected many good strokes. Scouts from this Province toward the enemy's frontiers have likewise been continuously employed and have rendered essential service . . . I shall signify His Majesty's approbation of Major and Captain Butler's conduct to them.[40]

Haldimand speaks of Captain Butler. The same week Butler signs himself "Ensign," but there always seems to have been confusion as to his rank.

On October 1, Butler wrote again to Gates:[41]

SIR: I beg you will pardon me in mentioning that from my close confinement and the discrepancies of the place, added to my situation, have greatly injured my health and depressed my Spirits. I therefore pray you will graciously consider me and grant me such release as your Benignity and goodness may point out — it would greatly relieve me were I indulged in being confined to a room in town, on giving security which could be demanded of me.

The multiplying of words or making declarations which I do not mean my Conscience and Honor forbids, but permit me to declare that the above will ever be gratefully and with thanks remembered.

[40] Haldimand Papers, B. 54, p. 155, Canadian Archives.
[41] Original letter, Gates Papers, N. Y. H. S.

The letter is written on the ordinary level of gentlemen's correspondence in the eighteenth century. It reached Gates about the time that he received word that Sir Henry Clinton had moved out of New York with 3,000 men and was threatening Putnam at Peekskill. The same day Burgoyne's army went on half rations, and Sir Henry Clinton, after burning Kingston, obligingly turned back to New York. But Gates had neither time nor inclination to listen to Walter Butler. All his time was taken up within his tent discussing the merits of the Revolution with one of Burgoyne's captured aids-de-camp.[42] Meanwhile Benedict Arnold, relieved of his command, but supported by the whole fighting element of the army and the brigade commanders, was pressing Burgoyne savagely into an inevitable surrender.

On the sixteenth of October Burgoyne signed the articles of his surrender. Hugh Hastings,[43] editor of the George Clinton Papers, says that that day "the civilized British enemy was superseded by the treacherous redskin and the merciless Tory." This was evidently also Trevelyan's view of it. The fact is that there is no evidence of a uniquely civilized warfare by Burgoyne or St. Leger, the British Regulars. It was all about the same; but, on the other hand, the British management of the war in northern New York was taken over by men who knew frontier and forest fighting, who were out to win the war, who would neither delude themselves that an army the size of Burgoyne's could be supplied, across such terrain as lay back of it, from a base two hundred and ten miles away, nor turn back from Kingston as Clinton did, or as Howe would have done. Trevelyan reminds us that "the Royal Army was attended by a train of loose women, mostly brought from Europe but, in part, recruited from the least reputable streets of certain American seaports." Camp followers were the custom of the time, but to bring them on a campaign of such physical difficulty seems more stupid than should have been expected from even Burgoyne, Howe, or Clinton.

[42] *The Revolutionary War*, p. 124.
[43] *Papers of George Clinton*, Vol. I, p. 161.

Trevelyan does not explain where Burgoyne had opportunity to recruit "in certain American seaports" but the point is a small one.[44]

The Butlers and Mason Bolton, the Niagara commander to whom Burgoyne's surrender left the prosecution of the war, were not so much merciless or "treacherous" as effective. We shall consider later what it would have meant to the American cause if the surrender of Burgoyne had brought peace to northern New York, and Washington could unmolested have supplied his army from the Mohawk granary.

On the day of Burgoyne's surrender the Claus-Johnson intrigue against the Butlers made another step forward. It was a good time. St. Leger was defeated and someone had to be blamed. The proud young Walter, with his evident contempt for the stodgy Claus, was not there to advise his conservative father. Claus wrote to Secretary Knox, at the War Office, in London,[45] that "Joseph [Brant] complained of being very scantily supplied by Col. Butler with ammunition." Butler thoroughly distrusted Brant's policy toward the Indians, and the fuss that London made over him may have been very irksome to one who knew him. The letter implies further that St. Leger's defeat was caused by his lack of artillery, which resulted from Butler's poor intelligence service. Knox is then reminded of the vast sums spent on the Indians by Butler for two years, and of a profit he "understands" Butler made from exchange, and concludes with the statement that "all the Rangers [Butler] can muster are not over 50."

But on November 6, came the long Claus letter[46] to Knox which in many ways is the most important piece of evidence in the history of the Butlers. In small part the letter has the following to say:

. . . My fifteen years Indian expenses, during which time I had a two

[44] It is all the more surprising that Burgoyne, to whom Marlborough's care for his communications on the march to the Danube and Blenheim must have been still the great textbook principle, should have acted in this infatuated way.
[45] New York Colonial Documents, Vol. VIII, p. 719.
[46] Ibid., p. 724.

years Indian war to manage and engage Indians against Indians did not amount to $\frac{1}{4}$ the sum of what I hear Mr. Butler's expenses do within the two years and that expended merely *to keep the Indians inactive* [47] contrary to their inclinations.

Claus had been at London while Butler was at Niagara and Guy Johnson and he plainly wanted the support of Secretary Knox against Guy Carleton and Butler. It is certainly plain from this letter that the Johnson Dynasty wanted the Indians let loose, a policy which had generally been charged against Butler, and that Butler spent great sums in maintaining at once their allegiance and their inactivity. The letter continues

It is the opinion of severall that had I not appeared at the expedition and Joseph [Brant] acted so indefatigably and cleverly with his party as to cause an emulation, the Six Nations would not have been encouraged to act, when the rebels advanced upon us, by Col. Butler. Joseph since his arrival from England has showed himself the most faithful and zealous subject his Majesty can have in America in Indian matters and deserves to be noticed as such.

The Butlers have been accused of pride and arrogance, but none of their letters has the unctuous self-praise of this Claus letter. "The Six Nations would not have been encouraged to act by Colonel Butler" surely means, considering the situation, that he would have been a traitor if it had not been for

Joseph [who, Claus continues], is perfectly acquainted with Mr. Butler's sentiments and conduct and disapproved of them; for which the latter dislikes him. I have fully wrote him and given him my opinion and sentiments how to act with the Six Nations and I am persuaded he will carry his point and bring them to action before Colonel Butler gets among them, they having partly engaged to me before I left Oswego to do so and be revenged upon the rebels. The Six Nations say our hatchet is dull on account of being restrained these two years from acting against the rebels.

This is indeed high intrigue. Butler acting under orders from Guy Carleton has restrained the Indians for two years. It is apparently his intention so to continue. He has seen their

[47] Author's italics.

utter instability at Oriskany against what Trevelyan would call
"grown men." Now with the connivance of Londoners who
had never seen any Indian but Brant who was a *cri* there,
painted by Romney, Major Butler's influence is to be secretly
undermined and the savages are to be incited to revenge. It
is a pretty business and the telling of it by Claus an oily
villainy. The Johnson Dynasty had taken Brant into itself,
though some said he was there by right of blood, certainly by
informal family connection. The Butlers plainly did not consider him as good as they were, and distrusted him into the
bargain. But the Butlers' "less luck" was out. The Johnsons
lost their lands, for which they were well compensated, and
young Butler his life. We shall hear more of the intrigue the
next winter.

Meanwhile the Albany imprisonment went on. We know no
details, but there is an entry in the Tryon County Minute
Book [48] for December 7th as follows:

Mrs. Butler, mother of Walter Butler, having through Mr. Yates
applied for leave to speak to her son in a private room and farther
that he might be confined therein, Resolved that as Mr. Butler was
made a prisoner by the Army of the United States that this Committee
cannot consistently grant Mrs. Butler's request.

Mrs. Butler was then forty-two. Her part in these troubled
years is a silent one. Her husband, the Major, had probably
slipped one of his runners through the lines into Albany. She
probably wanted to tell Walter what his father suggested as
to escape. Or it may have been that she wanted to see him alone
to hear of his sufferings in the jail. We have none of her
letters. Lady Johnson's and Molly Brant's are preserved, but
Catherine Butler was reticent like her husband and her son.
But a runner may have gone off to Major Butler, at Niagara,
that night with word that she had failed to see their son and
that some other method of communication must be found.

The next day, December 8, Schuyler himself interceded with
Gates, the Army Commander, for Walter Butler. He wrote:[49]

[48] Tryon County Minute Book, Schuyler Papers, N. Y. P. L., 879.
[49] Original letter, Gates Papers, N. Y. H. S.

Sir: I have received an application from young Butler couched in the most pathetic terms for release from his confinement, and begging my intervention in his favor. That he might be considered as a spy I never doubted and that he deserved to be put to death in consequence was certain but, as you have so happily terminated the campaign in this quarter, and that you can put it out of his power to do any dis-service to the public, I wish you would release him on parole or security which I believe he can find. Ten Broeck who was his fellow prisoner and in the same predicament may also on the same principles be entitled to your clemency, and I wish you to confer it.

As so often happens, Butler's letter to Schuyler is not found but there is no reason to doubt that the "discrepancies" of the Albany jail had affected his health and strength.

On the tenth there is an entry in the Tryon County Minute Book for the Albany Committee Chamber which reads, "General Gates having sent to this board a letter from General Schuyler recommending the liberation of Walter Butler and Peter Ten Broeck upon proper security and requesting the opinion of the Committee ordered thereupon that a letter be prepared to General Gates which was done in following words, to wit. . . ." [50] The letter is not given. It would be wonderful to know what they said.

Ten days later Guy Carleton signed a commission for Walter Butler to be a captain of the Corps of Rangers. The original of the commission is in the New York Public Library and is evidently the one taken from his body when he was killed at Canada Creek four years later. It is made out to "W. Butler, Esq., Captain in a Corps of Rangers to serve with the Indians during the Rebellion" signed by Sir Guy Carleton and Le Maitre, the aide-de-camp.[51]

On January 5, 1778, Butler wrote again to Schuyler asking to be paroled or exchanged. The letter is listed in the Schuyler calendar but is again marked missing.

He was allowed to live in a house in Albany about the twenty-sixth of February, but was not immediately transferred,

for he wrote on the twenty-seventh to Schuyler; "embraces
the first opportunity to offer his thanks to General Schuyler for
his generous assistance in procuring his enlargement from a
disagreeable prison." [52] This letter bears on the pleasant legend that Lafayette, who was then in Albany waiting to lead
an expedition against Canada, "was so impressed by him that
he secured his release." The story is given in most histories.
Unfortunately, for it would be delightful to have it true, there
seems to be no authority for it. [53] We do not know the condi-
tion of his transfer. From the above letters it would seem that
he gave a parole. If so, he broke it when he escaped and yet,
if that could be held against him, it seems incredible that his
detractors could have overlooked it.

At any rate he was transferred to some private house, and
Stone says [54] his hosts were Tories at heart. We have no
information about them. It is said that he succeeded in getting
his sentinel drunk and that a horse was awaiting him outside.
We know little. It was Saturday night and the high Albany
streets were probably full of burghers and their wives, whiffing
the first spring in the April night, gossiping about the smallpox that was like a cordon to the south across Westchester
and Connecticut. It is always difficult to remember that the
escapes and hurried journeys of history were made by living
men, not by dead figures from the past, that, as Walter Butler
stepped out of the house past the drunken sentinel, his heart
must have been hammering with the tension; he must have
wondered whether he could possibly get through. If they
caught him they would certainly bring him back to a firing
party. He was well known in the town. As he passed each knot
of gossips he must have wondered whether someone would
not recognize him and cry for the patrol.

In the British Museum there is the following original letter
from Walter Butler which appears to deal with the circum-

[52] Calendar of the Schuyler Papers, N. Y. P. L. Letter missing.
[53] It is not mentioned in Charlemagne Tower's *Lafayette in the Revolution*,
and Brand Whitlock, the biographer of Lafayette, wrote the present author that
in his entire research he had found no mention of it.
[54] W. L. Stone, *Life of Joseph Brant* (New York, 1838), Vol. I, p. 369.

stances of his imprisonment in Albany from August, 1777 till April 21, 1778. The date, as will be seen from the photostat, is 27th August, 1779.

Ranger's Barracks
27th August, 1779

HONOURED SIR,

Herewith you have a State[ment?] of Captain Ten Brock's conduct and the opinion of the Officers of the Corps thereon.

This behaviour of Captain Ten Brock's answers to his conduct when I came off. He then was confined in the same room as me in a better state of health than I ever knew him, at least much better than myself. He told me that he did not think we could succeed in making our escape and as he was not under sentence of Death like myself he would therefore wait and see whether he could not get exchanged. I told him in our situation I would not give my advice, but for my own part I was determined to make an attempt as my case was desperate. I at the same time told him that he was much more capable than myself to undertake the journey, and added that as his brothers and General Ten Brock had declared he should never have leave to join the Royal Army again he had very little prospect of having an exchange, therefore this was the only opportunity he ever would have again to effect escape. Still as matters stood he must judge for himself.

These matters I made you acquainted with on my meeting with you in the Indian Country last spring and in consequence thereof you empowered me to request Colonel Bolton would not fill the then vacant Company in favour of Captain Ten Brock, but on my arrival at Niagara I found the Company filled in his favour and as having no desire to injure him or any other man living, after having done my Duty have never moved the matter since.

I am, honoured Sir, Your dutiful and obedient Son,

WALTER BUTLER

Major John Butler

It is plain from the events of August, 1779, when the Sullivan Expedition was burning western New York, that the date of this letter must be an error. The battle of Newtown, between Sullivan's Army and the Loyalists and Indians under John Butler was fought on August 29, 1779. In a later chapter we shall quote Colonel Butler's report on that action

Rangers Barracks 27 Sep.
1779

Honoured Sir,

        herewith you have a State
of Capt Ten Broecks Conduct and the
Opinion of the Officers of the Corps thereon
This behaviour of Capt Ten Broeck answers
to his Conduct when I came off. he then
was Confined in the same Room with
me, and in a better state of Health
than, I ever knew him; at least much
better than myself —
he told me he did not think we could succeed
in making our Escape, and as he was not
under Sentence of Death like myself, he
would therefore wait and see whether he
                     —
as having no answer to p.......................
other man living, after having done
my duty, have never moved the matter
Since —

        I am, Honour Sir,

            Your dutiful and Obed.t

               Son

               Walter Butler

LETTER FROM WALTER BUTLER TO HIS FATHER

dated at Shechquago, August 31. In that he says in part: "On
the 27th instant one of our scouts came in and informed us
that [the enemy] were upon their march toward us in great
Force. . . . As my attention was entirely taken up with the
Indians I left the command of the Rangers to Captain Butler."
We therefore place Walter Butler with his father in the field
at Newtown awaiting Sullivan's attack on the day in which it
would appear that he was writing him a letter from the
Rangers Barracks at Niagara. It is true that the place is
not given as Niagara, but in the general correspondence of
the period the term invariably refers to Niagara.

As there is ample evidence that Walter Butler was in the
Newtown action it is reasonable to suppose that the letter is
misdated by Walter himself, since, even if there were a
"Ranger's Barracks" to write from at Newtown, it is hardly
likely that he would write his father, who was with him, such
a letter on such a night. The mistake in the date of the year
is of course not uncommon though, except for Deygert's May
6th letter after Oriskany, there has been no other noted in the
documents used in this book.

The matter, however, is more interesting than the mere
correction of a date in that it refers to an hitherto unknown
meeting between Walter Butler and his father "in the Indian
country" in the spring of '78, since "last spring" in the letter
must mean '78 not '79. It seems to be definitely established
that Butler left Albany and made straight for Quebec. His
father was at Niagara and he saw him there in June. It seems
very likely, therefore, from the words "in the Indian country"
that there had been an earlier meeting, since, if it referred to
the June meeting, he would have said "here" or "at Niagara."

The explanation may be this: Mrs. Butler may have received
money, through her husband's messengers, to secure the horse
for her son's escape; Colonel Butler may have arranged to be
at a rendezvous "in the Indian Country" to meet him; Mrs.
Butler may have been the go-between, and even, for that matter, have had some help from the Yates family, in whose plot
in St. George's Churchyard some Butler children had already

been buried. It is a reasonable speculation. The Butlers, father and son, were probably deeply attached to each other, and the old warrior may well have been waiting in some Indian hut for word of his wife, of how she looked and what the young children said, and how Deborah was grown, and of how they went sledding with Eve Yates.

The letter of course exemplifies the great defect of Walter Butler's character, which Robert W. Chambers has so perfectly summed up:[55]

In practically every one of Walter Butler's letters he has some personal grievance to air, some personal motive to urge. Except for the stereotyped "His Majesty's Service" there never is a word of loftier intent, nothing of either provincial or national consciousness, nothing of any moral aspiration, no hint of vision — compare his letters with letters from our line officers and from the general officers in our forces, such men as Schuyler, Heath, Greene, Knox, Scammell, Willett, Gansevoort. Always it is himself and his family who dominate his thoughts, his own grievances, his personal and restless ambitions. There is scarcely a kind word for anybody else, never any generous praise, only a selfish and gloomy preoccupation.

It is true of them all, but in this case the picture of poor Ten Broeck of the Rangers shut up with the wildcat Walter Butler in a cold room, his patriot brothers, including General Ten Broeck, refusing to let him be exchanged, while Butler taunts him with his better health and little spirit, has a somewhat amusing malice about it. They were probably both suffering from influenza most of the winter, arguing between chills or coughing fits as to which was better able to make an escape. Ten Broeck was probably growing cold on Loyalism and the poor devil must have suffered agonies with Walter Butler haranguing him respecting a devotion that he no longer cherished. Probably one blanket meant more to him than all the Butlers of Butlersbury and their cursed Rangers. One can imagine Ten Broeck's brothers sending him food and Butler arguing with him about eating rebel pottage.

What a sigh of relief he must have breathed that April

[55] Mr. Chambers had not seen this letter when the comment was written.

night when Walter Butler dramatically tightened his belt, felt
for his money and dagger, cocked his hat, and slipped through
the door silent as a ghost except for the faint jingle of his
spurs.

He went north out of the city. He may have had a moment's
farewell with his mother. She may have secured the horse.
There is no record of how he got out of Albany, or across the
Adirondacks still deep in late winter snows, alone and un-
aided, or of where he abandoned his horse, or how he lived.
Albany was still full of officers and men from Burgoyne's
army and one hundred and forty men were still in the jail.
Albany was demoralized with "the disaffected robbing the
well affected." On April 21, 1778, Ab'm Yates, Jun., wrote [56]
the Governor "News we have none, except a Disagreeable
Tale about the escape of Mr. Butler, who went off, I thinck,
on Saturday night. Could He be got again it would be a Lucky
Circumstance but I am afraid it will not be the case."

It was not the case, until, when his warfare was accomplished, they brought his scalp back with triumph and rejoicing.

[56] *Papers of George Clinton*, Vol. III, p. 204.

CHAPTER VI

THE CALDRON IN THE HILLS, 1778

Seventeen seventy-eight was the year in which the Butlers did the evil that lived after them. The Wyoming action was July 3 and Cherry Valley on a November day of rain and snow.

The rout of St. Leger and the surrender of Burgoyne gave the North a false sense of security. A royal army had surrendered to an embattled countryside. The threat of organized invasion was over and Lafayette was in Albany to head a great counter attack on Canada. Loyalists and Indians had both retreated from Fort Stanwix in confusion. The worst appeared to be over. A certain amount of sacrifice was still necessary for the patriot cause, but it had to do mainly with crops and cattle for Washington's army starving at Valley Forge. Such was the public feeling. But leaders like Schuyler knew the end was not yet; that if England herself could not invade again, the Loyalist corps at Niagara would still strike back, actually fighting for their homes and families. It must be remembered that the Loyalists who had gone to Canada to enlist were in most cases not accompanied by their families. It would have been almost impossible to get women and young children in any numbers through the forest belt west of Stanwix, unless under the protection of large forces, unharried and unpursued. Many individual women and children did get through; but the majority were necessarily in the Tryon and Schoharie hills at the mercy of their hostile neighbors. To understand the situation of these women and children it must be remembered that they were human beings, susceptible to fatigue, terror, and despair, like all refugees from war. Kirby, the Loyalist historian, puts the case quietly enough when he says [1] "multitudes of Loyalists were driven from their homes. They took to the woods and, after enduring all sorts of hardships and sufferings, arrived at Fort Niagara where they found refuge and defence from their implacable persecutors." These persecutors were not Washington or Schuyler or Allan McLane or Hamilton, but an illiterate and brutalized mob to whom their grief and suffering were a delight.

During the winter of '77-78, while Walter Butler was a prisoner in Albany, Washington's army was at Valley Forge. It was also the winter of the French alliance, signed in February, word of which did not reach Valley Forge until May 5. Butler's escape in April was across Champlain to the St. Lawrence, to Quebec and back to Niagara, to a captaincy in the Rangers; probably no other escape of the war gave equal evidence of one man's self-sufficiency. It is equalled only in the romantic tales of G. A. Henty, which so beguiled our boyhood.

On February 4 the French Cabinet decided on the alliance. [2] The next day Schuyler, thousands of miles away, wrote Congress [3] that he regretted he could not get the details of another treaty that was brewing at Niagara with the Indians, but that large presents were given them in compensation for the losses at Oriskany, and that the Onondagas had "declared against us." Four days later he wrote again

You will observe from the inclosed letter of Mr. Deane the interpreter that our opinion of the temper of the Senecas and Cayugas was but too well founded. These haughty nations cannot brook the disgraces which they sustained from the militia of Tryon County. . . . Their resentment has undoubtedly been highly irritated by the insidious acts and bribes of our enemies who, at a treaty held at Niagara, and which is just concluded, have had an opportunity to give an edge to their animosity. The Onondagas, we are apprehensive, will also be drawn in to manifest the same hostile disposition. From these unfavorable circumstances there is too much reason to believe that an expedition will be formed against the Western frontiers, of this State, Virginia and Pennsylvania . . . it is

[1] *Annals of Niagara*, p. 52.   [2] *The War of Independence*, p. 494.
[3] Original letters, Draper Notes 15S, p. 60.

our opinion that vigorous preparations ought to be made not only to defend the frontiers but to chastise those nations by carrying the war, if possible, into their country. Till they feel the power and the just resentment of the United States, there can be no safety for the defenceless inhabitants.

The Intelligence Section of the northern staff was well served. The whole Loyalist plan for the year 1778 lies in the sentence "an expedition will be formed against the frontiers of this state, Virginia and Pennsylvania." But all the spring nothing was done except to strengthen the forts and build one at Cherry Valley. Unpreparedness was the northern war policy. The punitive expedition recommended by Schuyler came eighteen months later.

On March 12 Guy Johnson [4] was at British Headquarters in New York and wrote Lord George Germaine from there that a runner had gotten through to him with despatches "from Colonel Bolton, commanding at Niagara and my deputy Mr. Butler." The despatches are a corroboration of the intelligence that had reached Schuyler. A phantom corps was massing at Niagara. Johnson observes that

Indians with small bodies of troops are often exposed to what appears to them as very discouraging difficulties; in which cases they cannot be expected to keep together like British troops nor can they ever do so after the beginning of October because of the hunting season.

Two weeks later James Deane, Schuyler's secret agent, wrote him [5] that he had

received undoubted intelligence that Joseph Brand is gone with a very large belt of wampums to the seven tribes in Canada. He is sent to call those Indians to Oswego, where Col. Butler is to meet them with what force he can collect of Indians . . . and to take part as soon as the season will permit.

Those responsible for the protection of the frontiers could scarcely have had fuller warning. On April 4 Benjamin Dickson wrote Schuyler that two friendly Indians had warned the

[4] Letter quoted in Ketchum's *History of Buffalo* (Buffalo, 1864), p. 300.
[5] Draper Scrapbooks, 15S, p. 65. The original letter was copied by Draper, "in the Rolls Office, Dept. of State," in Washington in 1860.

Cherry Valley inhabitants, and adjacent settlements, to remove from their habitations if they wished to escape danger as the enemy would be there in four weeks from March 28. "About 1500 Tories and Indians are assembled at Unadilla on the Susquehanna about forty miles of Cherry Valley."

Governor Clinton, in Albany, was seriously alarmed at the threatening news and more so that the Continental regiments were being ordered south, "Warren's regiment at Albany and Gansevoort's at Fort Schuyler excepted." He wrote General McDougall on April 18 that "the large stores of every kind which we have there and our extensive frontiers will lay much exposed not only to the common enemy who, if they should be joined by any of the Indian tribes, and the contrary is no way certain, will be too formidable for the militia to resist." [6]

We had observed that Washington, while giving his attention to the British main army, thought also of the frontiers and the grand strategy. But he expected the states to fight with their own militia for their frontiers, willing though he was to have a Continental staff aid them. He wisely refused to divide his own bayonet strength for this purpose and he was particularly critical of New York, as we shall see, for expecting it. Spring was at hand. Howe, with forces numbering 19,530,[7] would shortly move out of Philadelphia to give him battle, and Washington, with 11,800 men, weakened by the winter at Valley Forge, intended to have every Continental possible to face them, Gates, Putnam, and Governor Clinton notwithstanding.

No great army could come out of Niagara to strike Tryon and the Susquehanna. But the fact was that the Palatine militia, which with difficulty had been led to Oriskany instead of the harvest fields the previous summer, had no stomach to face any invasion. The reckless frontier tang of Boone and Morgan and Clark was not in their blood.

Hugh Hastings, the editor of the Clinton Papers, titles a deposition of April 17, 1778:

[6] *Papers of George Clinton*, Vol. III, p. 186.
[7] Ft. Greene, *The Revolutionary War*, p. 139.

The Wyoming Massacre Evidence to show it was planned as far back as February, 1778.

Of course it was not as a massacre but as a campaign to destroy and lay waste the country as a war measure, and to draw off Continentals for its protection. It was no "Tory and Indian Plot," as he calls it, but a well-planned campaign. If the Tryon-Susquehanna frontier could be continually distressed it meant a much less effective opposition to Sir William Howe. The crops of those valleys must be destroyed or carried off. A terrific problem in rations was facing the Canadian command. Niagara was not jammed yet with Indians and refugees as it was to be, but, to quote Haldimand's own words, "Every ounce of provisions they and we have consumed for the last eighteen months had been brought from England and transported not only to Niagara but to Detroit and numerous other posts in the interior." It is well to remember that the Rangers and the whole Niagara command were in what they conceived to be a death-struggle. It is absurd to suppose that the campaigns of '78 were undertaken to appease Walter Butler's desire for revenge. They were undertaken because the Continental Army had captured Burgoyne, rolled St. Leger back, all but ruined Howe at Germantown, and was grooming itself for "the Canadays."

Charles Smith, a Tory wrote Walter Butler on July 27, 1778 — and Governor Clinton captured the letter — that it was difficult to get recruits. "Men are struck with tarror, the Northern Army, I understand, having given them a sad stroke."

In Albany they were already busy with subscriptions for a statue of Honikol Herkimer; a Thomas Palmer was besieging the governor with demands for an export license for corn, and another man was disturbed because the barter of flour and salt was not better organized. But the whole frontier was writing in for help against the storm gathering in the West.

James Deane, the secret agent, wrote Schuyler again in May that the Oneidas, hitherto friendly to the patriot cause,

had gone to a council with "Mr. Butler and the Senecas at
Kanadasege. . . . I have not been able to procure any more
warriors to join Gen. Washington. Their apprehensions of
danger is such that they think it their duty to stay and protect
their women and children."

They were brewing strong medicine at Niagara, and at
great cost. Colonel Mason Bolton, the commandant, wrote
in the black despair over money matters that had characterized
the Crown's disbursing officers for thirty years:

I have drawn a bill of £14760-9-5 [nearly $74,000] on account of
sundries furnished Indians by Major Butler. Between us I am heartily
sick of bills and accounts and if the other posts are as expensive to govern
as this has been I think old England had done much better in letting the
savages take possession of them than to have put herself to half the enormous sums She has been at in keeping them.

They had been criticizing John Butler, and all the deputies,
for many years for their extravagances with the Indians, but
no one had found a cheaper way of securing their loyalty.

Walter Butler was meanwhile at Quebec resting and refit-
ting from the ardors of his escape. Claus, who was leading the
intrigue against Walter Butler and his father, wrote in great
disgust to Sir John Johnson:

Young Butler attends at Headquarters constantly though I cannot
perceive that there is any great notice taken of him; he says he wants
orders before he can proceed up the country. I should be sorry his flight
should occasion the death of any of our poor friends.[8]

There never seems to have been a time when the Johnson
Dynasty was too busy to write to each other, or their superiors,
about the Butlers and almost always to their derogation. This
letter is one of many overlooked by historians who speak of
the Johnsons and Butlers as though they were one. The Johnsons evidently had other friends whose safety was much more
valued than young Butler's. Apparently the Butlers countered
by never mentioning them. What Walter Butler said at his
trial about not knowing Colonel Weston or Fort Dayton

8 Claus Papers, Vol. II, p. 45.

accorded with his persistent attitude toward the Claus-Johnson whispering campaign. There is no doubt he did attend at G. H. Q. He had a very exalted, but not wholly unmerited, view of his own abilities and was extremely impatient of being ranked by seniority rather than merit. But anyone who could come alone across the Adirondacks, as he did, must have brought along military intelligence of great value, and his attendance may well have been at Carleton's orders.

By June 4, however, Walter Butler had gone from Quebec to Niagara, seen his father, and come back with information and many wants. Upon his return he wrote out in a beautifully concise *aide-memoire* what was to do. It is in the British Museum and reads as follows:

> Quebec
> 4th June, 1778
>
> Captain Butler is directed by Major Butler, Commandant of the Rangers and Deputy of the Indian Forces to communicate to His Excellency Sir Guy Carleton K.B. etc, that after the meeting with the Warriors of the Five Nations at Condassagoe he intends to proceed with them to the Banks of the Susquehana River to a place called Yondegalah (where he will be near the Frontiers of New York, Pennsylvania, and Jersey and have it in his power to supply his Corps and the Indians with provisions from the enemy) from whence it is his intention to fall on the enemy with the whole body of his Corps and the Warriors of the five Nations, and on such part of the New York Province as he finds the most likely he will be able to effect joining Sir Harry Clinton K.B. etc. and that in the meantime he will break up the back settlements of Pennsylvania and Jersey and the other parts of the Province of New York in order as it will distract the enemy; as to draw their attention from his main purpose. Major Butler is so happy to find the body of the five Nations and the Seneca in particular well effected to His Majesty's Government and desirous to contribute every assistance in their power to support his Armies in America.
>
> They declare their wounds to be as fresh as when acquired at Fort Handiver the last campaign, and they are determined to act with spirit in the present.
>
> The expenses of the Indian Department from the time of Major Butler joining Lt. Col. St. Leger and meeting Col. Claus at Oswego in the Summer 1776, then returning to the said place, were not included

in any Accounts of Major Butler or drawn for by him but in Col. Claus's. As to any money drawn for by Captain Tice Major Butler is quite ignorant of the intention for which it was drawn, or the use to which it was applied; excepting about £100 value given by Captain Tice to Indians at Niagara on his arrival through the Country from New York in 1776. The Indians to whom given Major Butler had rewarded sufficiently in his opinion for any services they had done. And had Captain Tice thought proper to have pointed out their deserts Major Butler, with the consent of the Commanding Officer, would have paid them proper attention. Captain Tice declared to Col. Butler that Sir William Howe had given him the Rank of Captain in his Army with the pay of 10/ per day and that he did not consider himself as belonging to this part of the Department and expected further no pay from Major Butler as Deputy Superintendant, therefore he was not returned in Major Butler's list of Indians Officers to his Excellency and not considered as an officer in his part of the Indian Department.

A company of Rangers filled with Canadians, Major Butler is of opinion, would in some measure remove from the minds of the Indians any ill suspicion they may entertain of the French.

The Rangers who have joined the Corps are nearly destitute of clothing and necessaries and having no Bounty allowed them confirmed by the General they being obliged to buy their own Arms brings them greatly in debt and subjects Major Butler to many losses either by their being killed or by natural Death.

The expenses of the Officers of the Rangers are obliged to be [illegible] in their present rout in hireing Horses, etc. to carry necessary things through Inland Country they may want, renders Butt and Forrage money necessary.

The Officers of the Indian Department having no Commissions or, in fact, anything to them, they act by authority, while if taken by the enemy will be considered in no other or better light than as Public Murderers and Highwaymen and treated as such.

A small Brass Gun could be of great service to Major Butler to dislodge the enemy from any House they may get in to. The Corps of the Rangers are much in wanting of a good Adjutant and Quarter Master.

The above is what I can at present recollect was mentioned to me by Major Butler to communicate to his Excellency Sir Guy Carleton, K.B. etc.

WALTER BUTLER
Captain of the Corps of Rangers

This is a singularly concise and effective memorandum, with its confirmation, from the other side, of Deane's report to Schuyler of the council fire at Canadasagoe, and its vivid threat "to break up the back settlements of Pennsylvania and Jersey." The question about Captain Tice's pay is to occur through most of the correspondence of the next eighteen months; and there is the question of the "small Brass Gun" or grasshopper which the Butlers always wanted but never got, although Sir John brought one on his invasion in '80.

The most important paragraph, however, is in regard to commissions for officers of the Indian Department. There was probably a clean-cut recollection of the "taking" at German Flats, and of threats to treat Tory officers as murderers if captured. In the Tryon County Minute for 1775 it is "resolved if in case Colonel Butler with his company or some of them should be taken up and found guilty they should be sent to the Provincial Congress as suspicious enemies to our country and its Borders to be then and there examined and tried." They were specifically not prisoners of war; and this resolution was never repealed. Hare, of the Rangers, was executed the next year to the grief of them all. The issue here is not clear. While Butler was a prisoner in Albany, Carleton signed a commission for him to be made a Captain of the Rangers, and John Butler was an officer of the Indian Department. Technically the situation was probably similar to what would happen if police officers in their own uniforms, instead of official army uniforms, took part in a war. Under the laws of war they might be liable to death as partisan irregulars. Guy Johnson in a letter of March, previously quoted, refers to John Butler as "my deputy, Mr. Butler," rather than as Major Butler, and it is probable that none of the Johnson Dynasty wanted the Butlers to be appointed to the army where the military channel was from Mason Bolton to Sir Guy Carleton or Haldimand, but kept as Indian officers under Guy Johnson, the Superintendant.

The whole Butler-Johnson-Claus relationship, which historians have referred to as friendly and intimate, is illuminated

with a different ray if we realize that the Butlers never
mention the Johnsons in their letters, and the Johnsons never
mention the Butlers, except to belittle or conspire against
them. The "friendship" was actually a feud. Its history is lost,
but it appears likely that the Dynasty composed of infinitely
smaller men than John Butler, and infinitely less brilliant
ones than Walter, saw their own overlordship of the Valley
and the superintendencies lost if these two enormously re-
sourceful and capable Butlers gained direct access to the Commander in Chief. It is obvious that Claus greatly preferred
to have Walter Butler stay in Albany, a prisoner. There is no
question of the value to the King's arms of this dashing young
officer, but only the question of Claus's preference. This jealousy was probably an old matter. Sir William, though for
family reasons he had made Guy Johnson his first deputy and
was succeeded by him, chose John Butler time and again
for the important missions, and the second generation must
have whispered together many a winter night at Johnson Hall
about the growing importance of Butler. This was their long-
awaited inning.

The day after Walter Butler drew up his memorandum at
Quebec, Colonel Jacob Klock at Palatine, New York, wrote
Governor Clinton that militia should be moved toward Cherry
Valley which was being threatened by Brant's movements. He
added that a force should move on Unadilla "drive the enemy
from thence and destroy the place," that it had always been
and still continues to be a common receptacle for all rascally
Tories and runaway negroes. Unadilla was on the Susquehanna River a little north of west from Kingston, New York,
a God-forsaken place, the rendezvous of criminals and deserters from both armies. It provided a base throughout the war
for the most murderous and partisan raiding. Even guerillas
must have a base of action and it was never wholly destroyed.
The same day Major Campbell wrote that Brant was "20
miles away, 700 head of cattle are feeding in a circumference
of ¾ of a mile at Cherry Valley." [9] So the warnings came but,

[9] *Papers of George Clinton*, Vol. III, p. 408.

as we shall see, they had been calling wolf from Cherry Valley for twenty years. Certainly the plan of Loyalist campaign was an open book.

Up to this time and on till November we hear nothing of Tory atrocities. Governor Clinton received a letter [10] June 8 from a man saying that Tory troops "took his grain and plundered his house and destroyed his furniture, broke his dores and windows and killed his hogs." but there is no mention of injury to women and children.

James Deane reported again, on the fifteenth of June, that the burden of the Kanadasaga council fire was to bring the Senecas into action, and that John Butler had been successful in collecting a considerable party "to join Joseph Brant upon the frontiers of this country." That was Monday night. On Wednesday, the seventeenth of June, Sir Henry Clinton, it will be remembered, evacuated Philadelphia, and started for New York with his column twelve miles long.

John Graves Simcoe, the Loyalist cavalry officer, later to be first governor of Upper Canada, was with him. Riddell, his biographer, states [11]

that it seemed to Simcoe likely that the British Army would leave America and the war be carried on in the West Indies; he accordingly applied for permission with his corps and other loyalists, to join Colonel John Butler who, with Rangers and Indians, was busy on the upper parts of the Delaware.

It was a particular mercy of Providence to the United States of America that the plan failed. The combined military vigor of Simcoe and the Butlers might well have driven the frontiers into a line running from Schenectady to Easton, Pennsylvania. They might not have held it permanently, or against the Continentals, but a success then would have unsettled Washington's whole western plan. It would have cut his communications with Lachlan McIntosh at Fort Pitt, and thus with George Rogers Clark. His army would have been weakened by having to face Clinton in front and Butler-Simcoe in the rear.

[10] *Ibid.*, p. 425.
[11] W. R. Riddell, *Life of John Graves Simcoe* (Toronto, 1926), p. 58.

As Clinton moved out of Philadelphia the whole Continental Army was put in motion, Washington eager to find the enemy and give him battle. Six brigades under Lee and Wayne filed off the same afternoon and the headquarters staff itself was out of Valley Forge at five the next morning. They were no ragged commandos, either, but a disciplined, hard-bitten army, singing to the cadence of marching feet, like all good infantry. They were at Coryell's Ferry of the Delaware on the twenty-first of June, roughly even with the British column, though north of it.

Communication with Governor Clinton, then at Pough-keepsie, was well maintained from General Headquarters, and there must have been tremendous excitement there as the expresses came in through the dust of a tropic hot wave. It was one hundred degrees at Monmouth. Few people then realized that weather comes from the west and that the fierce, dry heat that gripped the whole eastern seaboard had, a day or so before, burned the Mississippi Valley, which few men had ever seen, wilted Clark before Kaskaskia in Illinois, and made a furnace of Pittsburgh where Lachlan McIntosh, who later, in a duel, killed Button Gwinnett, a signer of the Declaration, had just succeeded Hand.

Each express from the South brought word that Washington racing Clinton to New Brunswick was gaining on him. Clinton, with eight miles less to go and several hours start, was slowing down as the Jersey militia broke down the bridges and Maxwell's brigade snapped at his flanks. Burgoyne had surrendered the previous fall and the whole country was set for Clinton's capitulation.

Little attention was paid in Albany or Poughkeepsie on the twenty-second to word from Klock, at Canajoharie, that Tryon was experiencing again "the cruelty of a restless enemy," that the settlements at Lake Otsego, between Cherry Valley and Cooperstown, were harried, eight men killed and fourteen carried away. Bigger game was afoot, and they were not greatly concerned that "Brandt boasted openly that he will be

joined at Unatelly by Buttler and that within eight days he
will return and lay the whole country waste."

An express came in that day from Gates to Governor Clinton with an excerpt from Washington's dispatch of the twentieth saying that Lee, with ten brigades, would cross the
Delaware that night and that Washington would "enter the
Jerseys tomorrow. By the last intelligence the enemy were
near Mount Holly."

Then, on the twenty-fourth of June, Clark in Illinois; Mc-
Intosh at Fort Pitt; Henry Laurens, President of Congress,
at Yorktown, disturbed that Burgoyne's captured standards
had never been brought to Congress; Washington at Hope-
well; Sir Henry Clinton ten miles east of Trenton; Butler,
near the Susquehanna's source: all must have paused from
arms and wars to watch the great cosmic drama of the sun's
total eclipse, visible that day throughout the theaters of the
war. But such things are soon forgotten and men's eyes turned
from the sky to the dusty roads of Jersey.

On the twenty-eighth Charles Lee, commanding the American advance, made leisurely contact with Clinton at Monmouth, behaved in inexplicable fashion, fell back in disorder
before Washington came up and lost the most marvelous
opportunity a soldier could desire to attack a marching column
impeded by baggage. The fruit of the whole winter's drilling
and organization was lost — but at least the Continental
Army was rid of Charles Lee. Washington's dispatch, dated
at Monmouth on the twenty-ninth, was forwarded by Gates to
Governor Clinton on the third of July to be received the following day.

The day before, unknown of course to the Governor, Butler
had struck Wyoming in the green heart of Pennsylvania.
Deane with his uncanny accuracy wrote General Schuyler from
Stanwix, on July 4, exactly what was happening:[12]

The Six Nations seem determined on a war with us. Forty warriors of
the Quiyaga tribe set out last week to attack the Frontiers of Pennsyl-

---

[12] Original letter, Library of Congress.

vania as I am informed by an Oneida Indian who saw them march out
of their castles . . . I have also an account which I believe may be
depended upon that Mr. Butler has lately been joined by a considerable
Body of Senecas and has marched to Tioga a place situated at the con-
fluence of the East and West Branch of the Susquehanna.

To understand the background of the Wyoming action it is
necessary to go back to the founding of that settlement in 1753
when, under a Connecticut charter, the Susquehanna Company
arranged to plant a colony there. The next year a James
Hamilton [13] wrote Sir William Johnson from Philadelphia
informing him that the unauthorized and disavowed (by Connecticut) settlement at Wyoming was bound to lead to "intes-
tine broils and endless disorders amongst us." The Connecticut
Yankees, however, made the settlement to the irritation of
the Pennsylvanians who regarded it as "unfair and illegal
encroachment." In 1762 two hundred Yankees came in and
built, and the next year the Six Nations came down, burned a
Delaware chief and let it be understood the settlers had done
it. The Delawares retaliated, killed thirty whites and the rest
fled.

Then in '68 the Pennsylvania proprietaries bought Wyoming directly from the Six Nations. The next year forty Yankees
came back and attacked the Pennsylvanians. A little war
started, scarcely larger than a hill-feud, known as the Yankee-
Pennamite War. The lawlessness, however, was so great that
General Gage was asked by Governor Penn, in 1770, to re-
store order with royal troops.

The Pennamites got the upper hand and were in control
until July 6, when seventy Yankees under Zebulon Butler besieged the fort, finally taking it on August 4 just as a relief
force came out from Philadelphia. This Zebulon Butler was
on the American side eight years later.

The little war went on until September 28, 1775, when the
"peaceful" place was attacked by Pennsylvania militia jealous
of the Connecticut prosperity. Men were killed and prisoners

---

[13] *Johnson Papers*, Vol. I, p. 396.

carried off. The Continental Congress distracted by the whole business called on both states to arbitrate.

With the coming of the Revolution, Lossing says,[14]

almost every original settler had espoused the cause of the Whigs. Interlopers, however, came in from the Hudson and Mohawk Valleys, exciting the indignation of the original settlers who, on the recommendation of the Congress, formed Committees of Vigilance to watch them. The newcomers were regarded as a colony of vipers. Several were arrested and sent to Connecticut.

The town then raised two companies of regulars which were attached to the Connecticut line. A Tory family, named Wintermoot, built a fort a little above the town and the justly suspicious settlers built one above it called Fort Jenkins. Loyalists from the neighborhood began to slip off to join John Butler. Others were banished to the Connecticut Mines, the prison at Simsbury, and the sinister terror and suspicion which so cruelly attends civil wars, religious wars, and witch-manias enveloped the valley. Sounds on the roads at night, heard through barred doors and windows, the hooded light in the field, were not friends or neighbors, but a man who lived in a lonely house in bitter loyalty to what cause no one knew. The little knot of men going north in the moonlight was a militia patrol going up the Susquehanna, or secret agents slipping out toward Niagara. There was something fearful in every footfall. The lone valley, pictured by so many as an Arcadia, was in reality a caldron in the hills boiling with greed and violence and fear.

The Loyalist war plan of '78 was definitely "to break up" the back settlements but, in doing this, there seems little doubt that the rescue of Loyalist families, not only of those men fighting in the Rangers, but of prisoners in Connecticut, was definitely intended. Kirby[15] states that "Butler proceeded to Wyoming with the main object of bringing in the families of the refugees to Niagara. Hundreds of women, old people and children had been left behind to the untender mercies of

---

[14] *Pictorial Field Book of the Revolution*, Vol. I, p. 347.
[15] William Kirby, *Annals of Niagara* (Lundy's Lane, 1896), p. 55.

the Rebels, and their rescue was ardently desired by the men at Niagara."

Though not the main object of the campaign it was an important factor. Every Loyalist foray had that as a subsidiary goal. It must be borne in mind that the Loyalists were not an alien crew of murderous wretches, but largely American-born men and women inevitably moved by love of their homes and children, filled with little plans and hopes not dissimilar to those of their patriot foes. No political bias is necessary to see that they came back to the Mohawk and the Susquehanna actually fighting for their homes and families like the Picardy regiments in 1918. This secondary purpose is corroborated constantly in the American archives themselves, Governor Clinton [16] writing May 29, 1780, at Fort George, with Sir John Johnson in rout before him:

They were much beat out and many of them lamed by their long march add to this they have taken with them much Plunder. Many women wives to Persons who formerly joined the enemy and their children, so that it is likely their march will be very slow and dilatory.

So much for the scene and the purpose of the action.

Eleven hundred men, red and white, came down the Susquehanna in canoes under Butler and camped, July 2, above Fort Jenkins. This is Lossing's figure. Richard Cartwright, escaped from the penalty of carousing in Albany, who was with the expedition gives the number as 574, of whom 110 were Rangers. Old Jelles Fonda wrote in his Journal,[17] July 2, twenty-eight years before, of a Council Fire near Stanwix with "Oneidas and Dascororas," and of how "Captain Butler sung the war song and threw the war belt but not one of the Oneidas stood up." This Captain Butler, now a Major, in his fifty-third year, seven years older than Washington, must have been of enormous vitality to come on this raid. The troops' hardships, and those of their leader, were of killing arduousness.

Lossing says "50 American Regulars opposed them" at

[16] *Papers of George Clinton*, Vol. V, p. 769.
[17] Original MSS of the Journal, N. Y. H. S.

Forty Fort, the lowest of the three forts. The Rangers took Fort Jenkins and occupied Wintermoot's without resistance. The Americans had appealed in vain to Washington for aid. It was Washington's wise and fixed policy not to undertake the defense of states or their frontiers. His duty was to face the British main army and his resources in men and materials were rarely sufficient for that. He believed in states' rights and equally in their obligations to defend themselves. However, some Wyoming men among the Continentals apparently did go back to meet the threat.

Forty Fort, the lowest of the three Wyoming posts, was under the joint command of Colonel Zebulon Butler and Colonel Denison. The Loyalists were at Wintermoot's. Forty Fort was full of refugees and a decision had to be made whether to receive the Loyalist attack there or go out to meet it. The country around was being laid waste by the Indians and John Butler sent in a flag to demand surrender. The Americans courageously decided to go out to fight. They made contact at Wintermoots in a short, sharp action at one o'clock, apparently outnumbered two to one by the Loyalists and Indians. John Butler had his left on Wintermoot's fort under his own command, Caldwell in the center and the Senecas on the right. The accounts of the battle are confusing, but it does appear that the Americans were commanded jointly by Denison and Zebulon Butler, with the inevitable disaster such dual control brings. The Loyalists extended their left and Denison, in endeavoring to change front under fire, a most difficult operation even for crack troops and highly skilled officers, appears to have been understood as ordering a retreat. There was a sudden break, the heart-chilling pause before flight, and the whole command gave way, some fleeing to Forty Fort, others to an island in the River and, according to Hildreth, "the surviving Continentals to avoid being taken embarked and escaped down the river."

Forty Fort was full of women and children, and Denison went bravely, if quite properly, back to defend them. Zebulon

Butler, with his wife on his horse behind him, deserted them and escaped to Wilkes-Barré. Butler was forty-seven years old, had fought in the French and Indian Wars, and the Havana expedition, and had been a colonel since March 13. It was his simple duty as an officer to go back to the Fort as Denison did.

Apparently the Rangers and Indians were on a great *battue* all night. No quarter was given. The witch, Catherine Montour, is alleged to have been there to spur the killing. Some relief reached the Fort during the night under John Franklin from Salem, and the next morning John Butler asked Denison to come to Wintermoot's to surrender, demanding also the surrender of the uxorious Zebulon Butler, then safe at Wilkes-Barré. The conditions of the surrender were agreed upon on July 4 as follows:[18]

1. That the inhabitants of the settlement lay down their arms and the garrisons be demolished.

2. That the inhabitants occupy their farms peaceably and the lives of the inhabitants be preserved entire and unhurt.

3. That the Continental Stores be delivered up.

4. That Major Butler will use his utmost influence that the private property of the inhabitants shall be preserved entire to them.

5. That the prisoners in Forty Fort be delivered up, and Samuel Finch, now in Major Butler's possession, be delivered up also.

6. That the property taken from the people called Tories, up the River, be made good and they to remain in peaceable possession of their farms, unmolested in a free trade in and throughout the state as far as lies in my power.

7. That the inhabitants that Colonel Denison now capitulates for, together with himself, do not take up arms during the present contest.

Before John Butler entered the Fort he ordered all liquor broken up to prevent the Indians getting it. He had been worrying about alcoholism in Indians for thirty years. Boyd, a British deserter, was found in the fort and executed by Butler's orders. No other lives were forfeited after the surrender.

---

[18] *Pictorial Field Book*, Vol. I, p. 358.

Colonel Denison [19] wrote to Jon[a] Trumbull on the twenty-eighth:

> At my return to the Fort foun that it was the minds of the grater part of the Peopl they present to capitulate with the enemy I went to there camp and was put to the disagreeable necessity of sineing the inclosed paper after which no person was hurt by the enemy untill after I left that plac the next day. I find that there is numbers of people in this state desire to take the advantage of our distressed situation to get Posesion of our settlement which things cannot be allowed.

There is nothing here condemnatory of the fighting methods of Butler's command, nor does it appear that the Whig Pennsylvanians were sympathetic to the point of forgetting the old land war. After the surrender it is said that the Indians broke over restraints and began to pillage the fort and the settlement the survivors finally fleeing in terror — many of them perishing in the panic-stricken flight. It does not appear that the Indians themselves killed any refugees after the surrender. That is not much to say. Driving them into a situation too difficult to be borne was terrible enough, and the shocked horror of two continents was the penalty, deserved or undeserved. Wyoming became a "massacre," worse in people's minds than the savage night attack of Grey's Redcoats on Wayne at Paoli. Perhaps half the infamy that has clouded the Butlers' name is from Wyoming. To the author it definitely seems undeserved considering the nature of war.

Campbell, a Scottish poet, wrote a long ballad of execration about it; certain writers have ignored the reasonable terms of surrender and quoted John Butler as telling Denison his terms were "the hatchet"; Brant is erroneously placed at the massacre and one of Draper's informants, faced with the fact of his absence replied: "He was here in spirit if not in person." [20] Lossing, by no means a friend of the Loyalists, says that survivors' accounts of the atrocities "were repeated everywhere in America and in Europe and remaining uncontradicted formed the material for the darkest chapter in the Revolution as

[19] Massachusetts Hist. Society, 2d Series, Vol. III, p. 342.
[20] Draper Collection, 4F, p. 200.

recorded by the earlier historians. No doubt the fugitives believed they were telling the truth." There are several books,
including Miner's *History of Wyoming*, with long accounts
of the massacres, and there is no reason to doubt that exaggeration and myth-making have gone into the story. An excellent example of this is an *Historical and Geographical Memoir
of the North American Continent and Its Nations and Tribes*,
published in Dublin, 1820,[21] which says:

> . . . of the butcheries perpetrated among the Colonists one in particular
> stained the British annals with indelible infamy. A band of 1600
> Indians and Royalists invaded the settlement at Wyoming . . . gaining
> possession of some forts by treacherous promises and of others by force,
> they put to death all the inhabitants of both sexes and every age, some
> thousands in number, enclosing some in buildings which they set on
> fire, and roasting others alive. They then maimed all the cattle and
> left them to expire in agonies.

Rupert Hughes [22] says, "even in John Marshall's time the
exaggeration of these tales of horrors was recognized in
the revision of his biography of Washington." John Butler
is portrayed as being refused knighthood for his conduct at
Wyoming [23] and Haldimand [24] as refusing to receive him. All
this is myth.

These appear to be the facts after the debacle of Denison's
troops at Wintermoot's fort. A savage pursuit of the fleeing
soldiers was prosecuted. Practically no quarter was given to
men in arms as has been the case in hundreds of actions, including those of the World War. That, after all, is a hazard of
war, however merciless it may seem. After the surrender Colonel Denison and Colonel John Franklin, who entered Forty
Fort with a relief party during the night, both agree that the
terms were lived up to and that John Butler exerted himself
to restrain the savages.[25]

There seems to have been reasonable quiet on the fourth,

[21] *Ibid.*, 4F, p. 215.
[22] *George Washington* (New York, 1930), Vol. II, p. 483.
[23] George Peck, *History of Wyoming* (New York, 1868), p. 97.
[24] Charles Miner, *History of Wyoming* (Philadelphia, 1845), p. 235-38.
[25] *Pictorial Field Book of the Revolution*, Vol. I, p. 285

after the surrender. None there knew it of course, but that day Kaskaskia, in Illinois, fell to the Virginians under George Rogers Clark. Denison was still there packing up and there must have been the usual lull after action, men smoking and cleaning rifles, sleeping, washing, gossiping, some doubtless claiming the old man was going east to strike Washington's flank, others with a rumor of a raid straight down to Philadelphia, some joined families who were to go off in the low-laden canoes to Tioga.

A runner apparently reached Major Butler on the fifth with word that a counterattack was forming to the southeast. He is said to have addressed his officers and Indians very earnestly, the latter in their own tongue, on their obligations under the surrender, and prepared then to fall back. He that day gave a warrant of immunity to Lieutenant Elisha Scovell and his company who had surrendered, promising that he and his people "shall live in quiet possession of their places with their families and shall be duly protected from insult." [26] The warrant is signed by John Butler and the Kayingwaurto, and sealed by the latter with the Totem of the Turtle Clan of the Seneca Nation. Appended to it is an inventory of 23 horses, 10 yoke of oxen, 9 sheep, 21 cows, and 28 hogs taken for his army.

The French fleet was off the Delaware capes on the eighth and, with that great news to break, Elias Boudinot, the all-around man of Washington's military family, wrote to Colonel Alexander Hamilton from Philadelphia,[27]

I am sorry to inform you that there is also intelligence of the settlement of Wyoming being cut off by Coll. Butler with about 1000 Indians, Tories and British troops. It is supposed that Carlisle will soon be the frontier of this State as the inhabitants are flying from all quarters.

Butler's forces reached Tioga, homeward bound, on the tenth, rested there four days and pushed on to Niagara accompanied by several Loyalist families from the Valley.[28] On the twelfth, while still at Tioga, John Butler wrote a report to

[26] *Papers of George Clinton*, Vol. III, p. 521.
[27] Charles Lee Papers, N. Y. H. S. *Collections*, 1871, Vol. II, 475.
[28] *Life and Letters of Richard Cartwright.*

Colonel Mason Bolton, commandant at Niagara, concluding it: "But what gives me the sincerest satisfaction is that I can, with great truth assure you that in the destruction of the settlement not a single person was hurt except such as were in arms, to these in truth the Indians gave no quarter."

Walter Butler was evidently still at Quebec, for Bolton, after getting this report, writes Le Maitre, the Adjutant there, in a postcript:[29] "I request you inform Capt. Butler of the Colonel's success."

Adam Crysler of the Rangers, who kept a diary[30] of his movements, laconically dismisses the whole campaign as follows: "In May 1778 I received Col. Butler's orders to come to Canatasagee; according I did and brought 19 men with me who are with Col. Butler's Rangers at present, at which time he made me Lieutenant; and from there I went under the command of Col. B. to Wyoming where we had an engagement with the rebels and killed 450; from there we went to Aughquagy." So the campaign ended.

In October Lord George Germaine wrote Sir Henry Clinton,[31] "I shall be glad to hear of the success of Colonel Butler in relieving and protecting His Majesty's faithful subjects on the back settlements in Pennsylvania." Clinton's report[32] was then on the way to him in the form of Major Butler's report to Lt. Colonel Bolton "which I received from General Haldimand a few days since, giving an account of the proceedings of the former upon the frontiers of Pennsylvania." That was September 15.

Germaine acknowledged it, November 4, from London. It is not hard to imagine that "uncomprehending" man sitting in Whitehall, the room acrid with the coal fire, the streets outside dark with fog and rain. The same day, D'Estaing with the French fleet, was moving out of Boston bound for Martinique and summer seas, and five thousand British soldiers

[29] Quoted in Miner's *History of Wyoming*, p. 253.
[30] Draper Collection, 14F, p. 12. Diary of Adam Crysler.
[31] Clements Collection, Sir Henry Clinton Papers, Dispatch No. 15.
[32] *Ibid.*, Dispatch No. 14.

were leaving New York for St. Lucia for the war in the West
Indies that Simcoe had foreseen. Germaine wrote,[33]

the success of Lt. Colonel Butler is distinguished for the few lives that
have been lost among the Rangers and Indians he commanded and for
his humanity in making those only his object who were in arms; and it
is much to the credit of the officers and Rangers of his Detachment that
they seem to partake of the spirit and perseverance which is common
to all the British officers and soldiers.

Germaine might have adverted to an effectiveness lacking at
Minden, when he, as Lord Sackville, did "not comprehend
how the movement [of the cavalry was] to be made." In all
the Royal and Continental posts there were letters about the
Butlers and few by them.

The Johnson Dynasty was at its malicious chatter too, Sir
John writing [34] Claus from Haldimand's headquarters, before
word came from Wyoming, that Haldimand

asked me yesterday what Butler would be about all this time; that he
thought he ought to strike a blow ere now. I told him I thought I
might venture to assure him that it was not his intention, that he would
remain where he was or thereabouts till he could join the army from
New York with safety or till it was too late to do anything.

How ceaselessly and mysteriously the Dynasty intrigued
against these Butlers!

The story of Wyoming comes to its last syllables in Sir
Henry Clinton's [35] *Historical Detail of the Seven Years' Campaigns in North America* where he appends Butler's report
and asks that it be weighed against the account "adopted by
all the writers on the American war for want of other information." He then deprecatingly concludes that he leaves judgment to others and himself has "only to lament the causes
which induced so much misery and Destruction to the human
Race."

Young Walter Butler, though, cried out bitterly against all
this in his famous letter written after Cherry Valley to Gen-

[33] *Ibid.*, Dispatch No. 16.   [34] *Story of Butler's Rangers*, p. 52.
[35] "An Historical Detail of Seven Years." MSS, Vol. I, p. 125.

eral James Clinton where he says, in his assured, hot-headed, but convincing way: "We deny any cruelties to have been committed at Wyoming either by whites or Indians; so far to the contrary that not a man, woman or child was hurt after the capitulation or a woman or child before it or after taken into captivity. Though should you call it Inhumanity the killing of men in arms in the field, we in that case plead guilty." [36]

[36] Original letter, Library of Congress.

When Klock wrote to Governor Clinton about Unadilla in June, 1778, he also said that "unless a body of troops is marched directly to Unadilla in order to drive the enemy from thence and destroy the place, the enemy will constantly make such depredations [from Unadilla] upon the settlements" that evacuation of the frontier would be the only remedy. On July 18 Brant sacked the little village of Andrustown, near the German Flats, where Walter Butler had been taken eleven months before. All Deane's warnings were being justified.

William Butler with some Pennsylvania troops, scarcely more than a posse, combing the Schoharie hills, picked up the discouraged Smith whose letter to Walter Butler had been captured. He was coming with a few Tories up the Hudson Valley to find the Loyalist bands who, with their red allies, were sifting through the forests of Tryon and Schoharie, with a pillar of fire behind them by night where the Palatine cabins were burning. Smith was killed and a Captain Long brought in his scalp.

Marinus Willett was chosen to lead the expedition against Unadilla but there was some indecision about it and the command went to William Butler who was an active and excellent officer. He was not related to the Loyalist Butlers, nor to Zebulon Butler one of the American commanders at Wyoming. He made war. There was a man named "Services, a noted villain"[1] and an uncle of Sir John Johnson,[2] who lived twenty-five miles from the Middle Fort and "who constantly supplied the enemy with necessaries." Butler sent out to get him. Services refused to surrender and was shot and killed. Caldwell

---

[1] *Papers of George Clinton*, Vol. III, p. 631.   [2] *Ibid.*, p. 505.

of the Rangers wrote John Butler, after the sack of the German Flats, "no word of Mrs. Butler, except that she was taken 3 weeks ago to Schenectady."

With Wyoming gone, Andrustown in ashes, and the German Flats to be struck next, it was plain that Cherry Valley would then be broken up. While John Butler was resting at Tioga, a prisoner,[3] Robert Jones, who was brought in from Brant's command, gave evidence that "Butler is not to come down to Minisink, as he understood from Brant, but was to go on an expedition against Cherry Valley . . . thinking it a favorable time for the purpose as he understood the times of the militia who guarded it is to expire next Friday."

Both sides were magnificently served by their scouts and spies. They seem to have been everywhere, one of Butler's evidently standing that same day at Henry Wisner's elbow, in Minisink, as he wrote Governor Clinton his astonishing letter:[4]

From a consideration of all these facts, evidencies, and circamstancies it apears to us not only necessary that a particular attention be paid to the present exigencies of our western affairs but also a well concerted plan either offensive or defensive be spedily put in execution for the safety and protection of our Frontiers. After we gained the intelligence by Capt. Cudebeck we thought best to dismis the whole of our regts. except one class from each company.

Surely the *non sequitur* has never had better illustration.

This sort of decision by the militia to go home, even, on one occasion, because it was raining, enraged Washington. He had written the previous year, deeply stirred, to the governors of New York and Massachustts, "It gives me inexpressible concern to have repeated information from the best authority that the committees of the different towns and districts in your state hire deserters from General Burgoyne's army and employ them as substitutes to excuse the personal service of the inhabitants." As Beard[5] says, "Masses of [the people] showed a remarkable affection for their homes and safety.

[3] *Papers of George Clinton*, Vol. III, p. 544.   [4] *Ibid.*, p. 539.
[5] *Rise of American Civilization*, Vol. I, p. 274.

By heroic efforts thirty or forty thousand privates out of
3,000,000 people could be kept in the field." James Duane
wrote Clinton "much more to be lamented is the unmanly
dread which our militia in general and the low Dutch more
especially entertain of these savages." [6]

The attack on Cherry Valley was not to be avoided by such
methods. Threats to that place of the lovely name were nothing new. Sir William Johnson, himself, had written Cadwallader Colden, April 28, 1764, "The inhabitants of Cherry
Valley are apprehensive that some sculking Indians may fall
upon Cherry Valley." [7] In November of '77 a German settler
wrote a long letter of warning to General Gates:

HONORABLE SIR: As we have sundry accounts that there is about
800 Tories and Indians embodied at Unadilla on the Susquehannah
River and they mean to take a stroke on our frontiers at Schohary and
others seize the Cherry Valley. . . . We have once before wrote your
Honor on this subject and now hopes you will take it under consideration and grant us speedy assistance by sending us a party of men to
assist us. . . . [8]

Then in March, '78, an appeal for aid was made to Lafayette
by the Cherry Valley Committee, James Wilson, Samuel
Campbell, and Samuel Clyde, "We are in dread every night
of being attacked." [9]

Finally Lafayette ordered a fort built there and the command of it was given a Colonel Alden. It was obviously a post
of danger and difficulty and the splendid Gansevoort, the de-
fender of Stanwix, sought the honor of its command. Through
stupidity in Albany, which left it practically defenceless, Gansevoort was refused the post. There is no question that had he
been in command the attack in November would have been
beaten off. Alden, little more a commander than the men who
appointed him, lost his life there, but with no particular credit
to himself, as we shall see.

[6] *Papers of George Clinton*, Vol. IV, p. 68.
[7] *Johnson Papers*, Vol. IV, p. 411.
[8] Original letters, Gates Papers, N. Y. H. S.
[9] *Papers of George Clinton*, Vol. III, p. 104.

Three times, at the end of May, expresses came into Albany from Klock at Canajoharie with warnings that the enemy was massing at Unadilla to strike Cherry Valley. But who cared for all that? Not even General Hand, back from Pittsburgh, to whom the last plea went on October 7.[10]

The Clinton Papers of these summer months are full of alarms and excursions. Much was afoot. The service of supply was at its eternal wrangle, the question of money pressed heavily on them, and there was also the very important question of civil peace. Indian and Loyalist raiding was a cause of incessant distress but it did not evoke, in all this time, accusations of atrocities against women and children. The destruction of property was enormous and, to a farmer who was losing home, barns, cattle, and crops, it may very well have seemed that life itself was lost. Schuyler wrote to Clinton[11] on July 20, "It is much to be lamented that the finest grain county in this state is on the point of being ruined," while Duane voiced the same fear, "the destruction of our western frontier is the destruction of our granary and will be severely felt.[12]

There is nothing here of atrocities, and, in fact, until Cherry Valley, there was no real complaint of them. But there was no civil peace. Governor Clinton wrote to Robert Livingston, July 22:[13] "I have myself taken great pains in concerting measures for apprehending the robbers who infest different parts of the country," and this is one of many letters. The state was full of bands of armed men who attacked lonely farmhouses or even small settlements, and it is not unlikely that many depredations laid to the Loyalist troops were the work of thieves.

The *Maryland Journal*, September 8, 1778, published a letter of August 9,[14] from Albany:

Robberies are rife, so rife that travelling in these parts is attended with danger. Many families plundered of their effects and otherways abused

---

[10] *Ibid.*, Vol. IV, p. 260.   [11] *Ibid.*, Vol. III, p. 565.
[12] *Ibid.*, Vol. IV, p. 68.   [13] *Ibid.*, Vol. III, p. 580.
[14] Draper MSS, 4F, p. 178.

by a band of ruffians who spread terror everywhere; we are daily picking them up; three men and two women under sentence of death and to be executed next week for these enormities.

It is a mistake to see the country of the Revolution neatly divided into two camps. There was a flow to life then as now. Men were fighting in the patriot armies or with the Loyalists, plowing their fields, tending their shops, and there were hundreds of ne'er-do-wells slouched over tavern-bars, doing odd jobs, seeking shabby favors from the governments, and other hundreds without allegiance to anyone, prowling dark roads, softly lifting the latch of town houses, going back with loot to the embraces of runaway girls.

Late in August Walter Butler came down from Quebec to Niagara ready to ride the whirlwind. He was second in command of the Rangers, senior to Caldwell who commanded the center at Wintermoot, eager to strike on his own. We know little of his summer in Quebec, but the next winter, when he went back there with dispatches, Haldimand had him write a diary of his movements along Ontario as part of the military intelligence to which later reference will be made, and it is thoroughly evident that, while young Butler thought he ought to have at least the command at Niagara, he did not win Haldimand's ill-will in making it plain, and he assuredly was eager to show the fighting stuff that was in him.

The news of the fall of Kaskaskia [15] could not then have been known in Quebec, as Hamilton did not learn of it in Detroit until August 6 when he started almost at once to the support of Vincennes. But the uneasiness about the West must have been extreme. Lachlan McIntosh had shoved down the Ohio and built a fort. The turning movement was developing, and runners must have come in every day with word of it. Peck, in his *History of Wyoming*, says: "Captain Walter Butler owed the Tryon County patriots a special spite on account of his imprisonment and, by way of taking vengeance upon them, he planned an expedition against Cherry Valley."

[15] James, *George Rogers Clark*, p. 131.

This is the opinion of all the secondary sources and is non-sense. The Niagara war plan, made early in the year, was to break up the back settlements. The Continental plan was to turn in the "upper posts." Success at Kaskaskia and Fort McIntosh on the one hand, and Wyoming and Cherry Valley on the other, were details in a much more massive scheme. A glance at the map will show Stanwix to have been a bad salient. The fighting in '78 was south and east of it. If its communications and supplies were cut off, which the fall of Fort Plain would achieve, it must ultimately fall and Niagara would have its advanced headquarters there instead of Oswego. Cherry Valley, to the east of Fort Plain, was not only a magazine of importance but its subjugation relieved a threat to the Tory nest at Unadilla, disturbed Fort Plain and Canajoharie, and definitely weakened Stanwix up the Mohawk to the northwest. This and no Monte-Cristo theatricality about revenge brought Walter Butler east from Niagara.

Germaine had written Sir Henry Clinton from London in March, "Should you not succeed in bringing Washington to a general and decisive action early in the season it is recommended not to pursue an offensive warfare against the interior but to attack the harbors along the coast between New York and Halifax." The Loyalists were left on their own. It was perhaps felt at Whitehall that there had not been a response, in '77, sufficient to warrant further effort on their behalf. If the men at Niagara wanted their homes back, and in many cases, particularly that of John Butler, their wives and children, they must go after them in arms. It cannot be too strongly emphasized that the fighting in the Valley in the autumn of '78 was not, as is usually stated, similar to forays by robber-barons, but a little war planned and waged by desperate and lonely men for the recovery of their homes. Even Lossing recognizes this where he says, "the recovery of the Mohawk Valley, where their property was situated, was an object too important to the Johnsons, Butlers, and the large number of refugees who accompanied them to Canada, not to induce extraordinary efforts for their attainment." This of course does not imply that the Americans were not fighting even more definitely for their homes, their wives and children, and their country, but simply that the Niagara corps were not alien invaders in the sense that Sheridan was in the Shenandoah eighty years afterwards. Captain Adam Crysler of the Rangers, a rough Indian fighter and a leader in all the invasions, was a man of substance in Schoharie. With each expedition he was coming back to his own, and the catalogue of his property is considerable.[16] He claimed £1381.4.4 for losses of:

A farm in Vrooman's Patent of 70 acres with improvements
$\frac{1}{4}$ of a sawmill
1 Grist mill
89 acres in Bouch's Patent
80 acres on Charlotte River

He was "much employed during the troubles and [went] through a great deal," and his mill was "burned down by the Indians understanding it to belong to a rebel."

General Stark wrote Washington from Albany, September, 14,[17]

Since my last Capt. MacKeen has returned from a Scout from the Unadilla and brought in three prisoners who inform that Butler and Brandt are determined to pay us another visit but if that should be the case I hope to be able to give a good account of them. I enclose you a copy of the orders I gave to Capt. McKeen for your approbation.

Surely there never was such thorough forewarning of any attack — or so little forearming. Everyone knew that the Loyalists would strike next at Cherry Valley, everyone — from the hapless farmers there to the militia and Continental staffs in Albany and up to the Commander in Chief in Headquarters at White Plains. In Albany, however, there appears to have been appalling ineptitude and disunity. Stark in the same letter says,

The Packet from the Committee of Congress is forwarded to Coll

[16] Loyalist Papers, Vol. XXX, p. 227, N. Y. P. L.
[17] Original letter, Congressional Library.

Alden (the Commander at Cherry Valley) but the Quarter Master General, with several assistants, were nine hours in providing an express, in the mean time, I was obliged to find another, and send the expresses away myself, in this manner is the Quarter Master General's Business carried on.

For that matter operations were carried on no better, but intelligence seems to have been superbly run.

It may have taken nine hours to enable the Quarter Master General to get an express out of Albany, but they came in fast enough.[18] On the eighteenth of September from Fisher at Caughnawaga, "The enemy have destroyed the whole German Flats and took with them all the cattle." On the nineteenth from Bellinger, "The enemy burned 63 Dwelling houses, 57 barns, with grain and fodder, 3 grist mills, 1 saw mill, took away 235 horses, 229 horned cattle, 269 sheep, killed and destroyed hogs and burned a great many outhouses. Two white men, 1 negro killed." No crimes yet reported against women and children.[19]

At last in the first days of October Albany struck back, William Butler being out for sixteen days burning and destroying the Indian castles near Unadilla. In his report to Governor Clinton from Schoharie, on October 28,[20] William Butler spoke of the success of his expedition and said, "I am well convinced that it has sufficiently secured these Frontiers from any further disturbances from the savages at least this winter; and it *will be ever, hereafter, difficult for them to distress these parts*." The report concludes with William Butler's journal of the sixteen days. The Indian villages, and they were real towns of stone houses with glass windows and brick chimneys, "the finest I have ever seen," were wiped out and the enemy's destruction at Andrustown and the German Flats duplicated. The report and the journal make no mention of the killing of Indian women and children, and the exact facts cannot be ascertained. Later, as we shall see, Walter Butler stated he was

[18] *Papers of George Clinton*, Vol. IV, p. 47.
[19] *Loc. cit.*
[20] *Ibid.*, p. 223.

unable to control the Indians at Cherry Valley because they were infuriated by the conduct of William Butler's troops at Unadilla.

As has been stated, the American dispatches themselves, up to this time, make no accusation against the Niagara troops and their red allies of crimes against women and children. Had they prevailed they certainly would have been mentioned. On the other hand it is not unreasonable to suppose that William Butler's frontiersmen had no high regard for Indian women and children, and the direct accusation is made that three Americans at Unadilla outraged and killed the young wife of a chief, Oneida Joseph.

The present author is naturally not to be understood as stating, or believing, that American soldiers in the Revolution were in the habit of raping enemy women, or that they were opposed by Galahads, white and red. In the special circumstances of the partisan fighting along the Mohawk in '78, however, the conclusions above seem to be fair. It certainly may be stated that frontiersmen in all wars and countries sanction conduct against colored races which they religiously condemn and ruthlessly take revenge for when employed against themselves. Furthermore, the destruction of property on a frontier, when it represents all that men possess, is so fearful a thing that it unbridles them for the most terrible and unrelated revenge. On whichever side a man may be, if he has seen his wealth destroyed, his home burned, his wife ill or dead from exposure, he will strike back with an almost studious cruelty even at the most innocent of his enemy's connections. Unadilla was worse than Andrustown, Cherry Valley than Unadilla, the Sullivan Expedition than Cherry Valley, and so up the stupid sequence of retaliation.

October ended then with the belief that the lesson had been taught at Unadilla. The season was late and, as Guy Johnson had said, the Indians had their winter hunting to think of. There had been constant rumors of the presence of Walter Butler in the Valley but no definite information about him, except that he was east of Niagara. Mason Bolton, the Ni-

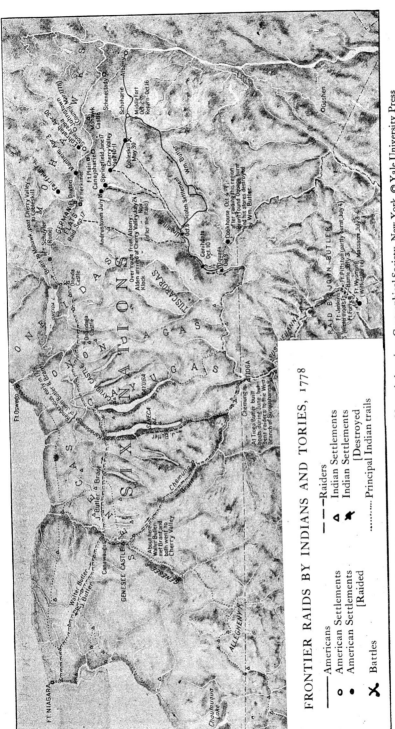

FRONTIER RAIDS BY INDIANS AND TORIES, 1778

Americans
○ American Settlements
● American Settlements [Raided
✕ Battles

--- Raiders
◁ Indian Settlements
✖ Indian Settlements [Destroyed
.... Principal Indian trails

Drawn expressly for *The Pageant of America* by Gregor Noetzel, American Geographical Society, New York. © Yale University Press

agara commandant, wrote General Haldimand on October
12 :[21]

Colonel Butler delivered to me the inclosed letters and will acquaint
your Excellency with the state of your Indian affairs as soon as he
receives a letter from his son, who is now with Sungerade endeavoring
to collect sufficient force to attack a body of 1400 rebels who have lately
advanced from Wyoming into the Indian country as far as Tioga.

It was about as far from the Cayuga Castle to Tioga, as from
Wyoming to Tioga, as Sungerade was probably at the Castle.

Walter Butler evidently moved south to meet the threat to
Tioga, and the Americans fell back to Wyoming; this we learn
from another Bolton letter written at Niagara on November
11, the day of Cherry Valley, of course without knowledge
of it. The letter says,[22]

From letters received from Captain Butler the rebels have thought
proper to retire from Tioga, leaving a garrison of five hundred men at
Wyoming, which they call regulars. The Senecas turned out four hundred fighting men. Captain Butler's little army of Rangers and Indians
amount to eight hundred, and from his last letter he intends to attack
Cherry Valley where the enemy have a number of cattle and a large
quantity of corn.

The fort at Cherry Valley, ordered by Lafayette the previous spring, was under the command of Colonel Ichabod
Alden, with about two hundred and fifty of the Massachussetts
line, and bore his name. The facts will not be understood if
this fort is understood to have been erected simply to protect
the defenseless people of Cherry Valley. The place, as a glance
at the map will show, was of great military value and a legitimate object of attack by an armed enemy. Captain Ballard, a
Continental officer serving there, speaks of it in his manuscript
memoir as "at that time one of the advanced posts of the army
in that direction, being connected with Albany by the interme-
diate post at Schoharie."[23]

Alden was a wretched officer. The principal mention of him
hitherto is by Gates who is distressed by the quarrelling be-

tween him and Anthony Wayne. Major Whiting, one of his officers, wrote General Hand at Schenectady, "when we were first attacked we had not a pound of bread per man in garrison. Had it not been for a barrel of powder, and half a box of cartridges belonging to the town our ammunition would have failed us." [24] It is inconceivable that there should have been such lack of fundamental precautions. Besides that Alden allowed officers of the garrison to live outside the fort, he himself among them, and also refused the townspeople permission to move themselves or their valuables into the fort. However, the little town seems to have gone pleasantly along, despite alarms, with its autumnal amusements. Alden's character and fate is curiously reminiscent of Rall, the Hessian commander killed at Trenton in the Christmas action of '76. One of his subalterns, William McKendry, kept a journal [25] of these days:

Nov. 1, 1778 — Some snow at this place
 "   2 & 3 — Nothing new
 "   4   — Capt. Hickling arrived at Cherry Valley
              with money for ye reg't
 "   5   — Nothing new
      6   "   "
      7   "   "
      8   "   "
      9   "   "
      10   "   "

Im Westen nichts neues indeed! Alden apparently said nothing to his officers of the dispatch that came in dated at Fort Schuyler on the sixth. [26]

We were just now informed by an Oneida Indian that yesterday an Onondaga Indian arrived at their castle from one of the branches of the Susquehanna, called the Tioga, that he was present at a great meeting of Indians and Tories at that place and their result was to attack

[24] Draper MSS, 5F, p. 44.
[25] Mass. Hist. Society *Collections*, 2d Series, Vol. II, p. 452.
[26] Wm. W. Campbell, *Annals of Tryon County* (New York, 1924, new Ed.), p. 102.

Cherry Valley and that young Butler was to head the Tories. I send you this information that you may be on your guard.

Alden acknowledged the warning on the eighth to the simple effect that he was much obliged for the information. He adds in a postcript that General Hand was that day at Cherry Valley. If the blue-nose Alden was not alarmed it is astonishing that General Hand, who was a rifleman, a former commander at Fort Pitt, and in a sense a frontiersman, should not have ordered the normal preparations made to receive an attack. He must have come out from Albany on an inspection trip, as he succeeded Stark in command at Albany as of that day, and it is strange that Major Whiting should have had to write him later of the lack of supplies at the fort.[27]

The fact, though, seems to have been that they were making war out of Niagara, and that in Albany they continued to regard the enemy effort as no more than the marauding of savage bandits. It is interesting to note that Colonel Bolton, a British regular, in the letter to Haldimand already quoted, describes the attacking force as "Captain Butler's little army of Rangers and Indians."

This little army is generally described as coming down from Niagara, meeting Brant, going to his winter quarters, persuading the noble Redskin against his will to turn back to the wanton massacre that followed. But on October 12, from Bolton's first letter to Haldimand already quoted, we place Walter Butler north of Tioga watching the American threat to it developing out of Wyoming. Captain Adam Crysler, of the Rangers, says in his Diary [28] for this general period, "I went under the command of Capt. Caldwell to the German Flats and destroyed the whole settlement and returned till we came to Chemung to Capt. Butler's and encamped under his command." It is evident from this, and from the evidence of the Sullivan Expedition the next year, that Niagara's ad-

[27] Blame certainly appears to attach to Hand in this case, the more so as he was an excellent officer, and was later made Adjutant General of the Army to succeed Scammell over Hamilton, and over Greene's and Knox's recommendation of Hamilton.   [28] Draper MSS, 14F, p. 12.

vanced headquarters under Walter Butler was at Chemung.

It is not clear why the proposed attack on Cherry Valley was not made earlier. Butler must have known that word of his plans was getting to Albany and was calculated to strengthen Alden's defense of Cherry Valley. He may have had to delay until he was sure the American advance from Wyoming would come to nothing. His vital line of retreat and communication to Niagara was through Tioga. If it were in American hands he was cut off. He may have waited to strike until the very lateness of the season convinced Alden and the townsmen that they were safe until spring. This, however, seems unlikely. Rains, cold, and hunger bore no more lightly on the Rangers than the Americans. It was a terrific march for seven hundred men down the Chemung River to the juncture with the Susquehanna and up it to Otsego Lake and on to Cherry Valley, probably over 150 miles of heavy going. Such a force could not live entirely on the country, and ammunition and military baggage would have to be carried. It seems almost sure that unknown circumstances held Walter Butler at Chemung much later than was intended. Woodsmen, such as the Rangers were, would not purposely wait till mid-November to attack Cherry Valley with a march of 300 miles to Niagara, through snowy forests and winter rivers, to follow. The chance of defeat always existed and it meant death to scores of them, if not in action then in flight through the snow.

Resistance at Fort Alden, after all the warning, was to be expected, with support from Fort Schuyler, Fort Plain, Schoharie, and Schenectady. Their own attack must be tip and run, lest they be cut off by the Continentals coming out of Schenectady, or William Butler's five hundred men [29] at Schoharie. If the little army of Rangers mustered 700 men that was their maximum; every death, every wound, every injury, every chill meant that much less. The Cherry Valley and Schoharie garrisons totalled 750 men, the latter still flushed with the Unadilla success, and support, to the extent of several thousand men, could be expected from various posts, including Van

[29] *Papers of George Clinton*, October Return, Vol. IV, p. 228.

Schaick's at Mount Johnson. In fact, after the action, the American command at Schenectady had over 1000 fresh troops in pursuit within two days.[30] Above all, Walter Butler must have been fully aware that there would be no element of surprise in his attack. The powerful Oneida nation was hostile to him, scrupulously loyal to the Congress, and had that month sent nine Ranger prisoners into Albany.[31] The family of Thomas Spencer, their interpreter and secret agent killed at Oriskany had a house in Cherry Valley.

If there is a parallel between Colonel Alden and Colonel Rall, the Hessian at Trenton, it is also evident that the raid on Cherry Valley, from a military point of view, was more reckless than Washington's Christmas attack in '76 across the Delaware. The chances of success were slim, and it would never have been attempted by a leader less brilliant or daring than Walter Butler. He must attack, win, and escape. The most complete victory would not obviate the terrific hardships of his inevitable retreat to Niagara. The gifts of personality which led to the outcry against his execution in '77 must have been all that led men to follow him on this forlorn hope. The idea that he struck Cherry Valley for revenge is absurd. The fact of this inevitable retreat bears further on the massacre which followed. It is inconceivable that with his mother and sisters in the enemy's hands, exposed to retaliation, he planned a massacre of innocents at Cherry Valley, and quite as impossible that he considered carrying them off to Niagara across a wilderness that he and his own hard-bitten Rangers could scarcely cross. He had Indians with him, it is true, but his father had had them at Wyoming and confined the killing to men in arms. But the "less luck" of his short life was out again.

It is probable that Butler had been in regular communication with Brant somewhere south of Unadilla, and that their junction at Oquago (Ogreago) now Windsor, New York, was a rendezvous. Lossing, who particularly insists on the revenge-motive, says [32] that they met near Genesee and that Butler was

<hr/>

[30] *Ibid.*, p. 284.   [31] *Ibid.*, p. 130.   [32] *Pictorial Field Book*, Vol. I, p. 268.

coming from Niagara. No authority is given and it is obvious from the Bolton letters that it is untrue. The rendezvous is given in the Draper Manuscripts, based on the Johnston Family Journal,[33] and fits in with what is known from military documents.

There has been much discussion as to what happened at the meeting. The general story is about as follows: Walter Butler, meeting Brant unexpectedly, announced his plan; Brant objected to it because the season was late — and he did not care to serve under Butler, but he finally agreed. There is no record in existence of what was said but it seems probable, as has been suggested, that the meeting was a rendezvous. Brant, Butler's senior, and soon to be made a Colonel, may have been surprised to learn that Butler did not intend to resign the command to him, or to divide it with him. There was no good feeling between them as the famous Claus letter showed. Brant had a bloody record beginning with the action at the Cedars. He had not been at Wyoming, and John Butler may well have told his son that his own control of the Indians there was due in part to Brant's absence. Brant had reported to Sir Guy Carleton, through Claus, that the Butlers were holding back the Indians, and that except for him the Indians would not have fought with St. Leger. He had had leave in England with Guy Johnson, a privilege that Walter Butler craved the whole war through. This is one of the frustrated hopes of his life; he apparently yearned to see the England he was fighting for, and never did. Brant may in addition have had actual difficulty in persuading his Indians to return to action, with the winter hunting calling them. But somehow out of this conflict of personal dislikes, ambitions, and ardors, the original objective was pursued and the march up the Susquehanna continued to an action the end of which Walter Butler could not foresee. All these military facts have been disregarded and the day remembered as a slaughter of inno-

[33] Published in the *Cherry Valley Gazette*, Oct. 21, 1858. Clipping in Draper MSS, 17F, p. 83.

cents with Walter Butler, in Lossing's phrase "the head and front of all the cruelty on that day." Fifty years later Timothy Dwight, the president of Yale, was to go there and invent his stories of Walter Butler's going from house to house, ordering the slaying of women and children in their beds, and all the histories were to quote his legend of Walter Butler's death, how he had begged for quarter, and how an Oneida had answered, "No, I give you Sherry Valley Quarters," — until a bloody myth enveloped his handsome head and men rejoiced that his mutilated body had been abandoned in the snows of Tryon.

In the meanwhile on the morning of November 8th, Alden, without acquainting all his officers with the situation, sent a Sergeant and twelve men out Beaver Dam Road on a scout, and a noncommissioned officer and five men out another road. The only other approach was by an Indian trail which Alden, unskilled in forest-lore, evidently thought unusable.[34]

The little army was ascending the Susquehanna. It was Walter Butler's first single command. This secretive young man, for all he wrote so well, had no time for the Journals that so many kept, Cartwright and Crysler and McKendry among them. Under orders next year he kept a journal as he crossed Lake Ontario, but we know nothing of what he thought as he watched the leaves and driftwood swirl down the river from Cherry Valley.

On the night of the tenth Alden's first scout was surprised and taken. A cold November rain had begun, and the Rangers must have cursed King, Country, and the Cause as the sleet cut their faces and dampened their powder, while they struggled through the dark woods to attack a Continental garrison, itself and its powder sheltered and dry. During the night the sleet turned to snow and the hearts of the soaking men must have sunk as they thought of the frozen trails back to Niagara.

Interrogation of the captured scout, however, put a different

[34] Draper MSS, 5F, p. 33, *New Jersey Gazette*, Dec. 31, 1778.

light on the situation. Butler until then could hardly have expected a different sort of resistance than Gansevoort had put up at Stanwix. It must have astonished him to learn from the prisoners that "the Col., Lieut-Col., Major, with other officers, and 40 privates lay at Mr. Wells house 400 yards from the great fort." [35] The map of Cherry Valley at the time of the massacre gives an excellent idea of the terrain. The contemporary report in the *New Jersey Gazette,* already referred to, says that the Rangers camped that night in the swamp back of the Wells house.

The attack did not break until eleven the next morning. The snow had again turned to rain and there was little visibility. The Rangers probably breakfasted on parched corn. McKendry describes the day in his Journal,

Alarm 11 oclock A.M. Mr. Hammell coming from the Beaver Dam was fired upon by ye Indians and was wounded he being on horse rode off and got clear it being half a mile from the fort. Immediately come on 442 Indians from the 5 Nations, 200 Tories attack'd Headquarters killed Colonel Alden, took Col. Stacy prisoner, attacked Fort Alden, after 3 retreated without success.

Just what happened it is of course impossible to tell. We do know, however, that Alden, Stacy, and evidently Whiting, the field officers of the garrison, were in the Wells house at the moment of the attack with a headquarters company. A Ranger gives their number as forty. Whiting in his report [36] to Hand says, besides Alden and Stacy, "one Lt., one Ens. the Surgeon's Mate and a few privates we had about 6 or 8 of the Reg't killed." It is evident that at least 20 soldiers and possibly forty were in the Wells house. Whiting says, "the Enemy surprised us. . . . They push'd vigorously for the fort and had it not been for great activity and alertness of the troops they had rushed within the lines."

This question of what happened at the Wells house, the scene of the major tragedy of the day, is of the utmost importance. Butler knew from the scout who was at the Wells house and

[35] Letter of Pollard, a Ranger. Draper Collection, Clark MSS, 49J, p. 18.
[36] *Papers of George Clinton,* Vol. IV, p. 286.

his plan should have been, and evidently was, to rush the fort itself and leave the Wells house to be covered by his supports. Inept as the command was, the soldiers in Fort Alden were Continentals and the attack was beaten off. It is important to know what action the Headquarters Company at the Wells house took, but there is no mention of this in the reports of either side, other than that Alden was killed while running to the Fort and Stacy captured. It is evident, however, that one of two things happened: either the company put up a fight there, or abandoned the house and its fourteen non-combatant inmates to the red enemy. If they stood and fought it probably came to a hand-to-hand conflict in which some of the domestic servants may have been killed; but how did it happen that Lt. Col. Stacy could surrender and his life be spared and the Wells family be slaughtered? If they abandoned the house at once apparently the Indians ran amok inside, seizing the opportunity when the Rangers were heavily engaged at the fort. The fighting went on till three-thirty in the afternoon.

No time is given for the killings in the town. The details of the day are of confused horror. There were evidently forty homes in Cherry Valley,[37] and thirty-one or thirty-two non-combatants [38] were slain during the day, thirteen of them in the Wells house. In only six other houses of the forty were people killed. This seems to be important in connection with Walter Butler's own responsibility for the massacre. While Lossing, Simms, and Campbell describe him as the instigator of it all, and while Dwight tells of his ordering babies killed, none of the four, in spite of their wealth of specific detail in other connections, ever gives the name of a family at whose murder he was present or a participant.

He had evidently not expected trouble with his Indians before night, and, in view of Wyoming, he may not have expected it at all, but word of the Wells and Mitchell murders

[37] *Papers of George Clinton*, Vol. IV, p. 410.
[38] *Annals of Tryon County*, p. 114 (32 killed); *Papers of George Clinton*, Vol. IV, p. 338 (33 captured).

apparently reached him at the fort shortly after the attack. He could certainly not break off his attack and permit a sortie. Pollard, the Ranger, says that Butler was at the fort and that the Wells murders were the work of Little Beard, an Indian, and that from the Wells house they spread through the town looting and killing. This was apparently somewhat before noon. Pollard then states, "Capt. McDonald with a party of Rangers was detached to save all the people he could, while Capt. Butler with one hundred Rangers lay within seventy yards of the fort keeping up a brisk fire."

The fort held out.

In the town Mrs. Dunlop was killed, three people at the Moore house, one at the Dickson, one at the Johnston, two at the Scott, five at the Mitchell, four at the Hubbard. Mrs. Mitchell and four children were killed and scalped. The husband had seen the Indians approaching, and according to Simms [39] "fled to a place of safety in the woods. On returning he found his wife and four children all tomahawked." Much sympathy went out to Mitchell but nothing has ever been said of his abandonment of his family for his own safety. He accused Newberry, a Ranger, of the murder of one of the children. But he did it the next year when Newberry and Hare of the Rangers were taken as spies and under sentence of death.

The secondary histories have strained so to blacken Walter Butler's name at Cherry Valley that at times they have lost all balance. Campbell,[40] for example, speaking of the Rev. M. Dunlap, *who was past seventy-five*,[41] at Cherry Valley says, "An Indian passing by pulled his hat from his head and ran away with it. . . . Another Indian carried away his wig, the rain falling upon his bare head. He was released a few days after but the shock was too violent. He died *about a year after*, though he could have borne up but a few years longer under the increasing infirmities of old age." Simms and Lossing and Mrs. William S. Little [42] all ponderously quote this further

---

[39] *Frontiersmen of New York*, Vol. II, p. 205.
[40] *Annals of Tryon County*, p. 105.   [41] Author's italics.
[42] Mrs. Wm. S. Little, *Story of the Massacre of Cherry Valley*. (Rochester, 1890.)

example of Walter Butler's ferocity. None of them mentions the Pollard letter which says, "Capt. Butler the first night by stealth sent Dunlap and daughter to the Fort."

The attack on the fort was broken off in the late afternoon. The town was in flames and probably twenty-five noncombatants had been murdered, others had fled to the woods. Many had been saved by Captain McDonnell's patrols, but the snow was bloody in the November twilight and Walter Butler as he fell back down the Beaver Dam Road must have cursed his luck and his red allies. He took forty noncombatant and military prisoners with him, and Lt. Col. Stacy, the second in command. They built a great fire and town cattle were doubtless slaughtered for food. Pollard says "the evening before the attack, the chiefs promised to observe the same humanity they had with Col. Butler," and now they thronged up and demanded all the prisoners be given them.

The Rangers and the white troops were greatly in the minority. It is hard to believe that the Indians were not incited by their great war chief, Joseph Brant, or that he could not have controlled them had he wished. Years later when Brant visited old John Fonda at Caughnawaga, Fonda censured him, Simms says,[43] for his cruelties at Cherry Valley. Brant "said the atrocities were mostly chargeable to Walter Butler." What more easy for a savage, who was to murder his own son, than to charge the dead Butler with his crimes?[44]

As the Indian demand for the prisoners was pressed Capt. Butler, according to Pollard, was obliged to comply to prevent their all being killed. No one seems to have been killed during the night. In the morning there was apparently a brief and futile attack on the fort and orders given for the long trek back to Niagara. Seventy-six years ago, that day, Queen Anne had ridden in state through the city of London to give thanks at St. Paul's for the great victory of James Butler, Duke of

[43] *Frontiersmen*, Vol. II, p. 210.
[44] Cf. *Annals of Tryon County*: "Colonel Butler alleged that Brant secretly incited the Indians in this massacre in order to stigmatize his son." The present author did not find Col. Butler's allegation, nor authority for the accusation but believes that both are in accord with the appearance of the facts.

Ormonde, in Spain. Walter Butler standing in the snow and
mud, the smell of burnt timbers and damp earth in his nostrils,
may have recalled it. His pride in the Ormonde Butlers was
very great and his disillusionment at the massacre and his
military failure must have been almost overwhelming.[45]

The garrison, McKendry says, "sent out and fetched in Col.
Alden and buried him under arms." Thirty-eight of the prisoners were sent back to the Fort in safety, but "Colonel
Campbell's wife and four children and James Moore's wife
and three daughters" were taken along in the retreat. In the
Cherry Valley Memorial [46] to Governor Clinton, dated
November 26, it is stated that Butler took with him thirty-
three prisoners but these were practically all Negro servants,
men and women, who probably went along voluntarily.

We come back here to the fact that Walter Butler's mother,
his aunt, Mrs. Sheehan, and the wives of several other officers
of the Rangers, were still prisoners in Albany. The taking of
Mrs. Campbell and Mrs. Moore as hostages for exchange
under the circumstances cannot be held against him. It was a
brutal business all around, but certainly the Albany Committee
of Safety moved first against enemy-women. It is interesting
to note that one of the Moore girls married an officer of the
Rangers at Niagara, who had been in the retreat that winter,
and that long afterwards, when Mrs. Campbell was united to
her children, she was evidently staying with Mrs. Butler who
had been finally released. There is even hostile evidence
that Walter Butler was willing to release the Campbells and
Moores: Colonel William Harper, writing to Governor Clinton [47] on December 2 of the "yousles molittie" (useless
militia), says that when Colonel Fisher reached Fort Alden
with a relief column

at the very time the prisoners arrived which the enemy sent back, and
informed us that Brant and Butler did propose to send back to rest of

[45] On the other hand, he may have been comforted by remembering the conduct of Ormonde's troops who "plundered Cadiz, sacked the churches with
heretical glee, raped women and nuns."
[46] *Papers of George Clinton*, Vol. IV, p. 338.
[47] *Ibid.*, p. 412.

the women and childring the next day, the wether being very bad and the distressed popell intreating that he [Fisher] would send out a party to meet them, if they shuld be dismissed . . . they could not be prevaled on so much as one man.

On the thirteenth Ten Broeck [48] in Albany ordered Van Schaack's, Lansing's, Schuyler's and Quackenboss's Regiments out toward Schoharie; and Van Woert's, McCrea's, Yates', and Schoonhaven's were started in support. Colonel Klock was "recommended to pursue them if he found it practicable." Colonel William Butler "marched with his regiment of Continental Troops and the Corps of Riflemen to the relief of the garrison of Fort Alden." But it was too late. The little army of "150 Tories, 50 British Troops and 600 Indians" was down the Susquehanna. Harper reported that "Two days after Cheryvaly was distresd Colonel Klock arrived thare . . . warmed himselfe and turned about, marched back without afording the distressed inhabitants the least asistance or release even to bury the dead." Governor Clinton himself forgot his horror of the murders and wrote John Jay five days after the massacre: "If the enemy are suffered to continue their depredations the consequences may be fatal, as this state will be disabled from furnishing any supplies to the army and hitherto they have depended upon it for bread."

Butler must have been almost back to Chemung when his runner reached Colonel Harper with a letter which Harper forwarded to Governor Clinton with a note saying:

You will see by the return the number and quality of the prisoners. Butler expects a number equal to those he sent back. . . . I was informed by several of the prisoners that Butler sade he would keep Mrs. Campbell and Mrs. Moore and thare childering till Mrs. Butler, Mrs. Wall, her nese, and his other friends are exchanged for them. I would therefore pray that Mrs. Butler, Mrs. Wall, Mrs. Strachan, Mrs. Clement, Mrs. Harkemer and as many of their families as will be equal to Mrs. More and her 3 childering and Mrs. Campble and her 4 childring may be exchanged for them.

[48] Ten Broeck's figures to Clinton, *Papers of George Clinton*, Vol. IV, p. 292.

Clinton received the letter on December 23 and said [49] that he could do nothing but had forwarded it to General Schuyler.

There is the following letter to Schuyler from Walter Butler, dated November 12:

CHERRY VALLEY

12th November, 1778

SIR: I am induced by humanity to permit the persons whose names sent you herewith to remain lest the inclemency of the season and their naked and helpless situation should prove fatal to them; and expect that you will realease an equal number of our people in your hands, amongst whom I expect you will permit Mrs. Butler and family to go to Canada, but if you insist upon it I do agree to send you an equal number of prisoners of yours taken either by the Rangers or Indians, and will leave it to you to name the persons. I have done everything in my power to restrain the fury of the Indians from hurting Women or Children or killing prisoners who fall into our hands, and would have more effectually prevented them but that they were so much incensed by the late destruction of their Village of Hughquay by your people, and shall always continue to act in that manner, as I look upon it beneath the character of a Soldier to wage War with Women and Children, and I am sure you are conscious the Colonel Butler or myself have no desire for your Women and Children to be hurt. But be assured Sir that if you persevere in detaining my Father's family with you that we shall no longer take the same pains to restrain the Indians from prisoners, Women or Children that we have hitherto done.

I am your most humble servant,

WALTER BUTLER,

Captain of the Rangers

General Schuyler [50]

Winter was too close for an exchange to take place. By Decem-

<hr/>

[49] *Papers of George Clinton*, Vol. IV, p. 415. The editor of the *Papers* marks the reference to Walter Butler's letter "not found," apparently overlooking Clinton's statement that he had sent it to Schuyler. Evidently it is the letter to Schuyler or one like it quoted above.

[50] Letter, British Museum. There is a doubt in my mind whether the letter recently found by Mr. James Brewster in the attic of the Union College Library is a copy or the original of this letter. I am inclined to believe it a copy. In any event it is dated November 12, 1778; not 1776 as was originally announced in the College Magazine.

ber first the Continental Scouts reported the snow a foot deep
in the woods, and McKendry's journal for November 15 says,
"A heavy snow storm fell two feet deep." But months afterwards couriers were still carrying dispatches about Cherry
Valley through woods, down to Crown Point, to New York,
across the sea, and out to the desolate posts at Detroit.

On February 4, 1779, Lieutenant Governor Hamilton at
Detroit received a letter from an Alexander Macomb saying:[51]

Captain Butler, Joseph Brant and their Rangers and Savages have
made cruel havoc on the Mohawk River — the fine settlement of
Cherry Valley is entirely destroy'd; men women and children all pro-
miscuously butchered by the savages, nor could Capt. Butler or the other
officers keep any restraint on them. I enclose you a letter from Mr.
Pollard to a young lad here, nam'd Geo. Forsith, which will give you a
good deal of news and of Butler's affair in particular.

The original Pollard letter is in the Draper Manuscripts and
has already been quoted in part. It concludes with the important words: "The bloody scene is almost past description. I
think it hath determined Captain Butler and McDonald from
ever having any more to do in such a service where savages
make the principal part of the army."

In January, Sir Henry Clinton [52] wrote Lord George
Germaine.

The Indians have again visited the Frontiers and surprised at Fort
Alden near Cherry Valley part of two Regiments, thirty or forty were
killed and six taken Prisoners, amongst them are the names of Field
officers. Our accounts are from Rebel papers and probably softened, we
therefore imagine they have suffered a great deal.

In February, McKendry, still at Cherry Valley, writes:

February 1 — Cold
    "   2 — Found Simeon. Hopkins dead in ye woods who
                was kill'd in the action of the 11 Nov. last.

Butler sent a runner ahead to Niagara from Unadilla on
the seventeenth of November with a report of the action for

[51] Draper Collection, Clark MSS.
[52] Original letters, Clements Library. Sir Henry Clinton Papers.

Mason Bolton. He says at the end, "I have much to lament that notwithstanding my utmost precautions and endeavour to save the women and children I could not prevent some of them falling unhappily to the fury of the savages." [53]

His letter of the twelfth to Schuyler, which Harper delivered to Governor Clinton, who sent it to Schuyler, who then gave it to Brigadier General James Clinton, was answered by him on January 1, under a flag, sent out under arms "that they may furnish themselves with Provisions," addressed "To Captain Walter Butler or any other British officer to whom it may be handed." The letter agrees to the exchange and says further

I am not informed if Mrs. Butler, her Famely and such others as will be given in exchange would chuse to move at this inclement season; if they do, they shall be sent, if not, they may remain until Spring and then may either go to Oswego or Canada at their option. . . .

Do not flatter yourself, sir, that your father's family have been detained on acc't of any consequence they were supposed to be of or that it is determined they should be exchanged in consideration of the threat contained in your letter. I should hope for the honor of civilized nations and the sake of human nature that the British officers had exerted themselves in restraining the Barbarities of the Savages . . . and that your Mother did not fall a sacrifice to the resentment of the survivors of the families who were so barbarously massacred is owing to the humane principles . . . [of our people]. [54]

There are two things of significance in James Clinton's fine letter: Whether Mrs. Butler was of consequence or not, she was not released until her son had hostages to trade; secondly, the letter was written after General Clinton had talked to survivors of the massacre, and if they had reported to him Walter Butler's own participation in the atrocities ascribed to him by the later historians, he would have had no hesitancy in accusing Butler of them.

Walter Butler replied at length in his famous letter of February 18:

[53] Haldimand Collection, Series B, Vol. 100, pp. 82-88, Canadian Archives.
[54] *Papers of George Clinton*, Vol. IV, p. 458.

18th February, 1779
Niagara

SIR: I have received a letter dated January last signed by you, in answer to mine of 12th November. It's contents I communicated to Lt. Col. Bolton the Commanding Officer of this Garrison — and by him I am directed to acquaint you that he has no objection an exchange of prisoners, as mentioned in your letter, should take place, but not being fully empowered by His Excellency General Haldimand to order the same immediately to be put into execution as they propose I should go down to the Commander in Chief for his directions in the matter. In the meantime Col. Butler (as he has done on every occasion) will make every effort in his power to have all the prisoners as well as those belonging to your Troops and the Women and Children in captivity among the different Indian Nations, collected, and sent in to this Post, to be forwarded to Crown Point should the exchange take place by the way of Canada or to Oswego if stated there. In either case Col. Bolton desires me to inform you that the prisoners shall receive from him what assistance their wants may require which prisoners have at all times received in this Post.

The disagreeable situation of your people in the Indian Village as well as ours among you will induce me to make all the expedition in my power to Canada in order that the exchange may be settled as soon as possible for the good of both. I make no doubt His Excellency General Haldimand will acquiesce in the proposed exchange — The season of the year renders it impossible to take place before the tenth or fifteenth of May next — However I shall write you by way of Crown Point General Haldimand's determination, as to what way of exchange would be most agreeable to him by May. I would wish Mrs. Butler and family, including Mrs. Sheehan and son and Mrs. Wall were permitted to go to Canada in Spring even should the exchange be fixed at Ontario.

It is not our present business, Sir, to enter into an altercation or to reflect on the conduct of either the British or Continental Forces or on that of each other, but since you have charged (on report I must suppose) the British Officers with inhumanity and Col. Butler and myself in particular; in justice to them and in vindication of his and my own Honour and Character I am in the disagreeable necessity to declare the charge unjust and void of Truth — and which can only tend to deceive the World — tho' a favourite cry of the Congress on every occasion whether founded on Truth or not.

We deny any *cruelties* to have been committed at Wyoman either by Whites or Indians; so far to the contrary that not a Man, Woman or Child was hurt after the capitulation or a Woman or Child before it or taken into captivity. Tho' should you call it *Inhumanity* the killing of *Men in Arms* in the Field, we in that case plead guilty.

The inhabitants killed at Chery Valley does not lay at my Door — my conscience aquits me. If any are guilty (as Accessories) it's yourselves, at least the conduct of some of your Officers. First. Col. Hartley of your Force sent to the Indians the enclosed, being a copy of his letter charging them with crimes they have never done and threatening them and their Villages with Fire and Sword and no Quarters.

The burning one of their Villages then inhabited only by a few families, your friends, who immagined they might remain in peace and friendship with you, till assured, a few hours before the arrival of your Troops, that they would not even get Quarters; took to the woods, and to complete the matter Col. Dennison and his bearing joined in arms with Col. Hartley after a solemn capitulation and engagements not to bear arms during the War. And Col. Dennison not performing a promise to release a certain number of Soldiers belonging to Col. Butler's Corps of Rangers, then prisoners among you, were the reasons assigned by the Indians to me after the destruction of Cherry Valley for their not acting in the same manner as at Wyoming — they added that being charged by their Enemies with what they have never done, and threatened by them; they had determined to convince you it was not fear that had prevented them from committing and they did not want spirit to put your threats against them in force against yourselves.

The prisoners sent back by me or any now in our or the Indians hands but must declare I did everything in my power to prevent the Indians killing the prisoners or taking the Women and Children captive or in any wise injuring them. Col. Stacey and several other Officers of yours when exchanged will aquit me and must further declare that they have received every assistance before and since arrival at this post, that could be got to relieve their wants. I must however take leave by the by to remark that I experienced no humanity or even common justice during my imprisonment among you.

I enclose a list of Officers and Privates whom I should be glad were exchanged, likewise a list of the families we expect these as well sent back as others in our hands you have likewise enclosed.

Col. Stacey and several Officers and others of your people are at this Post and have leave to write.

I am Sir your very humble Servant,

WALTER BUTLER
Captain of the Corps of the Rangers

Brigadier General Clinton
of the Continental Forces [55]

There was never any contradiction of this statement, either by the women later released or by Colonel Stacy. It is important evidence in Walter Butler's favor. Stacy was a prisoner in Quebec till the end of the war. McKendry says on February 12, "Sergeant Hunter escaped informs that Col. Stacy he was well and in good spirits in the hands of Col. Butler."

The list of the personnel of the Rangers to be sent back is available in the Ottawa Archives.[56] It is headed by "Peter Ten Broeck, Esq., Captain of the Corps of Rangers, 15 privates and a lieutenant, and 5 others taken variously at Unadilla, on the Delaware and at Tioga." Then there come the Loyalists' own families:

Colonel Butler's — Mrs. Butler, Mrs. Sheehan, Walter B.. Sheehan, Thomas, Andrew, Johnson and Deborah Butler and Mrs. Wall. Mr. McClennan's — Mrs. McClennan and three small children. Mr. Johan Jost Herkimer's — Mrs. Herkimer, Jane, Caty, Lourance, Mary, Jacob and Nicholas Herkimer,

and down the list.

There is "Mr. Henry Hare's — Mrs. Hare, Ally, John, Faulky, William, Peter, Barent and Caty Hare, children." Lieutenant Hare was executed as a spy the next year, accused of war crimes at Cherry Valley, and his wife, left destitute, pled with Governor Clinton for his life. It seems absurd to suppose that this man was guilty of atrocities with such hostages in his enemy's hands. Newberry, who suffered the same fate, and whom Governor Clinton in a letter to his wife called a murderer, is also on the list. "Wm. Newberry's — Mrs. New-

[55] Letter, British Museum.
[56] Haldimand Papers, Series B, Vol. 105, pp. 436-38, Canadian Archives.

berry and four small children." The workings of rumor, the spirit of the times, make it likely that when these Rangers were later taken on legitimate, if fatal, military espionage, their earlier residence in the Valley and their prominence made it easy to ascribe atrocities to them. They were caught and condemned. Guilty of espionage, it was so much the better if their executions could also be atonement for the massacre. No other evidence seems to have been brought against them. It is incredible that men, with wives and children who were devoted to them in prison, should have risked those lives by atrocities.

Walter Butler speaks in his letter to James Clinton of leaving at once to see Haldimand about the exchange. The secondary historians from Campbell down have asserted that "after the massacre at Cherry Valley he went to Quebec but Gen'l. Haldimand, Governor of Canada, gave out that he did not wish to see him." [57] On the contrary after his visit Haldimand wrote John Butler "I derived great pleasure in seeing Captain Butler who has given me a very satisfactory detail of his expedition. The prospect you have of recovering the liberty of your family is a sufficient motive for me to acquiesce in the exchange you propose." [58]

So much for the valley town named for its glory of wild-cherry orchards. The traditional American history has described the November action there as the work of murderous banditti. "Deeds of rapine, of murder, of [such] hellish hue cannot be related here," says Sabine,[59] and "sufficient [evidence] remains undoubted to stamp [Walter Butler's] conduct with the deepest, darkest, most damning guilt." "Butler, a nefarious scoundrel and murderer," says Hough,[60] "was the arch-fiend on the occasion and would listen to no appeals from Brant for mercy for these victims."

The facts in this chapter appear to the contrary: the attack

[57] *Annals of Tryon County*, p. 175.
[58] Haldimand Papers, Series B, Vol. 96, p. 162.
[59] Lorenzo Sabine, *Loyalists of the American Revolution* (Boston, 1864), Vol. I, p. 278.
[60] J. B. Hough, *Independence, A Story of the Revolution* (New York, 1893), p. 331.

was a military action against a fort and supply center defended by Continentals; it was part of the year's war plan at Niagara and known months ahead to our own northern command; it was made possible by the failure to push up from Wyoming to Chemung; it had every chance of disaster to the attacking force far from its base, surrounded by militia and Continental regiments, and with a hazardous line of retreat down the Susquehanna and up the Chemung, also known to the American command; it was made in conjunction with Indians who evidently behaved with reasonable humanity to noncombatants at Wyoming four months before; the warnings were all disregarded by Colonel Alden, the American commander, who could apparently have beaten off the attack without loss of man or woman or child had he not, with criminal negligence, failed to make any military preparation and refused the townspeople the protection of the fort; the little army under Walter Butler was joined by Brant and his Indians, and there, in a bloody mist, the story is lost, except that thirty-one people were murdered, thirteen in the first house, apparently before Butler could detach McDonnell from the fort to protect them. The fact is usually lost sight of that on November 26 the town asked bounty for 173 survivors [61] of the massacre. Bad as it was, it is evident that Butler did protect seven-eighths of the townspeople. There is the primary evidence of young Pollard's letter that Butler resolved never again to have anything to do with a service where Indians were in the majority.

His previous fighting had been before Montreal, at the Cedars, and at Oriskany, each time against men in arms. During the previous summer at Chemung he is accused of no crimes. There seems no doubt that the conduct of the savages came as a surprise and a horror to him. He writes the Canadian high command later that he hopes he may not have to serve again with them. His whole life was of "less luck." Here he could not say, "What though the field be lost, all is not lost." He came back to Niagara without a victory, and, though he

[61] *Papers of George Clinton*, Vol. IV, p. 338.

did not know it, his name was to be the most hated name in New York for a hundred and fifty years. It had gone badly and the Johnson Dynasty, snug and warm in Montreal, would have more to whisper and scribble about, against his promotion, against leave in England, against his right to command.

"Rakes of London" was a swinging theme of the time to come marching home with. It had a quickening beat and a promise of English leave, when the ice was out of the St. Lawrence, and the lucky ones went home to London. But, at Niagara, as the corps came in, they were more likely thumping out "Hollow Drum." The world must have seemed that to them.

Haldimand had seen that fall "the great advantage that might be derived from the establishment of a permanent settlement at Niagara," and six companies of Rangers were there in December to go into winter quarters on the west side of the river in the Rangers' Barracks, just built under the supervision of Colonel Butler.

The Rangers were fully mustered and equipped that December. Two of these companies were of "men speaking the Indian language and acquainted with their customs" and were to receive four shillings, New York currency, a day. The remaining companies "to be composed of people well acquainted with the woods in consideration of fatigues they were liable to undergo were to receive 2 shillings a day." It was high pay, and Haldimand estimated that the eight companies of Rangers cost as much as twenty companies of regular infantry.

Their uniform [it is reported] consisted of dark green coats faced with scarlet and lined the same, a waistcoat of green cloth and the buckskin Indian leggings reaching from the ankle to the waist, or the leather overalls worn by the American riflemen. Their caps were almost skull caps of black leather with a black leather cockade on the left side, and a brass plate in front embossed with the letters G R and the words Butler's Rangers. Their belts were of buff leather and crossed on the breast where they were held in place by a brass plate marked in the same manner and with the same words as the Cap plate.[62]

[62] Charles M. Lefferts, *Uniforms in the War of the American Revolution* (New York, 1926), p. 212.

As we read the roster of the Rangers the men become in-
dividualized and cease to be the "incarnate fiends" of the
secondary sources. It is easier to believe that a hundred name-
less Rangers were fiends than that:

Patrick Burke	John Clearwater
Laurence Van Allen	John Cornwall
Robert Campbell	Joseph Countryman
Roland McDonald	Abraham de Forest
Stephen Secord	Francis Elsworth
Andrew Hamilton	John Goodnight
William Atkinson	Richard Pierpont
Francis Chambers	John Stevens

— and "Richard Whittle, a tailor," were.[63]

The year was close to its end. James Clinton wrote Washington on December 18 from Albany [64] that smallpox had made
its appearance and that the inhabitants of Canajoharie were
much afflicted, and that Gansevoort's regiments had come into
Schenectady for inoculation. He goes on "as the snow is two
feet deep on the frontiers, I have ordered one hundred pair of
snowshoes . . . but every acc't seems to confirm the general
report that Butler and Brant with their banditti are moved to
Niagara." The day before Hamilton, the Governor of Detroit, reached Vincennes and settled down in the false security
that Clark would be held in Kaskaskia by the drowned lands
of the Wabash, no less than the Creole girls, who were infatuated by him and his men.

We know nothing of the Christmas of '78 at Fort Niagara,
but an old chronicler says that

There were congregated the leaders of fashion of those bands of murderers and miscreants who carried death and destruction into the remote
American settlements. There civilized Europe revelled with savage
America, and ladies of education and refinement mingled in the society
of those whose only distinction was to wield the bloody tomahawk and
scalping knife. There the squaws of the forests were raised to eminence
and the most unholy unions between them and officers of the highest rank

[63] Roster of Butler's Rangers, *New York Genealogical and Biographical
Record*, 1900.
[64] Original letter, Congressional Library.

smiled upon and countenanced. There they planned their forays and there they returned to Feast.[65]

It seems not unlikely after the snows and mud and long, lonely cold that the men of the Rangers must have wanted love after fighting, sleep after toil, port after stormy seas. There were 111 wives and 259 children at Niagara, though, to welcome some of them. The rest, and the handsome Walter Butler perhaps first among them, must have danced and drunk and lain with the slim Indian girls, or Canadiennes, down from Quebec, or the wives of other luckless men on duty in some distant upper post.

On Christmas Day Haldimand wrote Colonel Butler from Quebec

I have also received your letter of the 1st December enclosing Captain Butler's relation of his operations at Cherry Valley, the success of which had afforded great satisfaction if his endeavors to prevent the excess to which the Indians in their fury are so apt to run, had proved effective; it is, however, very much to his credit that he gave proofs of his own disapprobation of such proceedings.[66]

At the same hour, in distant Rhinebeck, Mrs. Montgomery, the young widow of General Montgomery, killed at Quebec on New Year's Eve three years before, in his thirty-eighth year, was writing Colonel Aaron Burr for help in getting her "shopping list" up from New York with the flag.[67] Down the river in New York, with the Christmas dinner done, Sir Henry Clinton, snug and warm, could think smugly of the Continentals on the windy hills of Westchester. Andrew Lang says, in *Pickle the Spy*,[68] that at the close of '78, in far-off Avignon, the young Pretender, Charles Edward Stuart, received an offer from America of a throne.[69] Lang says that Walter Scott told this to Washington Irving on the authority of a document of the Stuart papers at Windsor.

[65] S. De Veaux, *The Falls of Niagara or Tourists Guide* (Buffalo, 1839), p. 119. Unfortunately this purple passage in De Veaux's Guidebook [size 5x3] is all there is of comment on the Loyalist occupation.
[66] Haldimand Papers, 62B, p. 358, Canadian Archives.
[67] *Memoirs of Aaron Burr* (New York, 1836), Vol. I, p. 139.
[68] *Pickle the Spy*, p. 321.
[69] John Buchan's story, "Companions of the Marjolaine" in *The Moon Endureth*, deals with the incident.

The year 1779 was in the grand manner. If the main armies were deadlocked on the Hudson, a vast strategy was still worked out behind them, west and north, and an enormous territory beyond the Ohio was American when the bargaining for peace began.

A British expedition under Prevost laid Georgia waste in January; the French Alliance so far was a disappointment, D'Estaing, their admiral, doing little or nothing. Continental money and supplies had reached bottom, but the presence of George Rogers Clark and his rifles at Kaskaskia was to outweigh all these things. There was to be a major war effort, magnificently planned by Washington, through western New York and Pennsylvania. The heart of the storm was to be over the long northwestern flank.

Continental Headquarters was busy seven months on the Sullivan-Clinton plans. The British Headquarters staffs at Carleton Island in the St. Lawrence, at Niagara and Detroit, were in a frenzy for news of the real situation of Hamilton in Vincennes. The river paths and forest trails were thick with runners for both commands carrying urgent dispatches like the captured one from Sir John Johnson inscribed:

> His Majesty's Service to Coll. John Butler, Niagara.
> Night and Day to be forwarded.

Robber gangs, owing no allegiance, still infested New York State, Governor Clinton proclaiming early in the year that "the names of the Persons in the different gangs of Robers who invest this state and those who harbor and abet them," [1] must be discovered. Men were coming from Canada and

---

[1] *Papers of George Clinton*, Vol. IV, p. 776.

Niagara to the valley through the winter snows to see their families. There were upwards of three hundred disaffected families "back of us," Jelles Fonda writes Clinton, "mostly tenants of Sir John Johnson and Col. Butler, where the enemy frequently comes." [2]

There is a thrilling story in the *Pennsylvania Gazette* of April 21,[3] telling how, early in March:

Four armed men were discovered passing privately through the mountains in the eastern part of Sussex County. The inhabitants pursued them and having excellent dogs for tracking followed by different routes upwards of 30 miles, when they were discovered. Two of them made their escape, the other two were lodged in the provost of the Continental troops at Minisink. They proved to be spies sent from New York with dispatches to those infamous butchers Butler and Brant. One of the prisoners is named Robert Sand, formerly a Magistrate. No doubt but the Court Martial which is now trying them will honor them with a share of Continental hemp.

The Butlers at Niagara were still intent on getting Mrs. Butler and Deborah and the three boys out of Albany in exchange for the prisoners taken at Cherry Valley. In Walter Butler's long, indignant letter to General James Clinton it was explained that the Niagara command was not empowered to make the exchange and that it was thought best for him to go to Haldimand and lay the papers before him. Haldimand eventually approved of the exchange, but many months were to pass before it was consummated. Sir Henry Clinton heard of it, possibly from Continental sources, wrote Haldimand prohibiting all intercourse with rebels, to which the latter apologetically answered: "I have hitherto declined exchanging prisoners but I believe necessity will oblige me to it, having been pressed by Major Butler to effect an exchange of his wife and family." [4]

The posts are again full of word of the Butlers, and Canadian Headquarters full of whispers from the Johnson clan. Mason Bolton explains that he is sending Walter Butler to

[2] *Papers of George Clinton*, Vol. IV, p. 669.
[3] Draper Collection, 7F, p. 72.   [4] *Mich. Hist. Coll.*, Vol. XIX, p. 471.

G. H. Q. "at the Major's earnest request," and Haldimand says the same to Sir Henry Clinton. There is this mysterious reluctance on the part of everyone to help the Butlers, but none, as we shall see, to have them and their Rangers in the posts of danger.

On March 5, 1779, Colonel Bolton wrote Haldimand,

I consented (at the Major's earnest request) to Captain Butler's going to Canada in order to lay before your Excellency the letters sent here, as well as a copy of his answer to the one he received here from a Brigadier Clinton. . . . For further particulars I beg leave to refer you to Capt. Butler who has assured me he would not make any unnecessary delay and I have no reason to doubt it, for upon all occasions he seems to be extremely anxious to be employed and has taken great pains with the Rangers during the winter to prepare them for service early in the spring.[5]

This letter is of interest, not only as regards the Butlers, but in what it says about the writer, Mason Bolton.[6] He seems to have been most typical of the earnest servants of the Crown who conscientiously and ponderously went about their routine labors of administration, investigation, and report, mainly unaware or incredulous of the power and numbers of the self-confident men pushing west. These Crown agents, Bolton particularly, steeped in the thrift of European economies, seemed "appalled," in letter after letter, at the vast sums spent on the Indian alliance; amounts, a fraction of which would have bought them a Cotswold house and ease and hunting and country life, and their sons' sons after them. The brilliant ambitious "young Butler," bent on winning the war, must have been a puzzle to them. The letter goes on with news of the building of the block house and store at Niagara, and says that Bolton is consulting "every person here who could give me any information concerning the plan of Agriculture"; it adds that "David, the Mohawk, is gone by water

[5] Haldimand Papers, 96B, Vol. I, pp. 251-53.
[6] Severance, Old Trails of the Niagara Frontier, p. 54, says of him, "I do not know of any printed book which offers any information about Col. M. Bolton or the life he led here."

to observe Gen'l McIntosh's motions" (at Fort Pitt), that Butler will take down the Muster Rolls, "and also the accounts of what the new Barracks and Log houses amounts to."

The voyage to Carleton Island or Montreal from Niagara was an arduous one. Walter Butler took it several times and it seems usually to have worn him out so that the fever contracted in the Albany jail renewed its hold on him. The route lay along the north coast of Lake Ontario, a shore that was still but little known. Butler evidently kept rough notes on his journey for his own satisfaction, and wrote them out for the use of the intelligence packet after Haldimand had talked to him of the trip.

The journal, which is about 2,500 words, is full of the most specific cartographic detail and naval intelligence; the landsman who wrote it speaks of wind and water, storm and sky signs like a mariner; there is an eye for farming opportunities, for new naval stores — for shooting and fishing; time and distance are minutely gauged; all written with the beautiful simplicity of the Pauline voyage, long ago, from the coast of Asia toward Rome. But the journal is more than that: it is in that ancient English tradition beginning long ago with John Trevisa who wrote "The lond is noble, copious and riche of nobil welles and of nobil ryveres with plente of fische; many faire wodes and grete with wel many bestes, tame and wydde;" and down through all the varying line — Bacon with his Gardens, Walton, Evelyn, Hudson — of men who greatly love the land and the waters about it and the long skies above it.

Niagara, 8th March, 1779 — Three o'clock in the Afternoon. Set off for Canada in a Batteau — the weather Calm, the Season very forward and more than Common fine, no appearance of Snow, Ice or Frost. Rowed to the 12 Mile Pond — saw this evening a large flock of Pidgeons in trees and number of Geese and Ducks in the Pond. . . .

March 9 — At Six put off, the Wind and Swell high and ahead. . . When the wind increasing and no Harbour nearer than 40 Mile Creek made for the creek and was near striking on the Barr but the force of the waves on the Stern and working briskly of the Oars got into the River — the Lands in General Level, the higher on the East side —

Timber, Oak, Pine, and a few Chestnut trees, the place appears as
the head of the Lake though it runs for 40 miles Westerly beyond
this. . . . Saw a number of Blackbirds.

10th of March — This morning about 7, the weather being clear and
little or no wind, we saw the spray or Mist of the Fall of Niagara
bearing from this about South East. . .[7]

11th of March — Round this lake or Pond a quantity of Hay might
be made. Set in raining at 10 this morning, an hour before sun-set
A thunder burst with lightning and a heavy rain, a thick Fog and calm
tho' still a high swell, set off a little before sunset, half an hour out.
Fog clear'd off with a hard North west wind. Very squally.

. . . . Up this creek a Saw Mill might be erected having fine rapids
and good timber for boards. This creek in the Fall is fill'd with Salmon,
as all other of the large runs of water are in the Fall. . . .

12th of March — Continuing sailing down the Bay to the carrying
Place, unloaded the Boat, handed her over and loaded again in an hour
and a half. Toronto was built on a level spot of Ground nearly opposite
a long narrow neck or Point of land running 7 or 8 miles into the Lake
which forms a noble bay of nine miles deep, 2 or 3 miles from the
bottom of which on the North Side ships can ride in safety, it's strange
the French Built the Fort where they did and not where their shipping
were wont to lay. . . The Banck very high and steep being a mixture of
Clay and Chalk, nearly as hard as Free stone, it forms a Romantic
wild view — in many places appearing like Towers in ruin, the remains
of houses and relics of Chimnies. . . . The wind fair, sailed till 4,
rowed till dark, put in shore in a deep bay, where we found a fine
Creek, it's water as clear as crystal.

14th of March — . . . . Expresses in winter pass this lake on their
way to Canada. . . .

16th of March — Put off our boat very early. Much ice which had
formed last night. . . . Am told vessels can't sail out of Caderoghque
to the Lake but with a North or Northeast wind, an East and Southeast
and South wind are fair winds for ships once clear of the River, to
Niagara. . . . The little island opposite the Fort, improved in the French
time, is now covered with small trees.

The above are all the observations I made on the north shore of
Ontario, which would have been more perfect but for the severity of the

---

[7] In all the papers examined, whether contemporary or those of forty years
previous, this is the only mention of Niagara Falls.

weather, which prevented any taking notice of many parts of the shore, neither did I think those remarks would have been seen, or would have been more particular.

WALTER BUTLER [8]

Haldimand seems to have liked Walter Butler. Sir John Johnson says in a letter to Claus, "He [Haldimand] told me the other day that young Butler was a pretty, genteel man." Sir John adds: "I took the opportunity to give my opinion of him pretty freely." Haldimand wrote John Butler on April 8 in a letter [9] already quoted, of his pleasure and acquiescence in the exchange. On the eighteenth of April he wrote:

I have ordered your son to join you without delay; his former good conduct gives me room to expect he will exert himself much to the advantage of the service and to his own credit and honor by harrassing the rebels and thwarting as much as possible their plan of operation.

The letter incidentally crossed one to him from John Butler which said:

I have just received your Excellency's letter of the 25th December and shall punctually observe its contents. I ever have and always shall use my utmost endeavors to restrain the Indians from acts of cruelty and indiscriminate vengeance which both as a man and an officer I hold in abhorrence.

Much more was discussed than Cherry Valley and the exchange of prisoners. For twenty years the western strategists had conceived of Niagara, Fort Pitt, and Detroit as a unit. Independently each leader found his concept of the grand strategy focused and based on that triangle. Alvord,[10] quoting from the report of General Gage to the cabinet, April 3, 1767, says: "The opinion of the members of the Administration was that forts at Detroit, Michillimackinac, Niagara, either Ticonderoga or Crown Point, and in the Illinois country, should be

[8] British Museum, Addit MSS 21, 765, Transcript in the Public Archives at Ottawa. 105B, pp. 100-12. Reprinted *Canadian Historical Review*, Toronto, Dec., 1920.

[9] Haldimand Papers, Ser. 96B, Vol. I, p. 162-64.

[10] C. W. Alvord, *The Mississippi Valley in British Politics* (Cleveland, 1917), Vol. II, p. 31.

garrisoned." Braddock said to Benjamin Franklin:[11] "After taking Fort Duquesne [Fort Pitt] I am to proceed to Niagara." The rebellion of Pontiac[12] aimed simultaneously at the three corners of the Fort Pitt-Niagara-Detroit triangle. From the beginning Washington planned to reduce Detroit and Niagara as part of his grand strategy.[13] Charles Lee[14] wrote John Hancock, May 10, 1776, "May I urge to the Congress the absolute necessity of straining every nerve to possess themselves of Niagara at least, if not Detroit."

This strategy and the protection of the fur trade were evidently matters of discussion between Haldimand and young Butler. They did not know that Hamilton with sixty rank and file from the 8th or Kings (Walter Butler's former regiment), had already surrendered at Vincennes on February 25 "to a set of uncivilized Virginia woodsmen armed with rifles." They did know, however, that a threat to Detroit and the long northwestern arm was developing, and that assistance was needed. John Butler knew on April 2, at Niagara, that Hamilton was taken. Butler perhaps volunteered to go out with his Rangers. Evidently Haldimand could not or would not give a definite authority, though on April 18 he knew of Hamilton's "ill fortune," as he called it to De Peyster. The Johnson Dynasty had been poisoning his mind about the Butlers and the Rangers for months. The Johnsons had been in England and evidently were possessed of strong friends there. It may have seemed inexpedient to have any break with them — but something was afoot.

Walter Butler left Headquarters and started back to Niagara, writing Captain Le Maitre, of his old regiment, then Deputy Adjutant General from La Chine on April 29th: "It is of the last consequence to our interest in the Upper Country

[11] T. G. Frothingham, *Washington, Commander-in-Chief* (Boston, 1930), p. 16.
[12] Francis Parkman, *The Conspiracy of Pontiac* (Boston, 1879), Vol. II, 1 *et seq.*
[13] Washington to Schuyler, Nov. 5, 1775.
[14] *American Archives*, 4th Series, Vol. VI, p. 403.

the sending reinforcements immediately. The troops going up can take three months provisions." [15]

A runner from his father at Niagara had evidently met him at La Chine. (A Captain Chene at the same time was making for Detroit with word that Vincennes had been taken and Hamilton sent to Virginia a prisoner). Later, the same day, Butler wrote again to Le Maitre at some length:[16]

LA CHENE,

28th Apri, 1779

DEAR SIR,

I am thus far on my way to Niagara and should have been off a day sonner had St. George given me the assistance he might in procuring me carts.

Nothing new has happened since I had the pleasure of seeing you, but what you have more particular than me from above, except an attack on Oswagahie the 25th inst. The Commanding Officer was near being made a prisoner, two men killed and four Privates taken prisoner. This by a party of Onydais and a few Tuskaroras being among them. From these prisoners they will learn the strength of said Garrison and will be an inducement to their making another attempt on it, and I fear with more success if not immediately re-inforced.

Colonel Butler writes me the Rangers made prisoners on the Suskahanna in January 1778 are now in New York, whether by exchange or by consequence of the Capitulation made with Colonel Dennison at Wyoming he does not mention.

I received a letter from Mr. Guthrill, Surgeon to the Corps of the Rangers, mentioning the necessity of having a Surgeon appointed to the Six Nations, and that Colonel Butler wished it might take place, he at the same time to me in his letter wishes the General would appoint Mr. Guthrill. Allowance must, in my humble opinion, be made him for his extraordinary service in that way.

Notwithstanding the cold water that has been thrown on our Corps I shall not leave a stone unturned to do what in me lays tending to forward the service, and if I succeed in beating back the Rebels advanced against Detroit will determine the line of life I mean to follow — die the times permit just now my determination was taken.

I am convinced some people have endeavoured to prejudice the Gen-

eral against Colonel Butler and me particular to make Joseph say he
was not well used, but were it not for fear of giving the General cause
to think that I would be above entering into any such low dispute would
have convinced him it was false — and that he has been more notice
taken of than has been good for his own interest with his own people.

Captain Tice will deliver you this, who goes down in order to wait
on His Excellency for his orders. I mentioned to him Captain Tice's
desire to go on service but from what the General said it struck me
that he was not acquainted with Captain Tice or knew his services.
I therefore advised him to wait on His Excellency and apply to one of
the Gentlemen who had the honour to make one of General Carleton's
family in '75 for their informing the General relating to his conduct in
that year and since. As I have reason to be convinced you are a friend
to every man of merit and who has deserved well you would lend them
your aid, I make free to refer him to you, being assured you will do him
all the justice he deserves.

I shall take the very first opportunity of giving you any information
worthy of your notice. I must beg leave to declare how sensible I am
of the great attention you have on many occasions been pleased to show
me, which will make me take every opportunity to declare how much I
am,

>Dear Sir,
>Your obliged and real friend,
>WALTER BUTLER

Captain La Matre

The recommendation for that "man of merit," Gilbert Tice,
was one of the few Walter Butler ever gave anyone. He had
been Butler's commanding officer in that first engagement at
Montreal and for some reason his pay was in discussion most
of the war. His wife wrote him the charming letter already
quoted. She wrote him again about this time very seriously
quoting Acts iv, 31: "that where the apostles prai'd the place
was shaken a sure sign to those who fear and put their trust in
God; he will never forsake them." She concludes "This little
piece of pedantry the best of husbands will excuse in his tender
wife who ardently prays and constantly wishes your welfare."
Then apparently feeling that she had been too serious puts in
a flippant postcript beginning "Dear Tice."

It would be interesting to know exactly what is meant by the paragraph beginning "notwithstanding the cold water that has been thrown on our Corps." From earlier Johnson letters it is likely that the "cold water" was aimed at alleged military ineffectuality. Butler's failure to identify the people who are trying to prejudice the General against him may not mean he that did not know them. He must have heard the gossip around Headquarters. It is very likely that he really felt "above entering into any such low dispute" with men who, safe at Carleton Island, intrigued against the front. The main thing, though, is that he speaks of going out to Detroit. There was great worry there over the Clark expedition and they were calling frantically on Niagara for reinforcements. It was even rumored that there were 4,000 French soldiers at Vincennes with all D'Estaing's artillery![17] The stir along the Hudson as the Continentals began to move toward Easton may have come to their ears, and though they did not know it yet, Schuyler had written Washington two days before of the complete success of Colonel Van Schaick, who had moved out of Stanwix with 550 men and laid waste the Onondaga Castle.

It is interesting to note that at this time with young Butler volunteering for the post of danger in the West, and with Washington writing Sullivan, that "the Indians may have peace by delivering up Butler," Sir John Johnson writes Colonel Butler at Niagara to "send him 4 Bags of Paint," as though the old warrior were a sutler. At New Haven that spring they gave a dramatic presentation of the Tories and Indians at Wyoming and the worthy Dr. Stiles, President of Yale, "took the part of the blood-thirsty Colonel Butler." [18]

Lord George Germaine was writing Haldimand, with that incomprehensible fulsomeness of his, about Brant:

The astounding activity of Joseph Brant's enterprises and the important consequences with which they have been attended gave him a claim to every mark of our regard and which you think will be most pleasing to him. What has occurred to me as most likely to gratify him

[17] *Michigan Hist. Colls.*, Vol. X, p. 396.
[18] *Nathan Hale*, p. 33.

has been done, and enclosed herewith you will receive a commission signed by H. M. [His Majesty] appointing him a Colonel of Indians, and the brand [crest?] of the "Three Brothers." Store ship has a box with Prints taken from Lord Warwick's pictures of him, which he was particularly pleased with, some of which you will send into his Nation and dispose of the others in such manner as you shall think most honorable for him as a memorial of his services. [And then adds], Major Butler and his son appear also to have done good service and you will acquaint them that their care to prevent the Indians from molesting the Inhabitants unarmed is much approved of by the King.[19]

There is a certain irony in this making a colonel of an Indian, and then expressing the King's gratitude to a poor major and a lieutenant for their care in restraining the colonel's people. As Walter Butler well said of this Colonel, "He has been more notice taken of than has been good for his own interest with his own people."

Having reached Carleton Island on his journey back to Niagara Butler wrote, May tenth, to Haldimand:

CARLETON ISLAND
10th May, 1779

SIR,

Agreeable to your Excellency's direction I have made every inquiry I could in order to inform myself of such Accounts relating to the Enemy as may be depended on — but no arrivals from Niagara since Major Butler's last to your Excellency puts it out of my power to give any farther particulars of the Enemy at the Susquehanna or other matters from that quarter.

A prisoner brought in from Fort Handiver by Lt. Hare of the Indian Department informs that the Rebels have but three hundred men at that Post — we are farther informed by him that a body of the Enemy went down the Onida Lake in Batteaux and landed at this end of the Lake and marched to the Onandaga Village, where they found about thirty souls mostly Women and Children of that Nation, and led them into Captivity. Among the number I fear they have taken a child of Joseph Brant's. This stroke of theirs has every appearance as if they mean to take hold of Oswego for by having this Indian in their hands, they conjecture the Indians will not presume to molest them in such an

[19] Original Letter, Sir Henry Clinton Papers, Clements Collection.

enterprise. In my humble opinion this will have a great effect on the Indians either by enraging or intimidating them. Whatever effect it may have I hope it may not be the latter. Joseph is here with me and is much distressed about his Child. The Chiefs from Canada sent by your Excellency to the Onidas are here likewise and are to go up with me in the visit to Niagara. We have been waiting four days for a fair wind.

I am sorry to hear Killbuch a Chief among the Showanoes and Deleware has joined the Rebels at Fort Pitt and those parts. This Indian is a good warrior and may be of great hurt to us. Tho' I hope the Belts sent by the Five Nations to the Indians dwelling thereabouts may have a good effect and bring him and others to their Duty.

There is no foundation for the report of the Enemy having been at Oswego and by what the prisoner says was there any talk among them of such an intention. Lt. Hare is at present out with a party of Indians towards Oswegoe, who is to return here, by him we will learn if any movements have been made that may.

I am with much respect

Your Excellency's most obedient servant

WALTER BUTLER

Captain of the Corps of Rangers [20]

Back in Niagara Butler wrote [21] immediately to General James Clinton that relieved, happy letter the end of which is so charming:

SIR,

Agreeable to my letter directed to you of the 18th of February last, I were to acquaint you of His Excellency Genl. Haldimand's determination on the proposed exchange of Prisoners. I am so happy as to have His Excellency's Directions to inform you of his assent thereto, and that the same may take place by the way of Crown Point on the day of May next likewise that of Lt. Col. Stacy and others. Your officers and Soldiers, in our Hands will be given in exchange for an equal number of ours with you, (among which the officers and rangers mentioned in the list enclosed you, in my last, are to be included. The Commander in Chief has ordered all the Prisoners as well as those belonging to your Troops, as Inhabitants, or familes etc. at Niagara, or elsewhere immediately to Canada for the above purpose. I have by this opportunity wrote Mrs. Butler & Transmitted her some money, in order to enable

[20] "New Sources Sullivan-Clinton Campaign" *Quarterly Journal*, N. Y. State Hist. Assoc., Vol. X, No. 3.   [21] Canadian Archives, B 105, pp. 427-28.

her and family to come to Canada, which please permit to be delivered to her; if the season will admit. It will oblige me, and particularly the younger part of the family, their being allow'd to come immediately to Canada, as the children are to go to England in the first ships.

I am, Sir, your most obd't. and very Hble. Servt.
WALTER BUTLER,
Captain, Corps of Rangers

Addressed:
Brigadier General Clinton
Continental Forces
Albany

That ended the exchange negotiations. On May 13th John Butler who was out with his Rangers, southeast of Niagara at Genesee, captured a prisoner from near Fort Pitt who

says he saw a Circular letter from the Congress to the Inhabitants of the Frontiers to encourage them not to foresake their settlements — they promise that General Hand shall be sent with 3000 men up the Susquehanna and General Wayne with two regular regiments and a large body of Militia up the Allegany — he says they are preparing Boats upon the Allegany. . . . It seems to be the intention of the Rebels to erect a chain of Forts all along their frontiers.

It was the first stir of the Sullivan campaign. Butler was here still feeling his way through the rumors coming in. Sullivan, his antagonist, wrote to Washington on the 13th from Easton "They know of the expedition and are taking every steps to destroy the communications on the Susquehannah."

That same night Major Butler wrote [22] Bolton from Genesee, 350 miles from Sullivan, an unconscious confirmation saying:

I received a letter that a body of the rebels were on their way from Albany to make another attempt against the Indians — this news was brought him by a runner from Cayouga — This Intelligence has been but five days by the way. I shall march this morning with the party for Canadasaga.

This old fighter was amazingly informed at all times about his foes.

[22] "New Sources Sullivan-Clinton Campaign," p. 217 (both letters).

Two days later Brehm, Haldimand's A.D.C. who had come down to Niagara wrote him that "Captain Butler has promised to go out with a strong party toward the Tuscaroras by Col. Bolton's desire." On the twentieth of May, Walter Butler wrote to Haldimand that

Major Butler with the Corps had moved towards the Frontier . . . Col. Bolton has thought proper I should in a few days set off for Detroit with twenty-five Rangers and as many Indians as I can collect on the ground. . . . Could I prevail on Joseph Brant to accompany me with but a few of the Five Nations I flatter myself much might be done.[23]

There then follows the endless confusion about Capt. Tice's pay and the Ranger accounts. Bolton had informed John Butler that the "bounty money to the Rangers on enlistment [was] rather unreasonable and not agreeable to the Intentions of Gen'l. Carleton." [24] All through the war questions of the correspondence, Headquarters is writing in about money matters and there is the question of whether they can "draw for barrack accounts." The war was a terrific financial burden for both sides. Clark in the flush of his Vincennes victory found that his subsistence drafts on New Orleans had gone to protest. There is a two year cost of £2,378,429 mentioned in the British Headquarters Papers the next year and even the fur trade could not cover it.

On the 28th of May, as he was about to march to the westward, Walter Butler wrote Le Maitre again [25] of a paper in connection with the Tice pay which he had forgotten to enclose:

Some Indians came in just as I was sealing the letter troubling me for rum. . . . I expect soon to move to Detroit or Fort Pitt, whatever way it is my endeavors shall not be wanting to forward the service by what in me lays to preserve the Indians in our interest. *This kind of service is far from being agreeable to me but I shall not quit it unless I can with honor.*[26]

I am plagued with the families of Royalists who are ordered down. I pray the General will do something for these distressed people.

[23] "New Sources Sullivan-Clinton Campaign," p. 218.   [24] *Ibid.*, p. 217.
[25] Original letter, British Museum, D. 1.   [26] Author's italics.

Two days later intelligence got into New York that

the Chief of the Six Nations desired to let Sir Henry Clinton know that they had had no message from any General for a long time. They wished to know what quarter they were to give or what severity they were to exercise, that they understood he was displeas'd with their severities at Cherry Valley, and were sorry for it. That the rebels had destroyed their head town and killed their squaws and children and it was hard they should not retaliate. Brant and young Butler were gone to Detroit.[27]

It was blowing up to the south, east, and west. John Bowman,[28] with 160 Kentuckians, had already attacked the Indian town of Chillicothe. Logan, Harrod, and all the famous frontiersmen were with him, and, though beaten off, much plunder was taken. The turning movement was developing.

Six months before, in November, 1778, Washington had written Schuyler "Congress seems to have a strong desire to undertake an expedition to Canada." The elaborate letter is one of the many marvelous examples of Washington's ability to think in terms of a vast strategy, while considering every detail of the strategy. The conclusion of it is that by spring "the certain reduction of Niagara" must be accomplished, while Detroit must be threatened and, if at all possible, taken.

On May 31, 1779, after unresting work on his plan, Washington wrote to Sullivan:

This expedition you are appointed to command is to be directed against the hostile tribes of the Six Nations of Indians with their associates and adherents. The immediate objects are the total destruction and devastation of their settlements and the capture of as many prisoners of every sex and age as possible. It will be essential to ruin their crops in the ground and prevent their planting more.

This letter has been the basis of the general view that the expedition was "a punitive drive in retaliation for the outrages committed on the border settlements," although some writers,

---

[27] Clements Collection, Sir Henry Clinton Papers, Vol. CXV.
[28] Theodore Roosevelt, *The Winning of the West* (New York, 1895), Vol. II, p. 96.

like Greene and Johnston,[29] disregard it altogether and say that the only military events of the year in the North were Stony Point and Paulus Hook on the Hudson.

There is perhaps no wilderness of Revolutionary historical material easier to lose one's self in than is presented by the original sources of the '79 campaign. The State of New York at the centennial of that enterprise published a book [30] of 580 closely printed pages almost entirely made up of journals and letters of officers and men in Sullivan's army. There is primary material everywhere, and in 1929 Dr. Flick, the New York State Historian, issued his "New Sources — Sullivan-Clinton Campaign."[31] This last enormously valuable work makes clear the following points:

(1) By 1779 Washington saw that the war was pretty much deadlocked. He believed that peace was not far off. He saw that when the terms of settlement were drawn up, if the young nation got nothing but a strip of land along the Atlantic with no opportunity for expansion westward, the struggle would scarcely be worth its cost. Hence the Sullivan-Clinton Campaign and the expedition under George Rogers Clark farther westward were intended to stake down claims which would assure to the United States western New York and Pennsylvania and likewise the rich territory south of the Great Lakes farther west. Not many leaders of 1779 saw the great prize, but Washington, the Seer, did.

(2) The expedition was perhaps the most carefully planned offensive campaign in the Revolution. In geographic scope it covered immediately the major parts of Pennsylvania and New York and ultimately territory to the Mississippi. It was led by carefully selected officers and the troops were for the most part veterans.

(3) There were months of planning and gathering informa-

---

[29] Henry P. Johnston, *The Storming of Stony Point* (New York, 1900), p. 2: "1779 — a year without a pitched battle or a stirring campaign."

[30] *General John Sullivan's Indian Expedition, 1779.*

[31] *Quarterly Journal*, N. Y. State Hist. Assn., Vol. X, Nos. 3-4. See also the same author's *The Sullivan-Clinton Campaign of 1779* (ALBANY, 1929).

tion as to routes, water-levels, supplies, trails, seasons, settlements, transportation etc., during which Washington himself carried on an enormous correspondence with frontiersmen, rangers, scouts, travelling trappers, soldiers and missionaries. The culmination was his own sixteen-page questionnaire issued to General Hand, Colonels Cox, Stewart and Patterson.

(4) The territory invaded was an enormously important granary for the British "Upper Posts," and the base of all hostilities against our frontiers.

(5) The plan of the campaign was:

    a For Sullivan to go Northwest from Easton, past Wyoming to Tioga up the Chemung, through western New York to Niagara.

    b He was to rendezvous at Tioga with General James Clinton coming down the Susquehanna from Canajoharie with the New York brigade.

    c Van Schaick was to move through the Onondaga country, laying it waste from Stanwix (and did so in April).

    d Brodhead was to strike North from Fort Pitt toward the Genesee Castle and to be in at the attack on Niagara.

    e Clark at Vincennes was, in Forrest's phrase, "to move up, and fetch all he got."

(6) Each preliminary move in the campaign was known to Colonel John Butler almost immediately through his mysterious and amazingly efficient system of scouts, runners, spies and informants, and communicated by him to the Canadian High Command. His correct diagnosis of the intelligence brought in was unfailing.

For some reason Washington felt it necessary to offer the command of the force to General Gates, who (fortunately) declined it on account of his age. He was then fifty-seven. John Butler dominating the whole frontier and the tribes was fifty-four. Gates had been with Braddock and Washington on the Monongahela, and Pontiac with the French.

From May 28 to June 5 Butler wrote six letters to Bolton

or Haldimand tersely reporting the exact American disposi-
tions and objectives, the whole based on his interpretation of
rumors brought in by Indian runners. Time and again one
must wonder what it would have meant to Washington to
have had this thorough, skilled, dependable man with his brilliant, restless son on his side instead of Gates or Charles Lee,
or the long list of easily discouraged, incompetent, inexperienced men he had to contend with. "Some of her bravest leaders
spoke gloomily of the possibility of the Americans being driven
from the land [west of the Alleghanies]," as Roosevelt points
out.[32] Major Joseph Bowman, one of Clark's most trusted
officers, wrote [33] his friend Isaac Hite, "I am sensible that the
acting in a Public Compasity interfairs two much with our
Private affairs."

On May 28 Butler, who was at Canadasaga, wrote :[34]

The alarm spread among the Indians by the destruction of Onondaga
made it highly necessary for me to march into their country. . . . I have
got the families of the Onondagoes that have escaped to settle in the
different villages among the Senecas to plant their corn but have been
obliged to promise them. . . . a little provisions to help support them:
tho' I know the importance of the article of Provision, and how ill it can
be spared, I could not avoid doing this, as they have not been able to
bring off a single thing with them and we cannot let them starve. . . .
This evening came in an Indian who left Oneyda four days ago; just
before he left it he says there came in some Indians who had been
at Albany . . . there were great numbers of troops at Albany and
Schenectady and it was given out that they intended an expedition
against Niagara; and that at the same time a Body of Men from the
Susquehanna were to march into the Indian country. Tho there is no
great confidence to be put in many reports that the Indians bring in. . . .
I shall take such precautions that it will be next to impossible for
anybody of men to advance beyond Fort Stanwix or make any movement
on the Susquehanna without being made acquainted with it almost
immediately.

[32] *Winning of the West*, Vol. II, p. 92.
[33] Letter from Kaskaskia, copy in Draper Notes 4S. Original printed in
Virginia Magazine of History and Biography, Vol. XV, p. 211-13.
[34] "New Sources Sullivan-Clinton Campaign," p. 221.

Then there is the amazingly complete letter of June 1 to Bolton:[35]

Early this morning arrived a runner with the news that a body of the enemy were advancing. . . . The Bearer who is just come from the Mohawk River informs me that the Party who destroyed the Onondago village returned to Fort Stanwix . . . with about 35 Onondagoes and five or six Cayuga women and children. . . . I am told by a prisoner, brought in last Sunday, taken seven days before that at the German Flats, that the Rebels at Lake Otsego have been damming up the Lake and endeavoring by every method to raise the water sufficiently to the creek that leads into the Susquehanna to float their boats. Captain Butler writes me on the 29th inst that a runner came to him from Canawagaras informing that a party of Indians have . . . [seen] a large body of the rebels at Fort Pitt; they heard cannon and believe they are fixing a Post and then mean to come on.

The enemy must I should imagine have laid aside their designs against Detroit if they really mean to come into the Indian country in this Quarter and that they will I think is beyond a doubt. In this case if Captain McDonell is not able to drive off a great quantity of cattle and we cannot be largely supplied from Niagara I do not know what may be the consequences as it will be impossible without this to maintain any number of People together. . . .

P. S. A prisoner just arrived reports that the Rebels are still at Otsego; their numbers are some say 4000 others say 1500 [36] all Continental Troops commanded by Gen'l Clinton. They are waiting for Provisions and have been sometime employed in damming up the Lake to make the Creek passable for their boats if possible.

Examination of the American documents adds nothing to this enemy report of James Clinton's army, and the great engineering feat, unless it be the regiments: The Second New York (Philip Van Cortlandt's), The Third New York (Gansevoort's own), The Fourth and Fifth, Lamb's Artillery, and Harper's New York Volunteers.

June 3rd Butler slipped a runner through the "underground" for Sir Henry Clinton telling him that [37] reinforcements have been sent to Detroit. . . . The Indians desire them

---

[35] *Ibid.*, p. 223.   [36] There were actually 1,500.
[37] "New Sources Sullivan-Clinton Campaign," p. 219.

to acquaint Gen'l. Clinton that they were still firm friends . . . they had their spies upon the Mountains. . . . The provisions I have . . . will last us a day or two at the most. . . . Captain Butler's going out toward Presque Isle and Venango [38] may probably be of service. . . . I shall be obliged soon to send for more ammunition. . . . The Indians from the scarcity of Provisions consume more of it than ordinary by firing at every little Bird they see.

It was the same story of hunger or want both sides of the border. Clark was still at Vincennes with 350 barefoot men, powerless to move for want of supplies. Vincennes was scarcely able to feed its own inhabitants.[39] And then on the 5th,[40]

I have sent Aaron and David with two Parties down to the Mohawk River; They mean to go very low down and bring off a Prisoner that will be able to give us some certain Intelligence of what the Rebels are doing. Lt. H. Hare is with the one Party. . . .

Hare was going to his death a month later at a rope's end. It was a brave business.

It is apparent from all the documents that John Butler and his son were responsible for the whole territory from Albany to Presqu' Isle on Lake Erie, and even to Detroit. The Sullivan-Clinton-Brodhead effort was in effect aimed at them. At nameless campfires runners found them with rumor or dispatch or prisoner telling them of the hosts mustering to close in on them. There was something indomitable about these men living mostly on parched corn, in the rigors of the wilderness, that led them to stick it.

That same June day as Butler was sending Hare to his death, Schuyler wrote Washington [41] from Albany in his clear beautiful script, "The line of conduct which Your Excellency points out as necessary to be observed with the Indians meets our entire approbation. We shall immediately try to engage the Onondagas to bring off Brandt and Butler." [42]

It is evident that it had occurred to Washington or the

---

[38] Where Washington took Dinwiddie's ultimatum to St. Pierre ordering him to quit the Ohio country in '53.   [39] James, *George Rogers Clark*, p. 172.
[40] "New Sources Sullivan-Clinton Campaign," p. 218.
[41] Original letter, Congressional Library.   [42] See above, p. 70.

Headquarters Staff that liberty might be offered to the Onondagas taken by Van Schaick if they were willing to try to capture Butler. They would be received by him as allies in distress and might lure him into capture. Their wives and children were held as guaranty of their conduct. The plan did not come off. Butler makes no mention of such an attempt; he had cast his bread upon the waters for them and was secure. Washington's own suggestion of the ruse, however, is further evidence of the great importance laid on the Butlers by the American high command. It is almost safe to say that Washington paid more attention to their activities than to any enemy unit.

The Continental armies gathering for the rendezvous at Tioga were full of men new to Indian fighting, though hardened veterans. The great numbers of diaries kept give evidence of the fact that the zone northwest of Tioga was foreign land to them. It is particularly significant that, except for trained scouts and Morgan's Riflemen, the troops chosen for the force were those who would have been chosen to meet Cornwallis' Grenadiers. Washington had seen the Braddock expedition crushed, not because its units were veteran soldiers but because the advance was not screened by scouts. He was everlastingly aware of the worthlessness of militia. When there was fighting, whether in the misty streets of Germantown or the pathless wilderness, he wanted disciplined, well-drilled troops. And this was what he sent, so that in dispatch after dispatch from John Butler there was a rising note of alarm as he realized the Continentals were out.

Jones, the contemporary Loyalist historian, once a Judge of the Supreme Court of New York, says: "I have heard Colonel Butler compare it [opposition to the Sullivan command] to the driving of a wedge into a stick of oak. Nothing stopped or disturbed its [Sullivan's Army's] motion." [43]

Sullivan moved out of Wyoming on July 31, laying waste the country as he went, and met James Clinton near Tioga on

[43] *History of New York during the Revolutionary War*, Vol. II, p. 334.

August 19.[44] They had waited from June 1 to July 31 with maddening deliberation, but when their supplies and intelligence were ready, they marched; they had built a great military road and Clinton dammed a lake, though Washington apprehended "the worst consequences" from Clinton's great baggage train and reduced mobility. Governor Clinton, his brother, on July 30, attributed the success of Brant's raid on Minisink to "the uncountable delay of General Sullivan at Wyoming, we have had every reason to expect that long before this he would have been with his army in the Heart of the Enemy's country." In any event the delay made it possible for his army to live on the ripening garden-truck in the Indian country.

All the sixty days the Butlers watched them from the forests. On June 18 John Butler [45] had "procured the Releasement of a Mrs. Campbell and sent her with Mr. Seacord to Niagara." This was Colonel Campbell's wife taken from Cherry Valley. "If there is not a more convenient place," Butler says, "I have told her she might stay at my house."

He was then at Canadasaga, bedevilled with the necessity of keeping contact with the enemy's advance and being close enough to Genesee to feed his men from the dwindling magazine there. He heard on June 24 that "some persons at Niagara either out of jealousy or from some other motive have endeavored to persuade the Indians that they were imposed upon . . . and ought to demand £12 a head for their cattle." This was probably not the Dynasty, but jealousy of the high pay of the Rangers. He sent McDonnell raiding down the Susquehannah where the Americans had cattle. On July 3 he wrote [46] "It seems now beyond a doubt that the Rebels are coming up the Susquehanna." He had captured a deserter and gotten every detail of the commanders, men, and guns, massing at Wyoming.

It is interesting to compare Butler's deductions from his

[44] *General Sullivan's Indian Expedition.* "Journal of Col. Dearborn," 65-71.
[45] "New Sources of Sullivan-Clinton Campaign," p. 266.
[46] *Ibid.,* p. 266.

Intelligence service with that of Haldimand, his Commander in Chief. After reading the dispatches, the latter wrote [47] from Quebec, July 23, to Bolton, then at Niagara:

I have no idea that you can suffer from any attempt of the enemy. . . . It is impossible the Rebels can be in such force as has been represented by the deserters to Major Butler upon the Susquehanna. He would do well to send out intelligent white men to be satisfied of the truth of those reports. If anything is really intended against the Upper Country I am convinced Detroit is the object, and that they show themselves and spread reports of expeditions in your neighborhood merely to divert the Rangers and Indians from their main purpose — Major Butler should be aware of this.[47]

The "intelligent white men," Hare and Newberry, had been sent. On July 7 Butler got word of them. "One piece of intelligence I am much distressed at: Lt. Henry Hare and Serg't Newberry have had the misfortune to fall into the hands of the Rebels and were executed along with some other man." [48]

The execution stirred the Butlers and their Rangers deeply. Hare was an old neighbor: he owned three hundred acres of land in Tryon, bought from John Butler. His wife and children were prisoners in Albany along with Sergeant Newberry's family. They were on a scout and it is hard to see how a party of twenty-one men could be captured and have its leaders executed for espionage. But they needed victims in Albany and General James Clinton wrote his wife,

My dear, I hope you have received the things I sent you. . . . I have nothing further to acquaint you of except that we apparehended a certain Lt. Harry Hare and Sergeant Newberry who confessed they left the Seneca Country with 63 Indians to attack Schohary Cherry Valley and the Mohawk River. I had them tryed by a General Court Martial for spies who sentenced them both to be hanged which was done to the satisfaction of all the Inhabitants of that place as they were known to be very active in almost all the murders committed on these frontiers: they were inhabitants of Tryon County and had each a wife and several children who came to see them and beg their lives.[49]

[47] *Ibid.*, p. 274.   [48] *Ibid.*, p. 268.
[49] *Papers of George Clinton*, Vol. V, p. 122.

Campbell in his *Annals* calls Newberry the murderer of Mitchell's family at Cherry Valley. The evidence, if any, is flimsy. They were daring men and the evidence is in their favor, but wars take Hales and Andrés and fathers of families without discrimination.

Walter Butler heard the news at the Genesee the next day and wrote at once in high indignation to Brehm, Haldimand's A. D. C.:

Genesia River

8th August 1779

Captain Butler requests Captain Brehm will lay before His Excellency General Haldimand I beg to Lay before Y Excy the Fate of every officer and soldier serving on the Frontiers in those parts are to expect in case they should be so unfortunate as to fall into the enemies hands which will fully appear by the fate of Mr. Lt. Henry Hare, an officer in the Indian Department and Sergeant Newberry of my Rangers met with, taken on a Scout to Otsago Lake. They were no sooner taken but were immediately executed — likewise a Genteleman sent by Sir Henry Clinton to Colonel Butler with Dispatches was taken on his return from Colonel Butler and immediately executed.

The conduct of every officer both of the Rangers & Indian Dept., in exerting themselves on every occasion; to preserve the lives of Prisoners taken and also to treat them well; Particularly at Wyoming & Cherry Valley last Campaign, and this by Captain McDonell; should set the Rebels an example if they were men possessed of Humanity or common Justice, to do the like — as those Instances have had the contrary effect; some method should be taken to restrain the Rebels from such acts of Barbarism, or they will be under the necessity to do themselves justice — Mr. Hare has left a helpless wife and a number of small children, he had a Brother killed in His Majesty's service, a Captain in the Indian Dept., at Fort Stanwix in '77, who likewise left a wife and five small children — he has a Brother living, a Captain in the Corps of Rangers and a nephew, a Lieut. in said Corps, both men of merit. The Sergeant left a wife & Children —

Captain Brehm will likewise mention to the General, that had the Rangers and Indians which would be embodied sufficient Provisions to take them to the Frontiers they would be able to render Sir Harry Clinton most important Service in his expedition up the North River.

WALTER BUTLER [50]

---

[50] "New Sources of the Sullivan-Clinton Campaign," p. 277.

Haldimand thereupon refused parole to Continental officers in Montreal and there was an exchange of notes with Sir Henry Clinton, and through him with Washington, on the whole subject including Virginia's treatment of Hamilton after Vincennes. But Hare was dead and, the next year, in Montreal, Haldimand received "The Petition of Abigail Hare . . . a poor widow with six small children . . . the want of every necessary of life and the continual insults of the rebels obliged her to leave the Province of New York, and come off to this." [51] Haldimand granted her £20 a year but the house and acres on the Mohawk and her husband were gone. There would seem to be little doubt, though there is no reference to it, that the execution of their comrade left the Butlers indifferent to Boyd's death the next month.

On the night of July 16, while Clinton and Sullivan still waited, Wayne took Stony Point on the Hudson, greatly heartening the anxious men at Easton and demonstrating to Sir Henry Clinton that even without his best men Washington could dominate the Hudson. It was magnificently conceived and timed and of course beautifully executed by Wayne.

In his long letter [52] of July 21 to Haldimand, John Butler places Walter back at the Genesee Falls which was his advanced base. He speaks of a strong post at Cayuga and Chemung and adds, "should our services be required towards Detroit, Fort Pitt or Venango, there is no place we can be so centrical for either of those places."

The next day Joseph Brant attacked Minisink on the Delaware, far back of James Clinton's army and within striking distance across country of Continental General Headquarters at Morristown. It would seem evident that it was a diversion to draw off the invasion of the Indian country, and various historians so described it, but there is no mention of it in any of the Butler letters until August 4 when John Butler writes, "Dear Walter, a couple of Indians came in this evening from Joseph. He has been down to Minisink and I believe has met

[51] Original in possession of Robert W. Chambers.
[52] "New Sources of Sullivan-Clinton Campaign," p. 268.

with a disappointment." [53] Brant was disappointed though he
did write Bolton "we did not in the least injure women or children." He adds that they took only four scalps and three
prisoners, "owing to the many forts about the place into which
they were always ready to run like ground hogs." This is of
course bravado but a New York Militia officer did report
to Governor Clinton — "A party of 240 set out on Saturday
and marched that day within 2 miles of the place of action,
but the rain on Sunday made it imprudent to stay, as many
were not prepared to be out after such a wet day." [54]

On the 24th McDonnell, another "intelligent white men,"
such as Haldimand wanted sent out, reported that "The
enemy means to attack the Indian country from Wyoming
remains no longer in doubt." The commanders' names are
given and "the whole is said to consist of 8000 men, tho' I
cannot allow them above the half nor do I believe they have
that."[55] Haldimand had been beautifully served all spring by
the intelligence he put no credence in. This letter in fact
reached Butler with one from Haldimand telling him flatly to
procure "authentic accounts . . . not trusting to the reports
of Indians or deserters . . . it is impossible they can have nine
regiments, the cannon etc. reported."

To realize how slow the start of Sullivan was one must
realize that, on July 25, twenty years before, Sir William
Johnson had reported from Niagara, "This morning the Fort
surrendered by capitulation." Yet he and Sullivan had started
in the same month.

On July 31 Sullivan moved out of Wyoming, Hand's Light
Infantry in the van, Maxwell on the left flank and Poor on
the right with the 1st, 2nd, and 3rd New Hampshire, and the
6th Massachusetts, the Cherry Valley outfit, under Whiting,
the surviving field officer. Maxwell's brigade was formed of
New Jersey regiments, Hand's of Pennsylvania, the 4th and
11th, Proctor's artillery, militia, and Morgan's Riflemen,
and there were twelve hundred pack horses and seven hundred

---

[53] *Ibid.*, p. 278.   [54] *Papers of George Clinton*, Vol. V, p. 162.
[55] They had 2,500 men.

beef cattle. The way was hard, the weather warm and rainy, and stragglers numerous, some being cut off by the Indians and Rangers hovering around the army.

On August 8 they were at Standing Stone fifty-five miles from Wyoming, Sullivan ill and Maxwell in command; Walter Butler was still at Genesee, fuming about the way supplies were coming down from Niagara. He wrote [56] Mr. Gorin:

It is impossible for me to have the things sent in bulk here, and to be charged by me in my present situation and in fact in any way would I do it without two clerks. After you have charged, agreeable to the memorandum, the non-commissioned officers can divide the articles in small quantities. Please send me two bearskins. If Capt. Robinson gets up any port, please send me a barrel on my account. I am obliged to you for the hooks, for now it is that he that will not hunt or fish must not eat.

Give my best respects to Mrs. Robinson.

I am your very humble servant,

WALTER BUTLER

It is impossible not to like the writer of this human letter. A great campaign about to break and Niagara expecting him to distribute supplies as though he were in a quartermaster's depot. A great campaign about to break, and the young man who wore a gold-laced hat in the Wilderness sending for a barrel of port on his own account. But why the bearskins with the Continentals melting in the sultry August heat? The fish hooks were a life and death matter. John Butler had formed the post at Genesee partially because the fishing there would feed the men. There was a Captain Robinson at the fort to whom no respects are sent. Mrs. Robinson is the only lady mentioned in the letters of Walter Butler, and we know no more about her.

On the tenth Sullivan resumed command and was four miles from Tioga. They were coming on. The whole overture was in crescendo and both sides must have been glad to be through with waiting. John Butler wrote to Bolton from Canadasaga, that day, his brief warrior letter: "We mean

56 Ketchum, *History of Buffalo*, Appendix, letter quoted.

to make this our place of rendezvous and collect together as many as we can and give the enemy battle at all events." In the morning Sullivan forded the river at Tioga and the trumpets sounded for him on the other side.

That same day, as Walter Butler had prophesied in June, Colonel Brodhead moved out of Fort Pitt, up the Alleghany River, with 600 Continentals and some militia, headed for the Genesee. Colonel Butler warned [57] Walter that Sullivan was "very strong. . . . I think if it should be necessary for you to march it would be best to send off all the sick, along with the prisoners to Niagara, as we shall not be able to spare men to keep Post at the River." On the twelfth [58] he knew Sullivan had reached Tioga two days before, and he ordered Walter to "march immediately upon the receipt of this with every man you have got fit for duty and use all convenient speed till you reach this place. . . . I must desire of you to write to the Colonel and request him to send four or five boats to Genesee River for our use, and some provisions." The retreat he was later to make was masterly and the boats were the first preparation for it.

Brant at Chemung on the nineteenth wrote [59] Claus at Montreal, "there will be a battle either tomorrow or the day after . . . which we think will be a severe one. . . . Of course their intention is to exterminate the people of the Long House." There is a noble melancholy in the letter and it is Brant at his best. James Clinton had reached Tioga at ten that morning and the combined armies were about 4,000 men.

Butler was at Chucknut on the twenty-sixth, "Encamped within 14 miles of the enemy," who was laying waste the country. They had already burned Chemung where Brant's letter was written and Rowland Montour was harassing them. Bolton from the vantage ground of Niagara had evidently written Butler that the enemy were militia, as Butler replies [60]

[57] "New Sources Sullivan-Clinton Campaign," p. 279.
[58] Draper Collection, 9F, p. 207. Copy of original letter Draper reports belonging to Mr. Kirby.   [59] *Ibid.*
[60] "New Sources Sullivan-Clinton Campaign," p. 281.

indignantly, "You certainly must be misinformed in regard to these people, for from the accounts of every Prisoner that has been taken, they are some of the best Continental troops, commanded by the most active of the Rebel generals and not a regiment of militia among them." Butler was never wrong in this whole campaign but Bolton and Haldimand, hundreds of miles away, perhaps tutored by Johnson, always knew better. Haldimand, in fact, wrote [61] Bolton from Quebec the next day, the eve of the battle, though he did not know it, that Guy Johnson was going to Niagara.

I am apprehensive that some little misunderstanding may arise between Colonel Johnson and Major Butler relative to the Rangers. . . . I have particularly specified that they are immediately under the Command of Major Butler. . . . If, during the great resort of Indians at Niagara he [Johnson] may require, a Centry, or any little compliment, if you think it may effect the above purpose, I should wish he were gratified.

This letter, on the eve of the fierce Chemung action, covers the ground of the Dynasty's intrigue — Guy Johnson, the typical non-combatant, jealous of the kudos of his rank, jealous of the growing reputation of the Rangers as the crack troops, jealous of the growing dependence placed on John Butler by Haldimand and Bolton as it had been by the great Sir William. Bolton said in reply,

I am informed the Major has received letters acquainting him that Colonel Guy Johnson will certainly come to Niagara, in that case if he should apply to me for leave to go to Montreal I believe you will think it right not to refuse him.

The placid Bolton wanted no wars, big or little, at Niagara.

Sullivan went only five miles that day, being held up for hours by the jam of artillery in the woods. They destroyed eighty acres of corn in the morning and pushed ahead to within six miles of Butler's army in battle order. The next day, seeing no chance of checking Sullivan's advance, Major Butler wanted to fall back to a stronger position, but, in his official report, says that the Indians insisted on fighting at

Chemung. He threw up some breastworks and formed his line along a ridge, his left against a mountain, a creek in front of him and a defile on his right: McDonnell and Brant had the right, he took the center, and Walter Butler with Rangers and men of the 8th had the left. Officers and men were without blankets and had only corn to eat.

There was evidently the usual great difficulty of keeping the Indians in hand. Sullivan was pushing out his right to get around the mountain and cut off the retreat. Butler testifies to Brant's loyal support but says the Indians refused to understand the necessity of changing front. Poor, by "great prudence and good conduct," kept formation in the difficult movement to surround Butler's left. They got up the mountain, charged with bayonets, while the artillery opened on the main body. Butler says "the shells bursting beyond us made the Indians imagine the enemy had got their artillery around us and so startled and confused them that great part of them ran off . . . many made no halt, but proceeded immediately to their villages," like scared dogs running home. Butler was left with 250 Rangers and 15 men of the 8th, facing 4,000 of the flower of the Continental army. It is astonishing that he was able to draw off, as he did, to Nanticoke Town five miles away. Any pursuit should have gobbled up his whole force, but as he says "They move with the greatest caution and regularity and are more formidable than you seem to apprehend." The losses on either side were trifling, Butler admitting 5 men killed or taken and 3 wounded, Dearborn giving Sullivan's loss as 3 killed, 33 wounded. Butler closes his report "The consequences of this affair will be of the most serious nature unless there is speedily a large Reinforcement sent . . . the families will be flocking into Niagara to be supported."

Cartwright, Butler's secretary, says:[62]

General Sullivan by too great haste in firing his artillery in a manner forced his prey out of his hands; for had he delayed this till Poor got

---

[62] *Life and Letters of Richard Cartwright* (Toronto, 1876), p. 39.

around the mountain, it would have been impossible for Major Butler and party to have escaped and they all must have been killed or taken.

Sullivan, with such odds in his favor, appears to have failed. He did a great deal of complaining before and during the campaign and Washington, two weeks before, had so far lost his temper at Congress and Sullivan's complaints that he wrote the President of Congress "If almost the whole of the 2300 men are not effectually serviceable in action it must be General Sullivan's own fault."

James Clinton wrote [63] his brother the next night of the victory and said that the Rangers "had eaten nothing but corn for eight days past."

Sullivan pushed north burning and destroying, reaching the Seneca Castle on September 7, and "a very pretty town called Kaunandaguah" on the tenth, where Walter Butler and Rowland Montour were watching them. On the fourth, from Canadasaga, Butler urged Bolton to send boats to the Genesee to take off the sick.

Haldimand wrote Butler on the third a letter that must have infuriated the weary soldier, "The zeal you have already manifested for the King's Service will, I cannot doubt, continue to prompt you to advance it by a cordial assistance and mutual acquiescience with Sir John Johnson in every operation." [64] It is obvious that the Dynasty wanted the most powerful intercession before facing the war-worn Butlers, even when coming out, as in this case, with very late relief.

Bolton reported to Haldimand, on September 7th,[65] that a hundred Rangers at Canadasaga were down with fever and ague; Haldimand was getting relief together "at a risk of [their] perishing for want"; Bolton added that 1,000 men will not answer the purpose, though he sent out the Light Infantry Company of the King's Regiment to meet Butler on the Genesee and asked Detroit for the men he had loaned them. He was fearful that Niagara was doomed.

[63] *Papers of George Clinton*, Vol. V, p. 227.
[64] "New Sources on the Sullivan-Clinton Campaign," p. 286.
[65] *Ibid.*, p. 289.

On the eighth Butler reported,[66] "I endeavored but to no purpose to prevail upon the Indians to make a stand at Canadasagoe." Word of Brodhead's progess up the Alleghany had also reached him but he was still "in hopes I shall be able to persuade them to attack the rebels." On the thirteenth, with Sullivan's advance pushed almost to the Genesee Castle, Butler ambushed their advance of twenty-six men under a Lieutenant Boyd. Twenty-two were killed, and Boyd and a prisoner captured. The main body was two miles away and, at daybreak on the fourteenth, they entered Genesee, Butler evacuating it just ahead of them and falling back to Niagara. Sullivan, seventeen days out from Tioga, turned back toward Canadasaga. Niagara would almost certainly have fallen had he followed up, as Wayne probably would have done. It is impossible, however, to be sure that he could have fed the number of men necessary to subdue Niagara. He had made a waste of the gardens of the Long House and that was what he was sent to do. Brodhead had also turned back and had reached Fort Pitt that same day, failing of his objective, the rendezvous at Genesee, for want of competent guides, but loaded with furs and booty and waited on by the Wyandot warriors for whom the spell of an Iroquois alliance was forever shattered.

The next day George Rogers Clark reached the Falls of the Ohio and found the civil business of settling so active, that a march on Detroit was out of the question. De Peyster wrote Bolton that he would not weaken the garrison "till I am satisfied Mr. Clark is not meditating a stroke."

If neither Sullivan, Brodhead, nor Clark completed their assignments, the campaign was still a vast victory. Washington wrote to Laurens on the twenty-eighth with pardonable excess, "The Indians, men, women and children, flying before him to Niagara, distant more than 100 miles, in the utmost consternation, distress, and confusion, with the Butlers, Brant, and others in the lead."

The capture and horrible death of Lieutenant Boyd on the

[66] *Ibid.*, p. 291.

fourteenth is in a way the most famous incident of the campaign, but the discussion of it had best be left till later.[67]

Sir John Johnson had not yet reached Carleton Island on his way to Butler's relief by the twenty-third of September; Bolton wrote "to follow now is too late, to be of any consequence," but the Dynasty were already thinking about Sir John's invasion of the next year. In the South the same day the siege of Savannah was begun by allied French and Continentals.

October came, the year having fled swiftly from the day Walter Butler's march to Cherry Valley had begun in '78. Winter was closing in on the Northern lands. On the fourth Simon Girty won almost the only Royalist success of the year, when, on the Ohio beyond Cincinnati, he ambushed Colonel David Rogers coming up from New Orleans with 600,000 Spanish dollars lent to Clark by Galvez, Governor of New Orleans, on Virginia's security. Fifty-seven men were killed, the money captured and blankets and supplies for Brodhead's naked men at Fort Pitt were taken.

At Niagara the Rangers, as they recovered from the chills and fever of the summer fighting, were getting in supplies for the winter; their requisition [68] "of sundry articles wanted" was obviously made up in part by the young man who wanted a barrel of port for his own account:

60 doz. Handcfs, 30 dozen Shoe buckles, 30 dozen knee buckles, 30 dozen Sleeve do. 30 boxes of soap, 4 doz. chocolate, 300 lbs. coffee, 900 lbs. of tea, 30 barrels of Sugar, 3000 lbs. Loaf Sugar, 20 doz. Blacking Balls, 20 dozen Ivory combs, 30 dozen Horn Combs, 30 dozen Pomatum, 50 lbs. Hair Powder, 3 cwt. Starch, 1 cwt. Blue, 3000 lbs. Cheese, 3000 lbs. Tobacco, 6 Reams Writing Paper, 400 Quills, 12 Barrels of Molasses. There will also be Rum wanted if a greater quantity shou'd not be sent up than has already been done.

The composite picture of thirty dozen soaped, powdered and pomatumed Rangers, their linen starched and blued, their boots blacked, smoking their pipes, and sipping their tea,

[67] See Chapter XI.
[68] "New Sources on the Sullivan-Clinton Campaign," p. 292.

sweetened with lump sugar and laced with rum, as they wrote thirty dozen letters through the long winter evenings, is a delightful one, and there was pepper and cheese and mustard in the requisition, if one of them craved a midnight rarebit after a patrol in the soundless northern night with even the roar of the great falls frozen to silence. Even their enemies should not begrudge a little ease to the weary men who had retreated all summer before Sullivan's army, the fields and orchards ablaze behind them.

In October Haldimand, still worried as to what would happen when Butler and Guy Johnson met at Niagara, apparently at once fearful of offending Johnson and of Butler's accusing him bluntly of conspiracy, wrote [69] again on the seventeenth,

I am extremely sensible of the zeal and attention you have shown by forwarding the King's Service, while you have conducted the Department to which you belong and I cannot doubt that notwithstanding Col. Johnson's return to his duty, the same inclinations will prompt you to give him every advice and aid which your longer and more intimate knowledge of those officers enable you to afford for the advancement of the public good and common cause in which His Majesty's faithful subjects are embarked.

On the twenty-second of the month the New York legislature passed the Act of Attainder against "Sir John Johnson, Guy Johnson, Daniel Claus and John Butler, Esq. of the County of Tryon." The great landholders were penniless men; Butlersbury, Johnson Hall, Guy Park were lost. Plainly through all these events, great or trivial, the Continental power was growing. The British were pinned down. Enormous European enterprises were afoot against them. The Canadian command was at its wits' end for supplies for the starving Five Nations. Brodhead reported to Washington, November 10, that 2,000 Indians were living on a pittance at Niagara, afraid to venture outside the fort. The number may even have been higher.

On the anniversary of Cherry Valley, probably after Guy Johnson had reached Niagara, Butler wrote [70] Haldimand:

[69] *Ibid.*, p. 300.   [70] *Ibid.*, p. 305.

I beg leave to mention to your Excellency a promise made by Sir Guy Carleton signifying that from my long and approved services, joined to his good opinion of Captain Butler, he would give me the rank of Lt. Col. Commandant and him that of Major whenever there was a sufficient number of companies raised to admit of his doing so with propriety. This I am given to understand was approved of by Your Excellency and I hope will now be taken into consideration. . . . I would also beg permission for Captain Butler to go to England this fall if an opportunity offers as well as to procure proper arms, clothing, etc. for the Corps as to settle some family concerns.

It must have been apparent to the Butlers that much of the power of the Dynasty lay in the connections made in London, begun fifteen years before when the "dear child" John had gone there. They probably felt sure that Walter's looks and "pretty, genteel" manners would counteract the other's many visits. But no word came on this, as none had on the letter to James Clinton, saying that the young children were going to England in the first boats.

November 20 Walter wrote Haldimand: "I am sorry that it has not been in your power to procure the liberty of my family, but hope it may be done now from the late proposal of Schuyler." [71] Nothing had gone right. The anticipations of the spring for the reunion with Mrs. Butler and the young children whom Colonel Butler had not seen in four years, English leave, the disaster of the retreat from Chemung to Niagara, the reborn power of the Johnsons, the final loss of Butlersbury, all had gone with less luck. It was a gloomy Christmas at Niagara.

[71] *Ibid.,* p. 306.

Chapter IX

RED WAR IN THE VALLEY, 1780

Sir Henry Clinton went south to the Carolinas the day after Christmas, 1779, leaving the German, General Knyphausen, as commander in New York. The winter months of '80 were of a desperate cold. Knyphausen could have seen nothing worse in North Germany. *Rivington's Gazette* of February 16 reported that the artillery had come up from Staten Island across the ice. The cavalry were constantly in motion over the frozen harbor from the Battery and people walked across the ice from Long Island to Norwalk, Connecticut. In the North there was "such an amazing body of snow" that Governor Clinton could not summon the legislature.

The bearing of this terrific cold on the conduct of the Indians of the Five Nations is at once obvious and important. Sullivan's army had destroyed the whole great harvest, and thousands of Indians had, when they could, swarmed into Niagara to be fed. The rest were brought to the edge of starvation and hundreds must have perished in the forests. This being so, it was plain that those who could would strike back at the Tryon-Schoharie frontiers, as soon as the cold relaxed, mad with hunger and the bitter memories of Sullivan's devastation. No one could foresee the tragic link of the autumn's war and the winter's weather, but now it was plain that it was folly to have injured the Indians as Sullivan did, and then leave Niagara unscathed for them to refit, and strike back. To have injured them so dreadfully and not to have wiped them out was a colossal blunder.

The British too were bent on striking back. The long curve from Niagara to Pensacola, Florida, was alive with many enterprises. Haldimand's plans for De Peyster, the new commander at Detroit, called for the conquest of Illinois, the falls of the Ohio, Fort Pitt, and the Cumberland Valley. His instructions went out all winter through Niagara to Detroit where De Peyster, to Haldimand's amazement, spent £84,035[1] on presents and upkeep for his Red allies, and drank too, through the year, 17,520 gallons of rum, although "at Niagara where the expense of it is very considerable 10,000 gallons is the most has been expended."[2] Surely the scenes at Niagara that winter, as the runners went west with dispatches, must have been among the most thrilling and dramatic in our history: the huddle of cabins beside the frozen falls; the crunch of snowshoes as the lucky ones came out from the great fires to say goodbye to those going west; the ice-white stars sweeping over the unknown western lands; the savage winds out of Manitoba; the goodbye to the last picket, stiff and cold in his furs, but soon to be relieved; and the runners plunging alone into the trackless snow toward the "upper posts."

Walter Butler went out with one runner to Detroit before New Year's Day, and they wrote[3] back of him, "As Mr. Butler speaks French and seems very intelligent he has got orders to maintain the post of Miamis, if it be possible, with a few men during the winter." The heart chills in contemplation of this cold and lonely post, far west of Detroit, eleven hundred miles from Montreal. What superb courage it took to go there through a frozen wilderness. Perhaps it was for this post he had ordered the bearskins in August. Harry Hare's brother had been in Detroit, and like De Peyster was anxious to get away from it. Colonel Butler had gotten winter leave for him "to pass the winter at Three Rivers as he has a wife and family there." Walter Butler may have volunteered for the relief; some Rangers went with him as there was a whole dissatisfied company in Detroit who had been promised leave.[4]

Now as to the arc of Niagara-Pensacola: in the preceding

[1] James, *George Rogers Clark*, p. 198.
[2] Michigan Historical Collection, Haldimand to Lernoult.
[3] *Michigan Historical Collection*, Vol. XIX, p. 47.
[4] *Ibid.*, Vol. IX, p. 667.

August the Independence of the United States of America had been recognized in New Orleans by the Spanish Governor, Galvez. There was nothing sympathetic about the recognition. The British navy had New Orleans almost bottled up, and a great commerce was to be had up the river with the Americans on the Ohio. But early in February Galvez moved out of New Orleans and captured Mobile. There was a British post at Pensacola [5] under a General Campbell with 1,000 men, a third of them Maryland and Pennsylvania Loyalists, but they did not feel able to oppose Galvez. Probably, as we shall see, Campbell was waiting word from the North. At the same time with winter still heavy on the mountains James Robertson, Sevier, Shelby, and Donelson, together with Samuel Doak, a Princeton graduate who was to build the first college west of the Alleghanies, pushed out into the valley of the Cumberland and began permanent American settlements. There could hardly be a greater contrast than between these warlike and self-confident pioneers of Tennessee and Kentucky, eager to fight, and the run of Palatine peasants along the Mohawk, fearful of the Indians and the British. There were great rains all through late February in these western valleys, but no spring flood ever conquered a country as did the 20,000 people that swept over the mountains that springtime.

In February Walter Butler came all the way back to Montreal, exactly why it is not clear. He wrote[6] to Captain Mathews, Haldimand's secretary:

Montreal,
2nd February, 1780.

DEAR SIR:

I return you thanks for your kind favour; and must express my gratitude to His Excellency for his attention to the releasement of my Father's family; give me leave to add that as the General has expressed a desire to serve me I must likewise acknowledge the obligation I am under to him therefore, and will wait for his commands in anything he may please to point out for me.

---

[5] *George Rogers Clark*, p. 201.   [6] Original letter, British Museum.

I mentioned to Captain McDonell the distress of several men having families (whom I discharged last spring as having too large families) for the want of provisions, likewise that several men still of the Rangers, as having families, were sent down from Niagra in order to ease the Garrison in the article of Provisions, Flour is so high a price that they cannot afford to purchase it.

I have a man of the name of Pinsil who served formely in the Royal Americans, he has an old Mother who is upwards of 70 who he obliged to attend constantly; he says if he was allowed a little provision for her he could make out to save as much from his pay, would pay for some family taking charge of her. But otherwise he will be lost to the service. He is a man of good character and very fitted for the service he is in.

Pray when will the express go off for Niagra? If the General thinks proper had Captain Dame not best be sent? He expresses a desire to go. I, for my part, I think it would be the best thing he could do. I have paid a good deal of money for him but must stop my hand for a while.

I am, with my respects to Captain Peake,
>Dear Sir,
>Your obliged and obedient servant,
>WALTER BUTLER

Captain Mathews

It will be remembered that here was another year and Mrs. Butler and the young children were still in Continental hands. Two letters the following week from Haldimand make it probable that Walter Butler had come down about the exchange and his solicited promotion. Perhaps he had had news that the Dynasty were opposing both matters. Haldimand wrote [7] Mason Bolton from Quebec, February 12:

Major Butler's unswerving zeal for and attachment to the good of the King's Service, so often recommended by you in the arrangement of the Indian Department while under his direction, has induced me to promote him to the rank and pay of Lieutenant-Colonel, Commandant of his Corps of Rangers.

Haldimand somewhat cryptically adds that "this appointment [is made] from no other consideration than my desire to testify to Col. Butler my approbation of his conduct in the line

[7] Haldimand Papers, 96B, Vol. II, p. 178.

he has directed." This is half what Butler asked the previous November.

The same day Haldimand wrote [8] directly to John Butler, regarding his recommendation that Walter be given his majority; it is one of the most interesting letters in the correspondence, particularly showing how fixed the army has been about seniority, how loath in later years to promote Hamiltons, Pershings, MacArthurs over men "who have served a number of years."

Captain Butler's zeal and activity I am very sensible of and shall not be unmindful of them. I am sorry to observe to you that he rates his services very high and is a little inconsiderate in his expectations and request. He is a very young man and there are many experienced officers in this Province who have served a number of years that would be very thankful to enjoy his present rank and emoluments, and I cannot in justice to the service promote him over the heads of so many officers of merit and long service as compose the army of this province.

A flag shall be sent in the course of a few days requiring that Mrs. Butler and family be sent into this Province in exchange for Mr. Campbell's family recovered from Indians for that purpose.

This is of course an old, professional army speaking. In the new Continental army Alexander Hamilton, younger than Walter Butler, was a colonel, George Rogers Clark and Aaron Burr, both colonels, were his age. Butler probably felt that the ruin to his health, his trial and condemnation as a spy, his great Ranger service from Miami, Detroit, and Venango to Tioga and Cherry Valley, the fighting qualities of his own corps — almost, with the 8th Regiment, Canada's only defense — compensated for the fact that he had turned in no definite victory except Cherry Valley, marred by the killings there. Albany with its fear of him and with his menace to the service of supply of Washington's army would have felt him entitled to it.

The decision to pass him was known to Walter Butler in Montreal on February 21 and with it came news that must

8 *Ibid.*, Vol. I, p. 172.

have made him feel that there was deliberate intent to forget
him and his services. He wrote [9] Mathews again:

Montreal,
21st February, 1780

DEAR SIR,

I was informed three days ago that the Flag for Albany had passed
St. Johns. This alarmed me much as I wanted to send Mrs. Butler some
money, etc., to enable the Family's coming to this country. I made every
enquiry, and was very sorry to find it too true. How this can be rem-
edied I leave to your judgement who I give not a little trouble on every
occasion.

I should be wanting in every feeling did I not find myself sensible, in
a particular manner, of His Excellency's favour to my father in the
late promotion the General has seen fit to give him. At the same time I
must feel hurt that it was not convenient for the Commander in Chief
to have performed what he heretofor intended in my favour. Whether I
merited it more then, than now, I am not a proper judge. What fault
I have committed I am not sensible of.

Captain Dame is here waiting for orders to leave this for Niagra; if
he does not go soon the Creeks and run of water will be open which
will lengthen his journey.

We do very little else but feasting and dancing, it has nearly turned
my head. I find it as hard as scouting. In order to change the scheme
McDonell and me intend to make a tour of the Mountains every other
day on snow shoes.

Respectfully,
Your obliged friend,

WALTER BUTLER

It is almost inconceivable that the flag could have gone,
without word to him, except by intent. He was certainly, next
to the Johnsons, of the most prominent Royalist family; he
was in Montreal largely to expedite the flag and send the
money, and off it goes unknown to him. It can hardly have been
just chance. Was nothing ever to go right?

The last trivial paragraph is of vast interest. Legend
has him the despoiler of many women. We have heard only,

[9] Original letter, British Museum.

and that innocently enough, of Mrs. Robinson. Does he say this for its effect on Captain Mathews, or is he really sick of the town and the patter of people who want to ask him whether he was frightened that grim August morning when Willett came in his tent to say that he was to be hung as a spy, or what he thought of the dead women and children at Cherry Valley, and why the Rangers did not give Sullivan battle after Chemung, and those who jeered at the fighting qualities of the Continentals his father and he admire, and the people who would not understand that war was not like that candle-lit ballroom, brilliant with redcoats, and swords and ribbons, but an endless business of lonely marching, shooting, running, starving.

There is a letter from Jacob Bayley [10] at Newbury, Vermont, to Washington written this February which speaks of Butler as a menace. It is constantly a surprise to see the field of operations these Rangers covered. Bayley says

a Tory came to his friends and gave them warning to take care of themselves as a large Party under Col. Butler would be over to this River this winter. The Tories have done mischief a little above Charlestown have stole the Town's stock of ammunication. We have pretty certain intelligence from Fort Halifax on Kennebeck River informing that a letter was read there that great preparations were making in Canada to make a descent on this River. . . . Colo. Bellows has his regiment ready which is the lowest reg. we expect help from. . . . I would mention one thing more. I find at Darthmouth College four young men from Caughuawaga and St. Francois . . . Charity scholars who have been and are now Destitute of every support. . . . These scholars and the Indians have warded off the blow from us more than once. . . .

Newbury is in Vermont on the Connecticut River and was a headquarters of the Green Mountain Gang. It was perhaps natural that Tories should come in there. There was intriguing going on all winter, doubtless, with Ethan Allen, for Walter Butler was to declare later in the summer that he was ready to give up his prejudice against Allen and to fight with him. Both Washington and George Clinton were probably pleased

[10] Original Letter, Library of Congress.

to have Vermont and Maine worried about Royalists and
Indians. It would make it easier to call on them for men when
the Niagara raids began again. But from Newbury where
Bayley wrote it was nine hundred miles as the crow flies to the
Miami village where Walter Butler spent part of the winter.
It gives some idea of their tremendous energy. It is further
significant that we learn from a letter [11] of February 26 that
Captain Peter Ten Broeck, who was captured with Walter
Butler at Shoemaker's house in '77, and who had shared his
cell in Albany with him, but refused the risks of the escape,
was still a prisoner awaiting exchange.

The flag that went out of Montreal, February 21, evidently
did not carry the final arrangements for the exchange of Colonel Butler's family. The brother-in-law and the wife of Peter
Hansen, a prisoner at Montreal, wrote [12] him, March 4:

DEAR BROTHER,
    The Governor and Col. Van Schaick who commands here have prom-
ised to have you exchanged for one of Col. Butler's sons, Thomas or
Andrew. So I am in hopes you will come by this flag, who is going
to Canada for that purpose. If so I hope you will not fail to come to
your wife and children.

                                                    NELLES FONDA
    I have not heard from you in a long while but just find your name
mentioned in a letter from Col. Butler which affords me much joy to
find you was yet among the army. I trust you will try to send me a line.
Our old father is to be all well. Dear husband, your loving wife till
death,

                                                    RACHEL HANSEN

It is a terrible blow, of course, to any student of the Butler
mystery that no such letter, nor, in fact, any essentially intimate
letter from any of the Butlers was apparently ever captured or
preserved. It is obvious that the situation of Mrs. Butler
and the children was a ceaseless anxiety to both father and son,
but they never seem to have given in to lamentation. The vast
number of Revolutionary letters and documents that are available to scholars is a mystery in itself. How do they all happen

---

[11] *Papers of George Clinton*, Vol. V, p. 518.   [12] Claus Papers, p. 182.

to have been preserved? But since they were how does it happen that there are no *Butler Papers*?

The first notice that the Sullivan expedition was not the complete victory that had been expected came in March when Indians took the militia garrison in the North at Skenesborough, and burned a house in Tryon. It was a shock to Governor Clinton who wrote of "These early incursions of the savages instead of the overtures of peace which we had some reason to expect from them." Undoubtedly the highly capable Intelligence Section of the American staff made a first-class blunder in underrating the morale of the Five Nations. They ran from Sullivan's guns at Chemung but that was a special case. They seemed unable to adjust themselves to artillery fire. But, battle actions aside, they were a relentless, active, and savage foe who with empty bellies had brooded through the horrible cold of that winter on their wrongs.

On April 2 Joseph Brant opened hostilities with an attack near Harpersfield and then took some scalps and prisoners at his old haunt of Minisink. The next day the Sacandaga blockhouse miles away across the Mohawk, and over the next watershed, was attacked by a small Indian scout of seven, all of whom were killed by a relief party that came up. On April 24 seventy-nine Indians attacked Cherry Valley taking prisoners and scalps. The resistance to these small unorganized parties of starving men was itself desultory and unorganized. The Northern Command seemed to have learned nothing from the ravages of '79. No one knows why Bayley in the letter to Washington previously quoted should have said, "Two companies are put under the command of Major Whitcomb untill the last of March *when we think the Danger will be over untill June.*" [18] Why should anyone have thought that the Indians would wait through all the pretty days of April and May for their revenge. Across the Alleghanies the frontiersmen may have fought with a too-savage fury but at least they never fell into feeble self-delusions. They did not provoke retaliation; they made it as nearly impossible as they could.

[18] Author's italics.

May was a bad month for the Continental cause. On the seventh General Lincoln surrendered Charleston, South Carolina, the worst surrender in point of numbers the American arms have ever suffered. Almost simultaneously Colonel Harry Bird, with a murderous crew of a thousand Indians and 150 Rangers,[14] boiled out of Detroit, down the Maumee and the Miami to the Ohio, turning back to Detroit with a great line of prisoners — many women and children dying or being slain on the march. It was a horrible business for which Clark took the swift revenge he rejoiced in, as soon as word of it reached him. He was then somewhere near St. Louis operating against the expedition under Wabasha, Chief of the fierce Western Sioux, who, financed by Patrick Sinclair, of Machilimackinac, was to go down the Mississippi and join hands with Campbell coming up from Pensacola with his Loyalists. The plan failed and the arc from Niagara to Pensacola was almost wholly American. So much for the safety of the West "untill June."

The situation in Northern New York is covered by Colonel Van Schaick's letter to Governor Clinton of May 17: "The militia of Tryon County . . . are at present exceedingly dis-spirited and appear averse to adopting the measures necessary for repelling the Enemy. . . . It appears far from improbable that Schonectady will be our frontier to the westward." This last is almost unbelievably feeble when it is considered that Stanwix up the Mohawk was not even threatened and that Schenectady was "an easy day for a lady" from Albany. But Van Schaick goes on, "upwards of one hundred men have in a few days gone off from this and Tryon County and amongst those, some who were formerly good staunch whigs. It is confidently reported by the disaffected in Tryon County that Sir John Johnson is on his march to make an incursion." [15]

The report was correct. Sir John was coming up Lake Champlain to Crown Point and through the woods to the Sacandaga. He had four hundred Rangers and Greens and two

[14] James, *George Rogers Clark*, p. 209.
[15] *Papers of George Clinton*, Vol. V, p. 15.

hundred Indians and on Sunday night, the 21st of May, he entered the Johnstown settlements, and the next morning at daybreak laid Caughnawaga in ashes. Sir John himself was at Johnson Hall the next afternoon while half his force was down the river at Tripes Hill burning the district "except a few Tory houses." The aged and venerable Douw Fonda was brutally murdered that afternoon by Indians. Thirty-three years before, on May 16, Sir William Johnson had given him the King's Commission. Colonel Harper reported that night "Sir John thought proper to decamp before Sunset"; he fell back to Mayfield at the northwest corner of the vast Drowned Lands; he had splendid visibility across the Drowned Lands to the Maxon Range where his signalers could watch the whole valley. The valley was in great terror, Colonel Morgan Lewis reporting to the Governor on the 23rd,

They proceeded westward burning the houses and barns of the inhabitants and putting to death every male capable of bearing arms. It does not appear they have offered any violence to women or children. . . . Colonel Visscher was brought into Schenectady miserably wounded and scalped but not dead. . . . They [the Loyalists] shew a disposition tis said to fight. . . .[16]

Evidently neither of the Butlers was in this raid. There appears to be no mention of them in the dispatches of either side. Sir John probably wanted to show Haldimand what he could do by himself. Colonel Harper added a postcript to his dispatch saying "Sir John was heard to say that Butler was coming down the River; this comes by some of the prisoners who are returned." This sounds as though it was propaganda meant to be related by escaping prisoners. In any event it seems to confirm the absence of the Butlers. Militia forces were divided to meet the Butler advance and the confused commanders would no doubt have agreed, had they seen it, with Washington's philosophical observation to Governor Clinton the same day: "It is certainly to be lamented that we cannot oppose a sufficient force to every point upon which we are attacked."

[16] *Papers of George Clinton*, Vol. V, p. 743.

Colonel Klock, who had warmed himself in Cherry Valley after the massacre and then scuttled back to Fort Hunter, was greatly unsettled by the reports about Butler. He wrote General Ten Broeck on the twenty-third, "Brant and Butler are to attack on the south side of the River; spies have been seen on the south side of the River about an hour before night. . . . We momently expect to see all in flames." [17] He evidently had little confidence in Ten Broeck, to whom he was appealing for support, as he wrote [18] the same day to Governor Clinton begging for help, for "otherwise we shall be left a meal to our cruel enemy."

The phantom Butler never appeared though Clinton proved to Schuyler by deduction that "Fort Schuyler [formerly Stanwix] is actually besieged by a considerable Force, for, unless this is the case we must suppose Sir John a madman to set down and by unnecessary delay have it in our power to cut off his retreat." [19]

Sir John was still at Mayfield. On the twenty-seventh, however, he evacuated Mayfield, after giving Klock, Van Schaick, Lewis, Harper and the rest of them every chance to offer battle. He moved seven miles that day, and fourteen on the 28th, directing his course "high up the country by a back route that leads toward Crown Point." On the twenty-ninth Clinton wrote [20] the valedictory

They were by accounts we received from persons of veracity who were made prisoners and afterwards escaped much beat out and many of them lamed by their long march. Add to this they have taken with them much Plunder, many women, wives to Persons who formerly joined the enemy and their children, so that it is likely their march will be very slow and dilatory.

As has been repeatedly stated, the bringing off of their wives and children was one of the prime objectives of every Loyalist invasion, and that was undoubtedly the cause of Sir John's waiting five days at Mayfield, discouraging attacks

[17] *Papers of George Clinton*, Vol. V, p. 740-42.
[18] *Loc. cit.* [19] *Ibid.*, p. 755.
[20] *Papers of George Clinton*, Vol. V, p. 769.

by his well-spread rumors of Butler's presence to the west. Van Schaick started in restrained pursuit, the *New York Packet* at Fishkill, on June 8, reporting it and adding, "We hear the enemy had their feet much swelled by their long march."

There was a curious rumor during May of the flag that went out of Montreal unknown to Walter Butler. Bolton wrote [21] Haldimand that Mrs. Moore and Colonel Campbell's family, taken at Cherry Valley, were going back by way of Montreal, adding, "I am glad Your Excellency has given directions to prevent those families who are coming from Albany from paying us a visit as we find it a difficult matter to supply those already here with provisions." Such indifference to the feelings of his comrade, Colonel Butler, who had not seen his wife and children for five years, is almost unbelievable, except that for some reason the Butlers seemed to have aroused jealousy wherever they went.

Colonel Butler was certainly in Niagara shortly afterwards, because he was the bearer of Haldimand's letter to Bolton regarding his intention

of settling families at Niagara for the purpose of reclaiming and cultivating lands to be annexed to the fort. Lieutenant-Colonel Butler with whom I have conversed fully upon this subject has promised to give you every assistance in his power and from his knowledge of farming, his being upon the spot and his acquaintance and influence with those who may be found to settle I am persuaded you will find him very useful.

Schuyler's surprise that the Sullivan expedition had not finished Indian resistance for all time began, after Sir John's foray, to spread among men higher up; and the military importance of northern New York is further evidenced by the letter James Madison wrote to Thomas Jefferson from Philadelphia, June 2:

It appears from sundry accounts from the frontiers of New York and other Northern States that the savages are making the most distressing incursions under the direction of British agents, and that a considerable

21 *Mich. Hist. Coll.* Vol. XIX, p. 521.

force is assembling at Montreal for the purpose of wresting from us Fort Schuyler which covers the northwestern frontier of New York. It is probable the enemy will be but too successful in exciting their vindictive spirit against us, throughout the whole frontier of the United States. The expedition of General Sullivan against the Six Nations seems by its effects rather to have exasperated than to have terrified or disabled them.[22]

It was, indeed, "the whole frontier of the United States" that was blazing. One man, writing on the 13th of June from the Ohio, reports that "Butler it is said comes against Kentucky in great wrath, he boasts he will give no quarter, indeed what can be expected from a man that at Wyoming gave up his brother to be tortured and unfeeling enjoyed the sight."![23]

The American disasters of May ran on into June and there was a severe mutiny among the Continental troops in New Jersey early in the month. Knyphausen, hearing of it, thought he saw a chance to win the war in Clinton's absence. He came across the Jerseys with a flying column, only to be met by mutineers who, looking for trouble, turned on him — and back he went. Sir Henry Clinton, on his return from his successes in the South on the 22nd, started out to redeem the fiasco. The reliable Greene met him in front of Short Hills, piled him back to the Jersey beaches, and Clinton never crossed the Hudson again.

Haldimand and the British Headquarters in New York maintained excellent communication during this time both by land and water, and in the unpublished British Headquarters Papers [24] of the Rosenbach Collection there are a number of interesting letters, among them Haldimand's [25] from Quebec, July 6, to Knyphausen:

I wait with anxiety the arrival of the Provisions of which I have not yet had the least intelligence. Until it appears I cannot wish to increase

[22] *The Papers of James Madison* (New York, 1841), Vol. I, p. 47.

[23] *George Rogers Clark Papers, 1771-1781* (ed. J. A. James, Springfield, Ill., 1912), p. 425.

[24] Dr. Rosenbach very courteously allowed the author to examine and take notes from these magnificent manuscripts before their sale.

[25] British Head-Quarters Papers.

my force which I mean to do by raising some Companies of Canadians and Loyalists that daily come in from the Colonies, when I flatter myself I shall be in a situation to oppose any attempt that may be meditated against the Province. . . . The Rangers and Indians are harrassing with great success the back settlements of all the Provinces bordering upon this. Sir John Johnson is just returned from an incursion to the Mohawk River where he distressed the Rebel inhabitants considerably and brought away about 500 Loyalists fit to bear arms without the loss of a man. I have batteaux ready upon Lake Champlain to make a diversion in your favor should a French fleet appear in your quarter but want of all provisions will make it impossible for me to do more than to alarm the enemy in the neighborhood of Crown Point.

One of the most interesting points about letters of this sort is the thorough evidence it supplies of a war being waged by a staff, with each unit and its detail part of a larger scheme, in contrast to the idea that the fighting in Northern New York was a species of bushwhacking.

On the eleventh Haldimand wrote Sir Henry congratulating him on his Charlestown success, word of which he had only through "the channel of a Rebel newspaper." He wrote Knyphausen the same day [26] a letter interesting mainly in its brief light on the underground communication between New York and Quebec through the lines of the Continental Army.

I enclose to you [he says] a duplicate of a letter in cypher with which I dispatched the Runner who brought me yours of the 3rd of May. I hope he will arrive safe at his destiny and procure me the Pleasure of hearing soon again from you, Hoping in profitting of every occasion to justify respect and attention due His Majesty's Hessian Allies, etc. etc.

Runners went so regularly out of Quebec for New York (one was seen that rainy summer night in Albany by Dr. Stringer), across Champlain and down the Hudson past West Point, that one wonders whether Benedict Arnold may not have made their protection part of his service to the Crown.

Walter Butler was meanwhile at Niagara. He wrote [27] Captain Mathews from there about midsummer:

[26] British Head-Quarters Papers, Dispatch no. 27.
[27] Original letter, British Museum, A.D. 21765 F. 176.

Niagra,
20th July, 1780.

DEAR SIR,

I have been so busy since my arrival at this place that I have had very little time to write to my friends in Canada. I have received a number of recruits since my arrival which has enabled me to complete the 7th Company, and have a Sergeant, Corporal and thirteen for the 8th. From the parties out and from those I am about to send recruiting on the Frontiers I have the greatest reason to expect to complete the Corps this Summer, and further expect to be able to fill all the Companies and discharge any whose situation from having large families in Canada renders their remaining here not so convenient. We are very ill off for Barracks, the two buildings having but 20 rooms which you know is not sufficient for the Officers of 8 Companies agreeable to the regulations for quarters. We are endeavouring to repair the Huts and put the men into them, and are likewise building others as well for the Officers as for the men at our own expense. This we think hard and particularly so as we can't get a Board, Nails, or even Tools to assist us. We will want commissions for the 7th Company and others. I left a memorandum with you for, and were the General to send up commissions for the 8th in care to General Bolton I shall by the time they arrive be able to muster it complete. Every party gives us accounts of the distress of the enemy. Sergeant Bras of the Rangers writes from near Albany where he is recruiting that there was an action in the Jerseys between the Royal Army and General Washington in which the latter lost his Artillery, etc. This is said happened at Morristown, he adds that the Royal Army were on their way up the North River, his letter is dated 29th June last. I have offered to send out several parties of the Rangers but from their not being allowed I suppose they are kept for some other service.

McDonell has had his own trouble while he was out and at last could only get the Indians to go to Anyda, where they did not perform what they promised him. He was too ill with the Ague that he was in the necessity of having himself tied to his Horse. They killed their Horses and Dogs for food.

There are many Indians fitted out from this for War but agreeable to their general custom it is not all of them that go to their journey's end. Has nothing been done on my matter on which I wrote you? Pray drop me a line.

I am in haste,   Your obliged and respectful servant,

WALTER BUTLER

Cpt. Mathews

The action referred to is of course Sir Henry Clinton's retreat from Short Hills with Stark of Bennington in hot pursuit. The "matter on which I wrote you." What was it, English leave, the cause of his nonpromotion, what Johnson said when he got back of his showing compared to Butler's, what? The letter was written July 20 with no prospect of leaving Niagara. And this would appear to confirm Walter Butler's absence from Brant's sack of Canajoharie on August 1-2. None of the dispatches to Governor Clinton regarding this action — from General Ten Broeck, Colonel Wemple, or Colonel Clyde — mentions Walter Butler, and it becomes a matter of increasing mystery as to when Butler was in the Valley to commit the murders he is accused of.

Brant came into the Canajoharie settlements the first days of August and Colonel Wemple says [28] "Such a scean as we beheld since we left the river, passing dead bodies of men and children most cruilly murdered is not possible to be described." They appear further to have gone about the destruction of property with the thoroughness of Sullivan's troops, burning barns, churches, mills, houses, "farmers wagons and emplements they had to work with. Nothing left to support themselves on but what grean they have groing and that they are not abel to give for want of tools and very fue to be had here." Except that it was August they must have been as badly off as Brant's countrymen the year before.

A great chain of dramatic events followed this action in August; on the same day George Rogers Clark, having travelled seventy miles in four days of terrible going, burned the Indian capital of old Chillicothe in Ohio and pushed up to Piqua where he routed Simon Girty and his savages; the next day, the fourth, Benedict Arnold took command at West Point; on the tenth, Brant, moving with Clark's own swiftness, was on the Ohio,[29] below the mouth of the big Miami, where he defeated and captured Colonel Lochry with a hundred picked frontiersmen. The march had the incredible rush of one

[28] *Papers of George Clinton*, Vol. VI, pp. 80-81, 88.
[29] James, *George Rogers Clark*, p. 243.

of the great Montrose campaigns and the victory was decidedly over the best fighting stock in the West. Colonel
Lochry, while a prisoner, was murdered — but it must be
admitted Brant showed his mettle here against men in arms.
The same day, August 16, Cornwallis crushed Gates at Camden, South Carolina, then pushed north leaving the Carolinas
to a flood of Loyalists (under Patrick Ferguson), Creeks, and
Cherokees.

Desperate blows were being struck on both sides, but the
preponderance was with the British arms. Nevertheless a dispatch to Clinton on the 28th shows that Haldimand was considerably worried:[30]

The Trade fleet of 42 ships . . . was separated at sea . . . only 18
arrived . . . it is said 15 are taken . . . the fickle and perverse conduct
of the Indians prevented something great being effected . . . arrival of
7 French ships of the line and 600 troops at Rhode Island, a junction
of Spanish with a French fleet in the West Indies and other unfavorable
accounts. . . . A Scout from Mohawk River informs that the Oneidas
instead of joining their confederacy in the royal arms which they came
to Niagara to do have in a body seized the Mohawk land and are protecting their Harvest which is very plentiful for the use of the rebels.

Both sides were worried. Van Schaick reported to Governor
Clinton September 5 that even the garrison at Fort Schuyler
were "disaffected to their situation."

On September 17 Haldimand wrote [31] Germaine his care-
ful soldierly letter regarding his plans for Sir John's second
invasion. The purpose and scope of the expedition is beautifully stated. Secondary sources generally state that Sir John
came hundreds of miles with men and guns to get his family
plate and papers from Johnson Hall. It was apparently the
fashion in the last century to regard the Revolution as a series
of personal encounters — rather like tournaments on a large
scale. The fact was that the staffs of both sides were thorough,
soldierly, and excellently trained. The French fleet and army
were at Rhode Island. Haldimand wrote:

[30] British Head-Quarters Papers, Dispatch no. 28.
[31] *Mich. Hist. Coll.*, vol. X, p. 432.

In order in the meantime to divide the strength that may be brought against Sir H. Clinton, or to favor any operations his present situation may induce him to carry on and to give His Majesty's loyal subjects an opportunity of retiring from the Province I have fitted out two parties of about 600 men each, besides Indians, to penetrate into the enemy's by the Mohawk River and Lake George, the former being chiefly drawn from Niagara and to rendezvous at Oswego already marched under Sir John Johnson, the other I shall send across Lake Champlain so as to appear at the same time.

This was the seventeenth of September at Quebec. There were certainly great operations which Sir Henry Clinton's "present situation" induced him to, but nine days later they were cut short when Major André, his Adjutant General, was captured, and Benedict Arnold fled to New York, while Washington was coming from the War Council with the French at Hartford. André was tried and condemned on the twenty-sixth, the day that the Tennessee men were mustering to go to King's Mountain. It had been a close thing all down the long lines, but the game was up. Greene took temporary command at West Point, and on October 2 Major André was hung, to the grief of both armies.

The day before Schuyler reported to Governor Clinton that word had come in of the British advance up Champlain and also across Oneida Lake. They were coming from all directions, Houghton with a detachment of the 53d, the Shropshire lads of Housman's poem, striking at the upper Connecticut Valley. The main body, says Hough,[32] crossed over to the Valley of the Susquehanna. They here probably received reinforcements from Niagara by way of the Tioga route and proceeded up the eastern branch in the direction of Schoharie. Meanwhile Major Carleton's British force coming from the north took Fort George, and on the seventeenth Sir John burned "the whole of Schohary." There was a great west wind fanning the flames and the Loyalist army must have been delirious with the fierce joy of invasion, the autumn smell of the countryside, and the great hunter's moon, by whose light

[32] *The Northern Invasion of 1780*, p. 47.

Robert Van Rensselaer pushed forward his relief party.[33] He reached Canajoharie south of the Mohawk in close pursuit but they crossed the River ahead of him and burned Stone Arabia. Van Rensselaer was across the river at five-thirty in the afternoon with Sir John only a mile ahead and in full retreat, abandoning much of his baggage and plunder.

Neither side mentions Walter Butler as being part of the expedition. Word came, when Sir John was gone, of the tremendous victory of the Americans at King's Mountain on October 7, and on the twenty-second, leaving West Point to Heath, Greene went south to take command of the southern army and begin his superb campaign.

It is certain that John Butler was part of the invasion, because Haldimand reports to Germaine on November 20 that on October 31 Lt. Col. Butler "about forty miles from Niagra on his way from Oswego" picked up along the shore wreckage from the 16-gun schooner lost in the storm of that week. It was another bitter return to Niagara. The long awaited exchange was still uncompleted. For the fourth year he was back, unvictorious from the wars, to endure the long winter. A vast exhaustion and disenchantment must have been on them all. It had all gone badly — St. Leger, Wyoming, Cherry Valley, Newtown, and now this last useless maraud. So it must have seemed, though Madison had a letter from Washington that Schoharie, which had supplied 80,000 bushels of grain for the public use, was in ashes.[34]

Walter Butler in Montreal wrote [35] his friend:

> Montreal,
> 14th November 1780
>
> DEAR SIR,
> After the arrival of the post I leave this for Couteau du Lai where my Boat will meet me tomorrow morning. I shall make every effort to get to Niagra this fall and if my health will permit shall attempt in case the . . . are laid up to go round the Lake.

[33] *Papers of George Clinton*, Vol. VI, p. 306.
[34] Madison Papers, Nov. 14, 1780.
[35] British Museum, Ref. A.D. 21765, F. 187.

I wrote you on my way up from Quebec since this I have had letters from Colonel Butler that he has appointed Lt. Barnard Try, the oldest Lt. in the Rangers, Captain of one of the vacan Companies, and Lt. Tan is to be 1st Lt. Try is 1st Lt. since December 1777 this till the Commander in Chief's pleasure is known.

Sergeant Dairn of the Rangers that was, has come in from New York and has brought two of the Rangers prisoners with him.

I think it a hardship that Sir John Johnson has obtained leave to go to England and I was refused, my reasons and business on behalf of Lt. Colonel Butler was nearly the same as Sir John's.

I have heard nothing of the purchase, Mr. Ellice will pay the money when it is settled.

I am Dear Sir,

your Obliged and obedient servant,

WALTER BUTLER

P. S. Hanson was exchanged for Ensegn Shutan thinks it hard he is confined, if he and his brother would be permitted to be out to work with someone in Montreal who would not permit their having an opportunity to make off I should be obliged, as he was to be exchanged for part of our family.

CAPTAIN MATHEWS,
Secretary to the Commander in Chief,
Quebec.

Almost another year's end and still the exchange "was to be."

The reference to his health very possibly confirms the fact that he was not in the Invasion. The English leave was lost for another year, a year never to come. A year and two days and Haldimand will be writing his condolences to old John Butler on the death of so gallant a young officer. This same November 14, though, Claus writes to Guy Johnson:

DEAR BROTHER: Captain Butler once more moved the affair of his father's account of expenses given to me at Oswego in August 1777 when I thought I had fully explained myself in the matter. The Captain says now that if I gave a certificate how that article in my account was not paid that you would pay him and much more about Accounts.

The Dynasty held the strings of the vast purse of moneys

for the Superintendency and they seem to have known how to forget the accounts of other men.

Years before John Butler had written Sir William in his decent solid way that he had no desire that people should have to use a bad road if there was a good one. Now, on December 11, he wrote to Haldimand of the progress at the Niagara settlement. "I have got four or five families settled and they have built themselves homes." He liked to call the place Butlersbury.[36]

[36] Gilbert, the wanderings of whose family are so confusingly recorded, speaks of being at "Butlersbury, a small village built by Col. Butler . . . on opposite side of river to Niagara Fort." *The Captivity and Suffering of Benjamin Gilbert and His Family* (ed. Cleveland, 1904), p. 96.

CHAPTER X

"THE WINDS HAVE BEEN ADVERSE," OCTOBER, 1781

The western successes of the Americans in the fall of 1780 had not spread south or east. Washington had been bitterly disappointed in the faineant French forces; men, money, and munitions were down to nothing. It is a miracle that Sir Henry Clinton did not move out of New York and gobble up the whole hungry army. On New Year's Day, 1781, the entire Pennsylvania line consisting of 2,400 men — a fifth of the army — mutinied, and the New Jersey line shortly afterwards, but Clinton's agents, sent to buy them up, were hung and the army somehow held together.

Then on January 17 there was a turn in the South and Morgan of the Riflemen won a shrewd and smashing victory at the Cowpens over Tarleton and his Legion. At the end of the month Greene joined Morgan and took command of the southern army. It was the fifteenth of March at Guilford Court House that he began the series of brilliant, if inconclusive, battles from which he always drew off his army intact, inflicting mounting losses if not defeat on the British.

At Niagara there was silence. An Oneida Indian, escaped from that post, reported [1] that "when the snow will bear them . . . parties mean to intercept the provisions sent up to Fort Schuyler," and when asked "what expectation had Sir John, Brant and Butler in this last Execution," replied that "It was said they meant to destroy Schanectady which now will take them another Campaign."

In the previous October, however, General Schuyler had found "the conduct of some people to the eastward alarmingly mysterious; a flag under pretext of settling a cartel with Vermont has been on the grants. Allen has disbanded his militia."[2]

[1] *Papers of George Clinton*, Vol. VI, p. 483.
[2] *Ibid.*, p. 358.

The reference of course is to the Green Mountain Boys. In April, 1781, Ethan Allen was accused directly [3] of correspondence with the enemy and Colonel Warner stated that Allen had received two letters "one of which he burnt and one of the letters was from Beverly Robinson in New York," Sir Henry Clinton's chief of military intelligence. The Butlers knew and apparently shared the correspondence at Niagara, as we shall see, and for all their losses were not yet done with the war. Their patrols were pushing so close to Fort Pitt in the early spring that Brodhead was unwilling to send the promised reinforcements to Clark.[4] Washington even wrote Clark that an army under Sir John Johnson was coming out of Niagara against Fort Pitt and the western posts.

Walter Butler was in Quebec, May 6, and was called upon to explain his apparent disobedience to Haldimand's orders that he go to Niagara to sit on a general court-martial. Army orders are of course to be obeyed, not interpreted, but even for an army it seems surprising that an officer on mission, with leave, should suddenly be required to go five hundred miles by water to attend a court-martial not his own. Butler wrote [5] an extremely reasonable if not wholly soldierly account of his failure to obey:

Quebec,
6th May, 1781

SIR,

In compliance with His Excellency General Haldimand's orders signified by you requiring me to reduce to writing the reasons I have to assign for not immediately complying with your letter requiring me to repair to Niagra to attend a general Court Martial to be held there: —

Having Brigadier Powell's leave to go down in order to settle Regimental business of the Corps I belonged to, and other matters which immediately concerned myself; I drew Bills to the amount of Ten Thousand Pounds N. Y. Cy. at thirty days sight, a considerable amount of which was for sums in advance for the Corps by me and the Residue

---

[3] *Ibid.*, p. 776.   [4] James, *George Rogers Clark*, p. 237.
[5] Original Letter, P. R. O. Ref. 21734 F. 51 W. O. 28/4.

money belonging to them in my hands. I likewise had promised and given directions to the Officers commanding the Companies to draw on me for the payment of subsistance due the different Companies to the 24th April 1781 by the next opportunity; as not doubting my being able to have the subsistence by the time of payment mentioned. Thereto added a balance Mr. Ellice for subsistance issued to the Officers of the Rangers while in Canada on my Account, which I was in the necessity of making payment. The amount I have ready to show. Likewise Lieut. Colonel Butler having ordered out his private credit a complete stand of Arms and Accoutrements and this year's Clothing for his Corps without having any stoppages in his hands. To enable him to pay therefore which said Arms and clothing were ordered out in the very first running Ship for this Province, and Bills promised for payment on their landing. Further His Excellency having six months ago promised me a purchase of a Company in an established Regiment and directed me to have the money ready for the payment; This I complied with but finding it not taking place from it being unavoidable, I suppose, I was in the necessity to have same disposed of as I found the exact amount to near half of my pay. Those matters I could not do by second hand and should my Bills have been protested which must have been the consequence had I not come down I must have been ruined. — My having given up the paymastership to take place the 24th June rendered my settling every matter the more necessary. From these reasons, and from the impossibility of my being a Member of the Court and having no evidence I did presume should His Excellency still find my attendance requisite he would from my particular situation above mentioned pardon my having gone down and the more so as it cannot delay the Court but a few days if at all.

The above is the substance of what I have to say, and shall leave it to the Commander in Chief's justice to deal with me as he in his goodness shall see fit.

I am, with respect, Your most obedient servant,

WALTER BUTLER

Major Lernoult
Adjutant General

In the letter and those that follow there is a hint of another matter — "the purchase of a company in an established regiment." It seems reasonable to believe that two men as intelligent as the Butlers had begun to wonder what was the end of all the show. Everything they had had was lost. The war was to end sometime. Walter Butler, trained as a lawyer, probably had little taste left for a country practice in Canada, and in those days, after a commission was bought, the army offered a brilliant career. The "no principle" (as Ian Hamilton called it in his *Gallipoli Diary*), that they were not going to win, may have begun to take root. In any event Headquarters apparently decided to make clear to Butler that he was very much a cog in a wheel, for he wrote the next day — in reply to what, we do not know:

Quebec,
7th May, 1781

SIR,

I am sorry to find Brigadier General McLean has misrepresented what passed between me and him. The following is all which passed to the best of my knowledge, and can be qualified thereto: this I am more certain of, as then considering General McLean was not a friend of mine, was therefore at the time the more circumspect.

Immediately on my arrival at Montreal I waited on the Brigadier General McLean, sent in his servant to acquaint him I was in waiting, he came out, asked me — "If I had met Captain McDonell" to this I answered — "I had," he then asked me — "Do you know there is an order to send you to Court?" I said "I had the order in my pocket; but from my particular situation I was under the necessity to proceed to QUEBEC where I hoped from the reason I should offer and being incapable to sit as a member at the Court Martial and not being a Witness to it, to meet with His Excellency the Commander in Chief's pardon." Or words to this effect. This is all that passed between Brigadier General McLean and me, pro or con, on the subject.

He never showed me any order, or told me the consequence of my going down, as he says, or informed me that he in particular was ordered to stop me, as he has wrote you.

From what passed between us, I could not suppose but he alluded to the letter I told him I had received from you.

I am with respect, Your very humble,

WALTER BUTLER [6]

Major Lernoult

[6] Original letter, P. R. O. Ref. W. O. 28/4.

His dilemma at Montreal must have been real, and it is not impossible, in view of the Dynasty's many letters, that they may have suggested to the pipe-clayed McLean that discipline was being upset by this young Butler. The brief picture of McLean coming to his door, firing off questions, is very telling.[7]

This is all we learn of the incident. It must be admitted that from Walter Butler's first letter, wherein he said that Mr. De Lancey complained that he was abrupt with him, whereas he himself had not found himself treated with common decency by Mr. De Lancey, he was inclined to feel that insufficient regard was given him. Young men of unusual ability and promise usually resent the endless waiting for recognition far more bitterly than duller ones do.

Back in Montreal he wrote[8] his friend Mathews an interesting and convincing letter about the deserters and how McLean was subserving discipline:

Montreal,
15th May, 1781

DEAR SIR,

Last fall Lieut. Colonel Butler sent down two prisoners to Canada — Charles Hudman, for declaring himself a deserter from the 65th Regiment and demanding himself to be delivered up as such, after he having enlisted in a Rebel Regiment and taken by a party with me in Arms, on my way to Cherry Valley. He declared himself an Englishman and that he was forced into the Rebel service and begging to be admitted in the Corps of Rangers. I not knowing him to be a deserter enlisted him in the Corps of the Rangers and obtained his liberty from the Indians.

Thos. O'Conoly for attempting to desert, and sent down to Niagra a prisoner by Major Depeyster, therefore Brigadier McLean has their Crimes and notwithstanding enlisted the former in the 84th Regiment and the latter he has inlarged.

I spoke to him on this, he told me that they were not supplied with Clothing or Necessaries and was long confined, was his reasons for doing as he had done, I mentioned to him that these prisoners were sent down in order to be put aboard a Man of War or armed vessel.

---

[7] Compare Robert Graves' first lunch at the Royal Welch Mess in *Goodbye to All That.*   [8] Original letter P. R. O. Ref. W. O. 28/4.

Agreeable to what General Haldimand expressed formerly should be done with any of our people who should be in the same predicament of these two. I must observe that the allowing these people to go at large and to enter any other Regiment they pleased without making an example of them would encourage many to behave ill, and not be an encouragement for others to behave well. They have been and now are continued on our Muster Rolls and I thought the person who has the care of the prisoners would have supplied them with every requisite and whatever was the amount of their pay, I should be obliged to give an order to discharge the same.

I was just informed by one of my Non-Commissioned Officers that some of the men down with me observed that if any of them were desirous of leaving Niagra they had nothing to do but behave ill and then they would be sent down and they would join any other Regiment they pleased again. I could only wish these people were sent aboard some of His Majesty's Ships, this will set others behaving ill. Those men last fall had Clothing and Necessaries. What the Brigadier means by their not being supplied I know not. It must be more his fault than mine, for if he could order many to be supplied   an Officer was paid in advance surely he could see to his Soldiers securing the necessaries and subsistance.

I wish I knew what to do in this matter. I can't give up the man to the 84th Regiment.

I am, Your obliged servant,

WALTER BUTLER

This is a very human picture of soldiers' typical grumbling at Niagara, complaining that deserters could get out of Niagara, while they were stuck there, nothing to do, nowhere to go, no one to talk to.

On this trip Butler probably saw his mother and the young children. The date of their arrival in Canada is not definitely known, but was probably with the flag out of Skenesborough, November 15 the previous year. Incidentally there was a murderous raid on Cherry Valley in late April,[9] "8 killed and 14 prisoners taken," in which it is obvious from these letters he could not have participated.

On May 4 Schuyler had written [10] another long letter to

[9] *Papers of George Clinton*, Vol. VI, p. 812.   [10] *Ibid.*, p. 840.

Clinton on the "alarmingly mysterious" conduct of Vermont, wherein he said that "Ethan Allen openly invites the inhabitants on the east side of Hudson's River down to its banks to annex themselves to the Grants and give explicit assurances that they will not in that case be molested by the British." It would be fascinating to know more definitely of the workings of the Allen conspiracy. His correspondence with Beverly Robinson was known in Montreal and Niagara. There is a letter [11] from Governor Clinton to Heath at West Point, September 2, on the question of enemy communication from New York to Canada,

I am not acquainted with the enemy's present channel of Communication but I am led to believe it will be either through the Eastern Parts of this country and into West Chester and Smith's Close and so to Elizabeth Town or Paulus Hook on the west side of the river; on either route there are so many disposed to give their assistance that it is impossible to fix upon particular persons. The most probable way of intercepting them is to apprize the Magistrates and Militia Officers near the Line to have trusty Persons to watch the roads and no persons suffered to pass unless well known without being strictly examined. The communication for some time past from Canada to New York I have reason to believe has been principally through the Grants [Vermont] or across the Country by Niagara.

They knew at Niagara about Ethan Allen as Walter Butler wrote [12] Mathews:

Niagra,
30th May, 1781

DEAR SIR,

I arrived here some days ago in eight days from the time I left Montreal, the journey has fatigued me not a little and returned the Ague in me; but this I owe more to falling in the River than journeying; however I am getting better, and hope with care and the pleasure of thinking there may be something to be done in the action line, in some part of the Province, to get better of it, but I fear we shall be idle in this quarter. Clark is not in earnest — should Allen and his Green Mountain Lads return to their Duty; I could wish, if it would be for the good of the

[11] *Ibid.*, Vol. VII, p. 288.
[12] Original letter, British Museum, Ref. A.D. 21765 F. 217.

service, a few Companies of the Rangers were sent down there, I should like the service as being convinced we could be of very great service in that quarter, and I have now given over all those prejudices against serving with people who were formerly our enemies. The good of the service requires that we should give up sentiments of this kind.

Lt. Colonel Butler desires me to present his compliments to you and would be glad if a dozen Breeding Sows were sent down for the use of the Farmers. There is an old man in the Rangers, his name is Miet Thoners, tho' he is fit for service, Lt. Colonel Butler has permitted him to build a House and he is clearing a planting and turning Farmer, he wants permission to bring up his family from Masteries. This Colonel Butler would indulge him in if agreeable to His Excellency the Commander in Chief. They can be assisted by four of the Rangers who were left sick in Canada being — Philip Burt, James Crouder, Jacob Van Alstyne and Jacob Anguish, the latter likewise would be of use in the farming way if his family were allowed to come up, as the family he has is not large and is Indians.

A Smith will be requisite for mending and making at first the Ploughshares, Hoes and Axes, etc., for the Farmers; if one of the Rangers were allowed, or in fact any other Soldier, he can be assured the work at any fixed rate, but this Colonel Butler just now tells me he has wrote you.

We have had no accounts yet of the Success of our recruiting parties tho' in daily expectation of hearing from them. Lt. Bealt is gone into the New Jerseys if no misfortune misfalls him he must get a number of men.

I don't mean to apply again to His Excellency the General for the purchase of a Company, for on considering everything it would not be to my advantage. If he ever thinks me worthy of presenting to me an established Regiment it will be an act of his own without my application and therefore I must be solely obliged to him. But I can't help being surprised between you and me that Officers employed in the Indian Department in Canada who receive double pay and do no duty with their Regiment and as I know of have not done more than others, if so much, serving on like service for one pay, talk confidentially of being on the first promotion, and in fact one has succeeded, but doubtless they merit it, for my part I think so but not before many others I could name. Excuse this liberty.

I am your obliged friend,

WALTER BUTLER

Captain Mathews

It is interesting here to see the Rangers beginning to turn to "ploughshares, hoes and axes," and, as in a number of their letters, there is an interest in the small personal problems of their men that is at variance with the arrogant cruelty ascribed to them. This is the last Walter Butler letter but one. He had but five months to live.

He was afraid of being "idle in that quarter," but the same day Brodhead, who alone of the frontier commanders on either side had consistently wrong intelligence, wrote [13] Huntington, President of Congress, after stating that the hardships of the troops would shortly be too much for them.

The British force which, it is said, is to attack Fort Pitt will proceed from Niagara down the Alleghany River; consequently General Clark's expedition to the westward will by no means cover the principal settlements west of the mountains, and the same force with which we are threatened from Niagara may pursue him down the Ohio River unless a sufficient force can be raised to prevent their success in the attempt.

It sounded like good strategy but it was beyond the resources of Niagara.

The summer went on with ominous quiet. On July 13 Domine J. Van Gros returned from a tour of the Mohawk Valley and reported [14] to Governor Clinton:

I had almost forgot the repeated destructions this country has met with, if it had not been for the ruins, indicating that the inhabitants had had formerly the comfort of buildings . . . there is a prospect of as plentiful crops as has been in the memory of man.

August came and on the second Cornwallis entered Yorktown, Virginia. The same day Walter Butler wrote to Captain Mathews the last letter of which we have record. It is Butler to the life, summing up in a brief sentence his restless contempt for the noncombatants around him, and his pride in his Rangers. "The Rangers," he says, "are made drudges of for Mr. Stedman and others." Stedman was the storekeeper and portage-master at Niagara, who escaped in the massacre at Devil's Hole in September '63, and alleged for forty years

[13] Draper MSS 14S, p. 120.   [14] *Papers of George Clinton*, Vol. VII, p. 74.

afterwards the Indians had given him 5,000 acres of land because of it.

Haldimand, too, sent a dispatch [15] to Sir Henry Clinton on that day:

This is an extract of a letter I prepared to send, together with a full detail of all that has passed in The Affair of Vermont by a small schooner which I now cannot permit to sail, and in the meantime acquaint you that it appears to me infinitely more dangerous to yield to the delays urged by that people than to bring them to a declaration since from the best information these delays are only to procure time to strengthen themselves to act, no doubt in conjunction with Congress. They are busy forming magazines, have raised a considerable number of men and in a few months will be an important ally or a formidable enemy to either side. From the whole tenor of their conduct I cannot think they will adopt ours. To carry on the deception Ethan has quitted the service, but Ira goes Commissioner To Congress insted of coming here with the Flag, this to avoid the test of a controversy I think it cannot fail to produce.

That same night Haldimand wrote [16] again:

The difficulty of maintaining communication with Your Excellency I have always much regretted. It is peculiarly distressing at a time when there is every reason to believe some serious attempt against New York or this province is in agitation which early intelligence might avert.

They knew a great enterprise was afoot. On August first Haldimand had written [17] Clinton,

Tho' it is scarce possible the following report just received from an approved Loyalist in Albany should not have reached Your Excellency, yet the extreme difficulty our messengers find in escaping the vigilance of the enemy induces me to it.

The troops upon the Hudson and Mohawk Rivers are ordered immediately to Peakskill where a body of French troops are arrived. It is supposed an attack upon New York is intended. All the forces near the frontiers are ordered to move to the East Side of Hudson's River.

On August 11 Clinton was reinforced by 2,500 Hessians

[15] British Head-Quarters Papers.
[16] *Ibid.*, Dispatch 41.
[17] *Ibid.*, Dispatch 38.

giving him a strength in New York of 16,701 men. Heath was at West Point with 2,500 Continentals. Four days later Washington with that poised audacity which he seemed to possess beyond all other men made his superb decision to meet de Grasse on the Chesapeake and take Cornwallis. It was seventy-seven years almost to the day since Marlborough had gone to the Danube across Europe and won the Blenheim victory. As Washington was marching Clinton was conning the vast expense account sent from Whitehall showing that the war cost of 1780-81 was £2,378,429.

The French and Continentals were in motion southward on the 21st, and on the 27th there is a dramatic dispatch [18] from Heath at West Point to Governor Clinton, "The French army finished crossing at King's Ferry yesterday morning, Sunday." On the seventh of September "General Washington was at the head of Elk about noon. Cornwallis's whole army must fall into our hands," and on October 6 they began the first parallel before Yorktown. How trivial Guy Johnson's letter from Niagara, dated October 11, must have seemed to Germaine when with it came word that Cornwallis was taken! Johnson wrote "I hope shortly to reconcile the Indians to the plan of economy now entered upon, for reducing expenses, which however enormous was for a time unavoidable." [19]

There was to be still another battle in the Valley of the Mohawk before the end. With the dispatches that came to Governor Clinton from the South describing the net drawing in on Cornwallis, the distant alarms that preluded each northern invasion began to sound. In early September Col. Marinus Willett reported "that a large party were discovered by some Indians at Oneida, a part British with drums." [20] On the tenth of September Schuyler wrote [21] on a scrap of paper in great haste to Heath

It is given out that the enemy offended at having been duped by the Vermontese intend to attack them. . . . This gives me great reason

[18] *Papers of George Clinton*, Vol. VII, p. 262.
[19] Quoted in Ketchum, *History of Buffalo*, p. 356.
[20] *Papers of George Clinton*, Vol. VII, p. 304.   [21] *Ibid.*, p. 318.

to suspect that they mean to attack the Mohawk or this river. Yesterday two spies or British emissaries passed through the town and found means, although discovered, to escape.

On the seventh of September when Lieutenant Woodworth's party was ambushed west of Fort Plain it was reported that "the enemy are down in force," the next day, though, that was corrected to not "anything like so strong as was at first supposed," and the next day still less so. Continuous rumor followed that Sir John Johnson was coming for the Mohawk and Albany across Lake Champlain.

Stark wrote [22] Gansevoort, October 4, from Saratoga, "For God's sake hurry on with all the force you can," that the enemy were "in reality on this side of Lake George." Schuyler was so alarmed that he urged the Governor to go to Saratoga in person, and Heath to weaken the small command watching "Harry Clinton," as Heath called him. Heath did it too, sending the New Hampshire Continentals and some artillery [23] north on October 13.

No one should underestimate the terrific strain that George Clinton, Schuyler, Willett, and Heath were under. The "enemy's force," as Governor Clinton said, "is so formidable at New York and in such perfect readiness for some capital movement." There were of course an absurdly scanty force of Continentals facing them and even that had to be weakened to meet the new threat from the north. Whatever kept Sir Henry Clinton in New York with over 16,000 men no one knows. The double disaster at Yorktown and in the North, which was about to overtake the British arms, has come to be ascribed to Britain's growing European burdens. No one can compare the numbers here, and the one day's margin of flour Heath's army maintained, and ascribe it to that. If Sir Henry Clinton took West Point, or Albany, while Washington took Yorktown, it was only piece for piece. But nothing like that happened. A force came raging down from Canada, to make Haldimand's promised diversion; and Clinton waited, appar-

[22] *Papers of George Clinton*, Vol. VII, p. 391.   [23] *Ibid.*, p. 39.

ently unwilling, for once in the long tradition of British arms, to come out and fight.

They insisted in Albany that the attack was coming from the north. The force reported this side Lake George on the 11th, by Stark, was back at Crown Point on the 15th, according to Schuyler,[24] and Willett reported all quiet in Tryon that day, although the day before [25] there had been firing at the German Flats between Rensselaer's regiment and some Vermonters.

On the 19th Cornwallis surrendered at Yorktown.

The phantom army this side Lake George seemed to have vanished for several days but Lord Stirling reports them at Ticonderoga on the 24th. Heath complained on the 26th that "accounts from the northward are so vague and uncertain. At one time the enemy are beyond the lakes, at another this side the lakes, at another between them, and sometimes it is not known where they are." Part of them, about seven hundred, only 130 of whom were Indians, had come out of Oswego, on October 16, under Major Ross, commander at Bucks Island, with Walter Butler second in command. Colonel Willet himself later speaks of them as "a fine detachment," and Simms calls "Major Ross one of the most successful as well as humane invaders of Central New York." Moving across Oneida Lake with astonishing secrecy, since their final presence across from Johnstown was a surprise, they left their bateaux and provisions there under twenty lame men and came down to the river by way of Cherry Valley.[26]

The start was a poor one. We have Ross's own final report [27] to Haldimand after the retreat. Only a very few Indians came with the troops from Niagara and he found, when he was past the Oneida Lake,

the promis'd succour of Indians was a mere illusion for none ever appeared, the few that had join'd at Oswego were nothing more than the refuse of different tribes without a leading man amongst them, and so

[24] *Papers of George Clinton*, Vol. VII, p. 404.
[25] *Ibid.*, p. 407.   [26] *Ibid.*, p. 443.
[27] Haldimand Papers, 127B, p. 266.

early as that period began not only to make difficultys of everything
but to counteract and procrastinate whatever I proposed to them.

Ross goes on:

I sensibly felt my situation on an expedition where Indians were abso-
lutely necessary, nor was it less obvious to the troops, the officers
clamorous, particularly those from Niagara, even Indian officers declared
that Coll. Johnson had it in his power to send usefull Indian Chiefs
and warriors abounded in and near Niagara. Your Excellency knows he
had timely notice.

With heavy going through rain and mud they reached War-
rensbush, south of the Mohawk, and on the twenty-fifth they
were within twelve miles [28] of Schenectady. "The worst of
roads for fourteen miles," Ross says, "the troops laboured
hard to keep together and notwithstanding every exertion
several were obliged to be left behind." They set Warrens-
bush for seven miles in flames. "Near one hundred farms,
three mills and a large granary for publick service were
reduced to ashes."

Ross says he "could hear nothing of the troops at Crown
Point," but General Enos commanding the Vermonters near
Castletown reported to Stark at Saratoga that he heard them
"northward of Dead Creek near Tie [Ticonderoga] — the
beating of the Long Roll to the south of the Mount," [29] and
Tupper's regiment was deflected from the "pursuit" of Ross
to "tarry with" Stark.

The Loyalist force was now, as in all their invasions except
St. Leger's, practically surrounded. Again it was tip and run.
The northern invasions were like setting off to the Pole in
the nineteenth century. They must always turn back lest the
margin of safety vanish. Ross found his situation "criticall
and no time was to be lost to make good my retreat, from
prisoners and others I learned that the Rebels were on their
march from every Quarter, far superior to my numbers." If
he went back as he came, the Americans holding the river
could probably cut him off, and his boats and provisions at

[28] This is Ross's figure. Stirling in his dispatch of the 27th says 8 miles.
[29] *Papers of George Clinton*, Vol. VII, p. 449.

Canasayo might already be taken. He therefore decided to retreat toward Carleton Island and crossed the swollen Mohawk for Johnstown at one o'clock in the afternoon of the twenty-fifth of October.

It seems apparent from this quick retreat after burning only seven miles of the valley that a campaign had again broken down. The phantom force in the North, said to be under Sir John Johnson, was probably to have joined hands with him. Guy Johnson, another Dynast, had, in spite of "timely warning," apparently made no effort to get his levies up. The story of the Johnson intrigue, whatever its scope or intent, is so continuous as to leave little doubt of its motive.

Ross entered Johnstown about two in the afternoon after skirmishing with some militia. He

determined to take the woods and strike for the path, leading from the German Flats to [Carleton] Island. Some cattle were killed for the maintenance of the troops on the march, but our chief dependance was on horses — I at the same time sent out reconoitring parties to try to discover the motions of the enemy.

Then in the dismal rain of the end of a fall day just as they were entering the deeper gloom of the woods word came that Willett was on them. They were tired and wretched according to Ross's and Willett's accounts. The dismal nightfall coming on, miles of wilderness ahead of them — the whole situation must have brought their morale to a desperate ebb. It was growing colder too and there was a smell of snow in the air.

They gave battle in the woods. Ross by Willett's own acknowledgment broke the American right, but Willett on the left after losing a field piece held his own. Ross claims that as darkness came he was surrounding Willett and could have destroyed him but for the night. He states that prisoners say there were more than 1,200 men in pursuit of him "amongst whom were four hundred Continentals from Schenectady." No British officer failed to report to his superior when he met Continentals.

THE WINDS HAVE BEEN ADVERSE 241

On the 28th, after waiting for provisions, Willett started in pursuit. From the delay it would appear that Ross's claim of technical victory, or at least superiority, on the 25th was well founded. "To reap the full fruits of victory a vigorous pursuit must be made. The enemy must be allowed no more time than is positively unavoidable."[30]

"The 29th," Willett says, "we marched north upwards of twenty miles in a snowstorm and at eight o'clock A.M. of the thirtieth we fell in with the enemy." While Willett waited Ross had not gone far but had been lost seeking the trail north to the Saint Lawrence. "Contrary to expectations the Niagara Indians struck upon it at a different place to what was intended with a view to facilitate their own route, without any regard to our security." The three days, while they were lost, must have been almost unsupportable. They had been four days "with only half a pound of horse flesh for each man per day"; they must inevitably have lost blankets and equipments in the fight; they were cold and wet; the Indians were turned ugly; and the sense of winter and darkness coming over the earth was in the air. At any moment while they cursed the scouts, and tried to beat stragglers into line, the Continental rifles might open from the woods around them. Ross says the pursuit was in his camp soon after he set off and before the Indians left it. Three bateaux and horses were taken "from some remissness in not setting off."

Ross was making for Canada Creek which, if he could get across safely, might enable him to hold up the pursuit. He was unquestionably in full flight, the woods strewed, says Willett, "with the packs of the enemy, their horses abandoned except five far ahead with the wounded." There was no resistance, he says, before they reached Canada Creek, "their flight was performed in an Indian file upon a constant trot."

If Ross was to get away he must hold the enemy up at the ford of Canada Creek. The snow, now weighting the hemlock trees like some pretty scene of fairy lore, made the going

[30] Infantry Drill Regulations, p. 476.

heavier every minute for the worn-out men, and the pace could not be kept.

The rule for the withdrawal of a defeated force is very plain. "If an intact reserve remains it should be placed in a covering position to check the pursuit and thus enable the defeated troops to withdraw beyond reach of hostile fire." Ross states that it was "Captain Butler who commanded the Rangers covering the line of march." Next to the commanding officer it was the position of greatest responsibility. With Ross there were officers and men from the 8th Regiment, the 34th, the 84th, Johnson's Greens, Lake's corps, Jager's corps and Butler's Rangers. There was no question who was the best officer in the command.

The entire command got across the Creek at two o'clock with Walter Butler covering the ford. Willett's advance appeared as they drew off. Mist came down across the water, there was a burst of firing, with several men hit on either side. The Rangers' fire slackened and ceased, and after a pause the Continental Scouts, the Oneidas, then some troops, and finally Colonel Willett pushed through the chilling creek. There were several bodies on the opposite bank. One of them wore a gold-laced hat. They pulled it off and saw the bullet hole in the head, then someone, possibly Willett himself, recognized Walter Butler. He was evidently dying and an Oneida took his scalp, and the money from his wallet. Other troops were coming up. One of them, John Dusler, said afterwards he saw "a man the other side of the river holding up a commission and waiving it, said he had Butler's commission. That after this they all returned home." [31]

This was the end of it all, the bright soldierly hopes of the little boy who had seen the red-coat riders coming home twenty years before from Niagara, the cool effrontery of the young man who had walked into the enemy lines with a flag to get recruits; all the hopes for English leave, and promotion.

Lodowick Moyer, who was one of the pursuing party,

[31] Draper Collection, 3F, p. 53.

assured Simms [32] that he saw Butler's body as he came back from the chase and that it was never buried. The American reports make no mention of anything but the scalp which was taken to Albany. It is probable he was left lying there in the snow, no bearskins now to warm him. There is a legend that Tories brought his body secretly to St. George's Church, Schenectady, and that he is buried there. It seems unlikely: wolves were closing in on the armies.

Ross got away, many of his men left, in Willett's phrase, "to the compassion of a starving wilderness." He says in his report,

I cannot conclude without testifying to Your Excellency my sincere regret for the death of Captain Butler whose loss to the Service in General and to the Corps in particular is much to be lamented. The troops have suffered much in their limbs by the wetness of the weather and likewise by hunger all which they have endured with that fortitude which becomes soldiers. The troops from Niagara will embark for that place in a few days.

Colonel Butler must have been waiting anxiously for word of the expedition. He had just received Mathews' letter of November 1 pointing out the difficulties of making so young an officer as Walter Butler a major of the companies.

The Niagara troops arrived back there November 12, but rumor that young Butler had been killed in the covering action probably reached Colonel Butler before them. The scene is not difficult to reconstruct: terrified and hungry Indians coming through the snow to the fort; the usual wild rumors that the whole force had been captured or killed; Colonel Butler coming down in person to interrogate the prisoners in their own language; the inevitable question of when Captain Butler was last seen; the typically varying replies of frightened eyewitnesses, some that he was wounded, that he was with the advance guard, that Ross had sent him across for the boats, that he was killed at the ford of Canada Creek, and then man after man confirming the last till there seemed no possibility of error.

[32] *Frontiersmen of New York*, Vol. II, p. 549.

The arrival of the troops took away the last hope. Powell then in command at Niagara, wrote [33] Haldimand on the thirteenth: "I have the honor to inform you that the troops returned here yesterday from the expedition on the Mohawk River. Captain Butler who behaved very gallantly was unfortunately killed at the passage of Canada Creek." Powell had been at Cherry Valley and had married Miss Moore, who was carried off in the retreat.

Haldimand wrote [34] Ross from Headquarters at Quebec on the sixteenth of November: he said in part,

I read with much concern the fate of Cap'n Butler. He was a very active, promising officer, and one of those whose loss at all times, but particularly in the present, is much to be lamented: had the Indians done their duty it is probable this misfortune as well as other losses would have been prevented.

The same day he wrote Brigadier General Powell, then in command at Niagara:

You will of course hear fully from Major Ross the shameful, dastardly conduct of a people who cost Government to many thousands yearly — I cannot think of the subject with any degree of patience. To you and Colonel Butler I leave it to paint to them my displeasure . . . let them feel it in the distribution of presents.

Acquaint Colonel Butler that I most sincerely lament and condole with him the loss of Captain Butler. His good understanding, and the honorable cause in which his son fell, will assist in consoling him in this heavy misfortune.[35]

John Butler made no reply. He was evidently stricken by his loss, for the same November Colonel Alan MacLean, of the Highland Emigrants at Niagara, writes that he has been ill several weeks. "Butler recovers slowly. He is the only man here equal in any degree to the management of the Indians."

Whatever he wrote his wife, or she wrote him of the eldest son is unknown. Lodowich Moyer, a survivor, quoted [36] by

[33] Haldimand Papers, 96B, Vol. II, p. 33.   [34] Ibid., 124B, p. 69.
[35] Haldimand Papers, 128B, p. 289.
[36] Frontiersmen of New York, Vol. II, p. 549.

Simms said, "Colonel Butler offered a large sum to have his remains delivered in Canada but it was not done."

There was enormous rejoicing in New York for Walter Butler had become the embodiment in people's minds of all the horrors of civil war — of the unorganized bands of Tories and Indians that roved the valley murdering and burning. It appears that he came with St. Leger in '77, on his own luckless march to Cherry Valley in '78, and on the last invasion in '81, and was probably not otherwise in the Valley during the Revolution. The Americans make no accusations against Ross's men. Willett speaks of them as "such a fine detachment of troops." [37] But public opinion fixed on young Butler as the Devil, and made him part of every midnight murder of the long years.

The American command, as was fitting, exulted in his death. Lord Stirling himself, being anxious that Washington should realize that Stirling's own hand was in the Ross defeat, says, writing from "Rynbeck," November 20, that his congratulations on Yorktown were delayed because "[I have been] engaged on the Northern frontiers from which I have just returned." The letter [38] is a long and engrossing one. It reviews the rumors of the Champlain invasion, the fear that they would come "by Jessop's path down the North branch of the Hudson to Sacandaga and then to fall on the Mohawk River by Johnstown or to surprise Schenectada." He states further that Colonel Willett was "desir'd to look well to the westward." It rather appears that Stirling put this in as an after-thought, as the September-October dispatches have nothing to say of the west. It was only the beating of the Long Roll at "Ti" that they heard. The dispatch tells well and dramatically of the days from October 25 to 30, when Willett broke off the pursuit, leaving the enemy "in a miserable position without a morsel of provision and eight days march before them to get to any place of relief. Among their killed was their infamous partisan Walter Butler."

[37] *Papers of George Clinton*, Vol. VII, p. 474.
[38] Original letter, Congressional Library.

The news of it all spread slowly. Not until April 3,[39] the following year, was there "a rumor [in Detroit] that Cornwallis has surrendered, and the Six Nations offered to make peace." On Sunday, November 25, 1781, however, they knew in London that Cornwallis was taken, and Lord North cried out, "Oh, God, it is all over."

Lord Stirling's last paragraph in his dispatch might almost be a requiem for Walter Butler: "The winds have been adverse and the weather severely cold, the tops of mountains now in our view are white with snow, and the winds piercingly cold."

So the year was done with.[40]

[39] *Michigan Historical Collections*, Vol. X, p. 396.

[40] I have had the pleasure of exploring West Canada Creek with Mr. Pierrepont White, of Utica, New York, seeking the point between what is now Ohio City and Russia, above the junction with Black River, where the action is believed to have occurred. There are two possible fords which may have been used but local opinion inclines, and I believe it to be correct, to the ford known to local fishermen as Hess's Rift. To a certain degree dams and reservoirs have changed the look of West Canada Creek since the Revolution. It is a mistake to think of it as only a creek. It is a deep brown flood like "Iser rolling rapidly."

CHAPTER XI

THE BUTLERS OF THE SECONDARY SOURCES
AND ROMANCES

To understand the mystery of Walter Butler in the Revolution it is necessary to examine the group of books upon which so much of his ill-fame is based and which, though secondary sources themselves, have been the source for most of the standard histories.

Principal among these are *Travels in New England and New York* by Timothy Dwight, *Annals of Tryon County* by William Campbell, *The Pictorial Field Book of the American Revolution* by Benson J. Lossing, *The History of Herkimer County* by Nathaniel Benton, *The Frontiersmen of New York* by Jeptha R. Simms, and his other book *Schoharie County and the Border Wars of New York*. This is not a complete bibliography; there are similar books — Barber & Howe's *Historical Collections*, Peck's *Wyoming*, and others — but it is the main body of New York lore. The publication dates are roughly from 1821, Dwight's date, to 1882.

It is perhaps an ungrateful business to condemn these histories. The Revolution was still close in point of time when they were written, and the work that went into them was enormous; Lossing, for example, travelling thousands of miles to every battlefield of the Revolution to draw pictures and make his copious notes. But the point of view of them all is naïve and provincial, the facts often carelessly stated or untrue, the conclusions unctuous and hypocritical, and the Revolution little more than an unorganized feud between wicked Tories and godly Americans. The whole war is seen in the most personal terms, the writers apparently unaware that the art of war is one of the oldest in the world, possibly third after hunting and painting. War, in a general way, has been waged along the same lines since Xerxes came west and Hannibal north, east, and south. The art of war had a great renascence under the organizing genius of Gustavus Adolphus, another under Marlborough, and the American Revolution on both sides was waged in the light of these lessons. But it is a fact that they were writing of its most violently personal phase, the civil war in northern New York between old friends and neighbors, supplemented by the savage Iroquois whom the Tories made their allies. It must also be admitted in their favor that their books are no more personalized than Draper's standard and original work on King's Mountain.

Roosevelt in his *Winning of the West* has an excellent paragraph on works of this sort. He says:

During the early part of the [nineteenth] century our more pretentious historians in addition to their mortal dulness felt it undignified to notice the deeds of mere Indian fighters. The men who wrote history for the mass of our people, not for the scholars, although they preserved much important matter, had not been educated up to the point of appreciating the value of evidence and accepted undoubted facts and absurd traditions with equal good faith. . . . At this day it is a difficult and often an impossible task to tell which of the statements to accept and which to reject. Many of the earliest writers lived when young among the old companions of the leading pioneers and long afterwards wrote down from memory the stories the old men had told them. They were usually utterly inexperienced in wild backwoods life [and] accordingly accepted the wildest stories of frontier warfare.

The source of these books was almost entirely the stories of eyewitnesses, or their descendants; the use of documentary evidence was apparently unknown, and it never seems to have occurred to these writers that any survivor of the Revolution to whom they talked was capable of having forgotten, of being mistaken, or of deliberately making up a good story.

David Elerson, the famous rifleman of Morgan's corps, was ninety-five when Simms had an interview with him. Simms never questions whether the events of Elerson's youth might not then have been a little hazy to him, or even in retrospect have become more and more magnificent. He explains this by saying, "I have confined my inquiries in matters of importance principally to individuals sustaining a character of conscientious regard for the truth."

Campbell, who wrote his *Annals of Tryon County* a hundred years ago, in speaking of documentary evidence says, "Every person will readily perceive how difficult it is to collect materials for even such a sketch where the few tattered and moth-eaten documents are to be sought for among many persons." Of course now, after a hundred years, the almost perfect state of preservation of original Revolutionary documents is a constant amazement to the student and in 1831 they must have been almost like new, so good was the ink and paper.

All this would not be important were it not that these writers have given a character to Walter Butler which the primary sources make exceedingly doubtful that he possessed. These writers speak with great vehemence of the "diabolical cruelties of Walter Butler." "he out-herods Herod in his cruelty," he had "a tiger-like cruelty," "the cowardly cruelty and meanness of Walter N. Butler [made] Brant almost a saint when compared with [him]." These phrases are but summaries of their accusations. The great part of the mystery is why they chose him as their victim. Myths grow rapidly and the ascribing of unbelievable cruelties to unknown enemy leaders is one of the oldest processes in history. A name is sometimes enough for men to fasten on. Budenny, the Soviet cavalry leader in the Polish War of 1920, was known around the world in a day or so. Suddenly everyone knew him and his powers and his savagery, or thought they did.

There were years of bitter feeling between the Palatines and the landed gentry in the Mohawk Valley. The hatred of the Butlers antedated the Revolution in part, and, among the peasantry, was in large measure the hatred of the under dog for the acquisitive.

The war in the Mohawk Valley was in many families, like the Ten Broecks and Herkimers, brother against brother, and always neighbor against neighbor. With the courts and former magistrates, of whom John Butler was one, gone away, it was a great opportunity for ne'er-do-wells and desperadoes to engage in murder and looting, in barter in scalps with Indians, and this they did. Wives and children of the Loyalists, left in the Valley, were the object of American persecution, and suffered greatly.

It is of course impossible now to assess the guilt fairly but it certainly must be the fact that not every American was a selfless patriot, nor every Loyalist a murderer of babies. Yet this in effect is what these books have claimed, and called Walter Butler "the archfiend" of them all. If this were the case there would be abundant evidence of it in the primary sources and there is none, although the standard historians have accepted it as true, relying on the authors that we have mentioned.

The first thing these good men did was to change the villain's name to Walter N. Butler; no one knew why unless it sounded better in calling him the "infamous Walter N. Butler." Initials were coming into fashion when they wrote and someone simply tacked it on.

President Dwight began the myth-making. In his story of Cherry Valley, Walter Butler ordered a woman lying in childbed to be butchered but this was prevented by Brant. Of course if such a thing had occurred it would have been mentioned in the dispatches to Governor Clinton. Dwight goes on to say [1] that John Butler "is consigned to immortal infamy by the baseness, treachery, and cruelty with which he betrayed Colonel Zebulon Butler at Fort Kingston and butchered and burned the garrisons of men, women and children." This is apparently a confused version of Wyoming but certainly there was no betrayal of Zebulon Butler there, as he galloped off safely to Wilkes-Barré with his wife before the fort surrendered.

Dwight then dramatically relates that, after Cherry Valley,

[1] *Travels in New England and New York*, Vol. III, p. 191.

Walter Butler sacked Fort Plain and was wounded "by two Indian chiefs of the Oneida tribe. When his enemies came up, he begged for quarter but one of them, with a hoarse and terrible voice, cried out "Sherry Valley" and dispatched him instantly with a tomahawk." This places Walter Butler's death after Cherry Valley in '78, three years before the fact, and though Simms, Benton, and Lossing all adopted and amplified the tale of his crying for quarter and receiving "Sherry Valley quarters," till the school histories had it, none of them mentioned the error in time and place. The story was myth-making at its worst.

Van Tyne [2] points out that after Lexington "stories grew with the flying hours. By evening of the nineteenth of April Amos Farnsworth was ready to believe that he went into a house where blood was half over shoes. Men's names were blackened in a day, and were not to be cleared of infamy for several generations." So it was in Northern New York, with the Butlers dripping with the blood of innocents.

Campbell in his *Annals*, among his many errors, has the Canada Creek action on August 22, instead of October 30, and apparently did so in order to be able to say that Marinus Willett, who died when he was ninety, passed away on the anniversary of the action.

Simms was the type of man who believed in the good old times. He felt the country was going to the dogs and observes in his *Schoharie County* that "the feeding of candy and sweetmeats to children has tended more than most people imagine to destroy the vigor of our race." He also felt strongly about tobacco, remarking that "its fumes I do not scruple to believe, would ascend to heaven [from an altar] with as grateful an odor as from the lips of that individual whose taste is so perverted as to smoke it." The sequence in most of these books is maddening. If anything, it is geographical. The writer goes from place to place recording all that ever happened there, even though any single event may, for its understanding, need

[2] *The American Revolution*, p. 5.

to be placed elsewhere. But Simms finds his sequence in interviewing individuals. When he met anyone he interrogated him and recorded what he said, whatever various times and places were involved. Like all the others he is unable to place Walter Butler in any incident, except the military actions referred to, but the implication is that he was present at them all.

The books are far from worthless, the material in them is stupendous, but it is very possible that their atmosphere is more that of Simms' time than of the Revolution. Simms regards John Butler's lingering death "by the most acute suffering" long after the war as "punishment in this life for cruelties in the Revolution." What then of Anthony Wayne's death?

Sir John Johnson's invasion of 1780, according to Simms, is by way of Genesee to Tioga and up the Susquehanna while in reality it was from the North, but more important are his stories of how a sow crossed a river and walked a hundred miles home, and how a man held the lower jaw of a bear open until his son shot, how a man tomahawked a bear, how a panther was decoyed by a dummy, how a man held a wildcat by its paws, how Major Van Vechten served rattlesnakes at banquets, how Marinus Willett had a son by a widow at Fort Plain, and how Isaac Potts heard Washington praying at Valley Forge.

William L. Stone, who wrote a *Life of Brant* and one of Sir William Johnson, is one of the secondardy sources. He uses the "Sherry Valley quarters" story, but he admits that Dwight's diary was the source of this important evidence. Stone is less unctuous than some of his group but not much more thorough. He erroneously places Sir John and Guy Johnson at the Chemung, or Newtown, action in '79, adding in a footnote, "Sir John was certainly there and the author has somewhere seen the name of Guy Johnson." Neither was there, as the Haldimand-Bolton letters show. He ascribes the 1780 invasion to Sir John's desire to get his silver plate from Johnson Hall, and apparently actually believes that with a great empire fighting for its life they could furnish, equip, and maintain in the field a thousand men for such a purpose. Stone, with the group's vehemence, says it was one of the most murderous expeditions, and then, stopping to think, adds "murderous in its character but few were killed."

Peck's *Wyoming* has the legend of Colonel Butler applying "to the British government to be knighted" but failing, a story apparently based on a misunderstanding of Butler's routine application to the Government for compensation, as offered, after the loss of his estates in Tryon. He thinks "the Wyoming massacre was not aggravated by manifold more horrors than it has been our painful task to record thanks to [Walter Butler's] imprisonment in Albany." Lossing had the same belief. The escape from Albany had of course been three months before Wyoming.

Based evidently on the authority of one of these writers Frothingham, in a recent book, *Washington, Commander-In-Chief*, calls Wyoming "a massacre of men, women and children with revolting tortures of the hapless settlers."

Benton, who wrote the *History of Herkimer County*, made a real attempt in it to sift the evidence surrounding the death of Walter Butler, particularly as the stories had been affected by the Dwight legend. He presents and examines a number of versions and gives at least a slight impression of wanting the facts.

It is not worth while to examine all the "eyewitness" stories, except to discredit Dwight's tale of "Sherry Valley quarters." In the case of Butler, as in that of John Wilkes Booth, there were many who claimed the honor of having fired the shot. He was shot from his horse, on his knees getting a drink of water, alone, with his men, and hiding behind a tree, and many claimed to have done it.

Lossing, whose *Pictorial Field Books* are so well known, was perhaps the most unctuous of the lot. There never lived another man surely who believed as much that was told him! Tories with him were malignant or snivelling except that extraordinary few whose "opinions were courteously but firmly expressed; they took every opportunity to dissuade their friends and neighbors from participation in the rebellion; and by all their words and acts discouraged the insurgent movement. But they shouldered no musket, girded on no sword, piloted no expeditions against the republicans. They were passive, noble-minded men and deserve our respect." Surely, though, the companionship of the Rangers would have been pleasanter than these courteous pacifists, if such there were. There were frequent cases of cannibalism among Tories according to him.

It seems unnecessary to examine the secondary sources more thoroughly than this, except in the case of the death of Lieutenant Boyd, the commander of Sullivan's scouts near Genesee in '79. In General Sullivan's Report [3] he states that Boyd with twenty volunteers "mistook the road in the night, and at daybreak fell in with a castle six miles higher up than Genesee. Here they saw a few Indians killed and scalped two, the rest fled." Boyd was then surrounded, wounded, and taken. Later that day General Hand's outfit came on his horribly mutilated and decapitated body. This was September 14.

The secondary sources in general agree as to what happened:[4]

Brant left Boyd and his companion in the care of Col. Butler. The latter, as soon as Brant had left them, commenced an interrogation to obtain a statement of the number, situation, and intentions of the army under Sullivan, and threatened them in case they hesitated or prevaricated in their answers to deliver them up immediately to be massacred by the Indians who, in Brant's absence, and with the encouragement of their more savage commander, Butler, were ready to commit the greatest cruelties. . . . They [i.e., Boyd and the soldier] refused to give Butler the desired information. Upon their refusal, burning with revenge, Butler hastened to put his threat into execution. He delivered them to some of their most ferocious enemies.

Simms adds:[5] "To those Indian cruelties we must suppose Butler was not only a witness but that they were rendered the

[3] *General John Sullivan's Expedition*, p. 300.

[4] For example J. B. Wilkinson's *Annals of Binghamton* (Binghamton, 1840), p. 96.

[5] *Schoharie County*, p. 313.

more inhuman in the hope of gratifying his revengeful disposition."

In a letter [6] of the same day, September 14, from Buffalo Creek, John Butler reported to Mason Bolton the capture of Boyd and a private saying,

The officer who is a very intelligent person says their army consists of near 5000 Continental Troops, 1500 of which are Riflemen commanded by General Sullivan and Brigadiers Hand, Poor and Clinton. They have but a month's provision and intend, according to his account, to come no further than Genesee.

This letter does not sound like a fabrication. There is no further mention of Boyd in the Loyalist dispatches. Practically all the journals of American officers speak of finding Boyd's body and many list the mutilations. None of them mentions either of the Butlers as a witness or accessory.

Simms, Wilkinson, and Campbell all detail the mutilations. It is obvious that one, at least, is impossible — Boyd's walking around the tree after an incision had been made in his abdomen and his intestines fastened to the tree — and from what we know of atrocities in wartime it is not likely that any of the mutilations were under-stated.

But, though the torture may have been milder than was reported, it is bad enough that a Continental officer, after being questioned before Butler, should have lost his life. Colonel Butler, however, cannot be held entirely responsible for his execution. It can hardly be contended that there were no cases where Continental officers were safely entrusted to Indians, and on the other hand the killing of prisoners going back from the lines is neither a new nor an old custom in any army, but depends frequently on the weariness or spirit of the guard. Certainly Butler did not provide proper guards for Boyd or he would not have been killed. It is possible, as has been stated, that the fate of Hare and Newberry, of his regiment, prompted him to let Boyd take his chances with the Senecas. Boyd was said [7] to have been desperate, having

---

[6] "New Sources on the Sullivan-Clinton Campaign," p. 296.
[7] *Schoharie County*, p. 300.

left a girl pregnant and pleading for marriage at Clinton's base. Butler may, of course, have been directly responsible for Boyd's death, but it seems very doubtful. He had great respect for the Continentals, knew their superiority and that they would certainly retaliate on his own officers. There is no mention of such retaliation, and it would almost certainly have occurred if they had held Butler responsible. How then has the story grown up? This may be in part the answer: Arthur Campbell's letter of June 13, 1780,[8] says that Butler "comes against Kentucky in greath wrath, he boasts he will give no Quarter, indeed what can be expected from a man that at Wyoming give up his Brother to be tortured and unfeeling enjoyed the sight." Here we see the beginning of the confusion. John Butler of course had no brother at Wyoming but was opposed to Zebulon Butler, who escaped, and to Colonel Dennison. John Butler's grandmother was a Dennison and they may have been related.

With the Americans in the fort at Wyoming in '78, however, there was a man named Boyd, a deserter from Niagara, whom Butler had ordered executed when he was taken. The man naturally pleaded for his life but Butler evidently felt that desertion was so on the increase that an example was necessary. War being what it is he cannot be condemned for that. As the hasty historians of the early nineteenth century read these accounts, Boyd, the British deserter, merges with Boyd, the Continental, killed while a prisoner at Genesee in '79, and Butler becomes the instigator of another atrocity.

All these books are crowded with unrelated incidents through hundreds of pages. There must be thousands of characters in them, eyewitnesses and their children's children after them. Much in them is true, much false, but, false or true, they have been indiscriminately used as authoritative sources on the Revolution. Their mass, if nothing else, makes them important, but there is no evidence that any of the authors had ever heard the word "credibility."

[8] *George Rogers Clark Papers, 1771-1781*, p. 425.

Far different are the romances of the Revolution in New York, *In the Valley*, by Harold Frederic, published in 1890, and perhaps the earliest first-rate historical novel, except Cooper's, written in this country, and the five novels by Robert W. Chambers. Frederic's story begins in the Mohawk region, November 13, 1757, as word comes that "the French are in the Valley." It is told by Douw Mauverensen, the adopted son of one Thomas Stewart, of the landed gentry of Tryon. The hero was a boy of eight in 1757, and Walter Butler, his playmate, was probably five.[9]

Mauverensen tells his life story from that night until 1782, with the history of the years woven almost perfectly into his romance. He does have Cornwallis surrender a year late, in '82, but otherwise is almost letter perfect, and certainly so in the fidelity of his minor detail. He tells early of John Johnson "so ignorant as scarcely to be able to tell the difference between the Dutch and the Germans," and of young Butler who appears "of a better sort mentally but he too never cared to read much." The outdoor life of the boyhood of that day is told with great charm and detail, the coming of autumn with the pigeons darkening the sky, and the October husking of the "white corn, swollen and hulled by being boiled in lye of wood-ashes, spooned steaming into our porringers of milk." He tells of how the "bush-bauer peasants" of the Palatine were gradually preceded in the Valley by Scotch and Irish and English, the Campbells and Clydes of Cherry Valley, and the Butlers, and of how these last looked down on the "Dutch and German cobblers," to the great Sir William's disgust.

Walter Butler and he "always liked each other, doubtless in that we were both of a solemn and meditative nature. We had not much else in common, it is true, for he was filled to the nostrils with pride about the Ormond-Butlers." He tells of how, at a garden party at Johnson Hall, they are talking of the Boston people and Walter Butler bursts "out against

[9] Harold Frederic evidently thought Walter Butler at least eight, an apparent impossibility in view of his mother's birth year, 1735.

them with eager bitterness" and a great lady says to him
" 'Bravo! Admirable! Always be in a rage, Mr. Butler, it suits
you so much. Isn't he handsome, Daisy, with his feathers all
on end?' "

The Valley, says a character in the book, "left no place for
a free yeomanry." The Johnsons and the Butlers, father and
son, "have no restraining notion of public interest. Their
sole idea is to play the aristocrat, to surround themselves with
menials, to make their neighbor concede and do them reverence. It is a reflection of their old Gaelic tribal system."

The hero quarrels with his foster father and goes to work
in Albany where, with the Schuylers, Van Renesselaers, and
Peter Gansevoort, he finds "educated and refined gentlemen
not inferior in any way to the Johnsons and Butlers. If they
did not drink as deep they read a good deal more, and were
masters of as courteous and distinguished a manner." There he
attends "a gathering at the Patroon's House," which is surely
one of the greatest period scenes in our literature, with
Schuyler there, about to go to the first Continental Congress;
the nonagenarian Cadwallader Colden; John Johnson, already
at odds with his dead father's faithful tenantry; Stephen
Watts, wounded later at Oriskany; young De Lancey; and
"the dignified, sober figure of Abraham Ten Broeck," uncle
and guardian of the boy host, the Young Patroon.

Then there comes the rumor of war and that Walter Butler
will call the wild Indians "from the headwaters of the Three
Rivers and from the Lake plains beyond to coerce the settlements if the Valley tribes prove to have been too much spoiled
by the missionaries."

The hero goes on Montgomery's expedition to Quebec.
Then he tells in moving fashion of the mustering of the
Mohawk men to meet St. Leger coming down the river, and he
walks in the dusk with Honikol Herkimer the night before
Oriskany, when the grim old warrior is accused of being a
Tory. Oriskany is told with thrilling but faultless accuracy,
ending with "honor and glory to the rude, unlettered, great-
souled yeomen of the Mohawk Valley who braved death in

the wildwood gulch that Congress and the free colonies might live."

The story ends as word comes

of the violent death of Walter Butler, slain on the bank of the East Canada Creek by the Oneida chief Skenandoah. Both Daisy and I had known him from childhood, and had in the old days been fond of him. Yet there had been so much innocent blood upon those delicate hands of his, before they clutched the gravel on the lonely forest stream's edge in their death grasp, that we could scarcely wish him alive again.

It was high romance. But greater was to follow.

In 1901 Robert W. Chambers published *Cardigan*, the first of his five tales of the Revolution in Tryon. In them he *created* a third Walter Butler who is the villain of all five tales. There is the Walter N. Butler of the secondary sources, possibly the Walter Butler of this present book, and the Walter Butler of the Chambers novels, with his "amber eyes, which all men now know see as well by dark as by the light of the sun," his melancholy, his beauty, his savagery, a person of such fascinating evilness that one is reminded of no one so much as the beautiful and corrupt Henri, duc de Guise, the leader of the St. Bartholomew Massacre.

In the first line of his first preface, that of *Cardigan*, Mr. Chambers says, "Those who read this romance for the sake of what history it may contain will find the histories from which I have helped myself more profitable." In none of them, however, is there more scrupulous care for detail, for accuracy, for the atmosphere of the times, and certainly no one living is more deeply versed in the Revolutionary lore of New York. But there are also "simple folk who read romance for its own useless sake," and for these Mr. Chambers has unfortunately written. Unfortunately, because no one but a student of Tryon and the Revolution can possibly appreciate the saturation of knowledge, along with the great dramatic sense, which has gone into these novels.

The hero of *In the Valley* is a Dutchman, and his story, for all its alarms, is a peaceful, proper tale. Not so the Chambers tales told by the sons of wild Irish gentlemen like Michael

Cardigan and George Ormond, or Frenchmen like Carus Renault, or Scotchmen like John Drogue, Lord Stormont, and Euan Loskiel.

As he started to write these books, on a fair April day of 1900, there were still gold-green pike in the Vlaie water beyond his great house at Broadalbin, and the site of Summer House Point, beloved by Sir William, was still called by its first name. Now all is gone and a vast lake is spread over the mysterious channels of the Drowned Lands, and Thendara, where Walter Butler came too late, is gone forever beneath the deep waters.

Cardigan is the first of Mr. Chambers' cycle, and it opens on May Day, 1774, with a holiday in the schoolroom at Johnson Hall, which is full of Sir William's wards and bastards. Captain Butler has just consented to instruct them all till the new schoolmaster comes. He is a learned youth and Sir William Johnson's secretary. The hero, young Michael Cardigan, is freed from schoolroom discipline by Sir William, and for some light affront challenges Walter Butler to fight. "A year runs," says Butler, bidding him wait, "like a spotted fawn in cherry-time."

There are days of divine outdoors in the Tryon spring, robins rippling their lovely curfew call, crickets awakening under the plank walk, the great Sir William lost in meditation. There is much coming and going of Sir William's Highlanders, a stir in the mails about the Boston people, a strange western Indian from the Cayugas who speaks, with belts, of Cresap's men pushing into his people's lands beyond Fort Pitt, "turning the savages against the colonies by his crazy pranks on the Ohio." There is a scene of the most simple but moving splendor, when Sir William Johnson, speaking like John of Gaunt of old, tells the boy, Michael Cardigan, that "Should He in His wisdom demand that I choose (between the King who has honored me and mine own people in this dear land) and if the sorrow kills me not — then I shall choose."

A great press of officers and Indians comes to Johnson Hall for the council fires, and presently Lord Dunmore, the

Royal Governor of Virginia, appears and there are sham battles with the drums of the Royal Americans beating, "Down, Derry, Down," and a new, barbarous tune, lately in vogue, called "Yankee Doodle."

Then comes the great scene in Sir William's library, from whose windows today one may look on the blockhouse and the place of the Council Fires, with the room jammed with Johnsons, Indians, Dunmore and his staff, Tryon, who was to burn Fairfield to Washington's grim amusement, and the Butlers, father and son. Here Sir William, the greatest servant of the Crown in North America, speaks to simpering Dunmore with the vast authority of his person and position, telling him, and England, that if England used red savages against the Boston men, then woe unto her. Walter Butler speaks up for the use of the Iroquois; Sir William replies that he will try to pacify his wards, the Indians, and asks, "How then can you propose to let loose these Indians on our people?" Tempers mount until Sir William, with Lord Dunmore's war-to-be in mind, says that he intends to protect his distant Cayugas, come what may.

It is apparent that Lord Dunmore and Walter Butler have instigated Cresap at Fort Pitt to take what he wants from the Cayugas. Young Butler is called upon to deliver his keys as Sir William's secretary, and Michael Cardigan is sent to Fort Pitt. He must have taken the same bitter route that James Clinton and Brodhead took in '79 — Johnstown to Cherry Valley to Tioga, up past Chemung to the Alleghany, down past Venango to Fort Pitt — to "show Cresap what a fool he is."

He is wounded there in defense of his lady, and Walter Butler who went after him is beaten up. Cardigan comes back to Johnstown, in a coma after his wounds, and awakes to find his sweetheart gone away, Sir William dead, after that horrible July day when he spoke with belts to the Six Nations, and the heart gone out from Johnson Hall; the Dynasty, Guy, Sir John, and Claus, have taken it over, and are arming for the wars.

Cardigan goes to Boston in search of his frail, sweet love, Felicity, whom Walter Butler desires. He is caught outside General Gage's house in company with a highwayman, is imprisoned and condemned to death. He escapes on that great night, the nineteenth of April, '75; rides out of Boston ahead of the British columns, sees the silversmith, Revere, galloping on to wake the Minute-men; comes to his lost love's house, meets Butler there (and who knows but he was), spares his life, though "the haze that the moon spun in the garden grew red like that fearsome light which tinges the smoke of burning houses, and I [Cardigan] remembered the dream I had of him, long ago, when I saw him in the forest with blood on him and fresh scalps at his belt"; sees Lexington and Concord and Prescott and Lord Percy, Hotspur's great-great-grandson, leading the bleeding redcoats back.

Cardigan comes back to Johnstown with his bride, Felicity, to rest till June when, in the darkness of the village streets, he begins to hear rumors from the North about Walter Butler, and he lies close to his young wife's breast till, at last, in one dim morning he awakes to see Felicity leaning from the casement calling out in a strange, frightened voice:

"Michael! Michael! They are coming over the hills. Footfalls in the hills! Out of the morning men are coming.". . . For a long time we stood silent, the village slept below us; the stillness of the dawn remained unbroken, save by a golden-robin's note, fluting from a spectral elm.

Then, after a time, they hear a roar of voices below them and the cry that Cresap is on the hills with five hundred men of Maryland. Cardigan throws his long rifle on his shoulder and runs swiftly through the garden.

Suddenly, as though by magic summoned, the whole street was filled with riflemen, marching swiftly and silently, with moccasined feet, their racoon caps pushed back, the green thrums tossing on sleeve and thigh. On they came, rank on rank, like brown deer herding through a rock run; and, on the hunting shirts, lettered in white across each breast, [he] read: Liberty or Death.

The book ends as Cardigan joins the riflemen bound for Washington's Army at Cambridge.

Then came *The Little Red Foot*, a story beginning with the funeral of Sir William Johnson, which all the gentry attended, and John Butler's "dark, graceful son Walter — he of the melancholy golden eyes — an attorney then and sick of a wound which, some said, had been taken in a duel with Michael Cardigan near Fort Pitt."

The teller of the tale is young John Drogue, a Scotchman, "Brent-meester to Sir William," and to him John Butler's letter on good roads and bad would have been referred. Drogue tells of how he went to his cabin in Fonda's Bush, after the funeral; of how there came the news of Lexington and the Johnson intrigues, and all but Sir John vanished north in the night; and, with Mr. Chambers' inimitable perfection of detail, of how, "on a bitter day in early winter, an express passed through Fonda's Bush" calling out the Mohawk regiment, who, on snowshoes, "were scarce in sight of Johnstown steeples when the drums of an Albany battalion were heard; and we saw, across the snow, their long brown muskets slanting and heard their bugle-horn on the Johnstown road."

In the spring he dines at Johnson Hall, and Sir John is there, and Henry Hare — later to be hung — and there is talk of "the gallantries of such men as Sir John and Walter Butler . . . [with] young girls, the daughters of tenants, settlers, farmers." Hiakatoo, the fierce Seneca is there, and, riding away, he meets patriot patrols on the road and sees Iroquois signal flames, thin and high, burning against the stars above Maxon.

Later when Colonel Dayton occupies the Hall he goes out with Nick Stoner (the stones of whose cabin are on Mr. Chambers' lands today) on a scout up the Valley of the Sacandaga, "where the great Iroquois War Trail runs through the dusk of primeval woods." There they meet a young war party of Oneidas by a stream where you can stand today in woods that were standing then, and there Nick Stoner plays on his fife the quaint and sad refrain, from the raids of '56:

> Lord Loudon he weareth a fine red coat
> And red is his ladye's foot-mantelle
> Red flyeth ye flagge from his pleasure-boat,
> And red is the wine he loves so well
> But oh! for the dead at Minden Town —
> Naked and bloody and black with soot,
> Where the Lenni-Lenape and the French came down
> To paint them all with the Little Red Foot.

The horror of Indian and Tory warfare comes down on the Valley, the particular horror that no one knows who is friend or foe. Drogue is wounded and recuperates, there passes at Summer House, Sir William's pleasance, a winter

of blue and silver; and the Vlaie Water ran fathomless purple between its unstained snows . . . nothing living stirred on that dead white waste save those little grey and whining birds which creep all day up and down tree-trunks; no signal smoke stained the peaks; the deer yarded on Maxon.

Spring comes with "one grim lank Forest Runner sprawled on the settle by the kitchen table, smoking his bitter Indian Tobacco and drinking rum-and-water well sugared . . . [telling how] near Niagara [he] saw Butler Rangers manoeuvering on snow-shoes, with drums and curly bugle horns," how St. Leger and Burgoyne were coming, and how he saw Simon Girty (who was to take 600,000 Spanish dollars on the Ohio) and Newberry too (who was hung in '79) in war paint "Eating half raw venison, guts and all." Then the "blue-eyed Indians" and the Redmen begin to appear in the Drowned Lands — Harry Hare among them in his green Ranger uniform — and they burn Summer House, "staining the dark water with a prophecy of blood." The tale goes on that dark summer of Oriskany, the capture of Walter Butler, the hero's transfer to Washington's army, his return to Tryon in '80, when Sir John lays Caughnawaga in ashes, and his troops, or his allies, murder the aged Douw Fonda. It is superb romance and much of it sound history that lives and moves.

The year after *Cardigan* came *The Maid-At-Arms*, perhaps the best of them all, though *The Reckoning*, is war and arms as Walter Scott might have liked to write it. It is, says the author, merely an attempt "to paint a patroon family disturbed by the approaching rumble of battle."

This book particularly tells of Broadalbin Bush, Chambers' own lands, and is written with a deep and passionate love of that gentle valley.

One George Ormond, a cousin of the Butlers, from the walled lanes of St. Augustine, Florida, comes north, in the summer of '77, stirred with the thought of war, and the decision as to his loyalty. He is kin to the Varicks who live in a manor house in the Sacandaga Valley. The Valley is full of rumors of what the Johnsons and Butlers and the rest of the landed gentry will do against the growing strength of the Continentals. The night he reaches the Varick's there is to be a great Tory company at dinner. Walter Butler,

a dark graceful young man . . . in a very elegant black-and-orange uniform without gorget . . . light as a panther . . . [with] cruelty in his almost perfect features, which were smooth as a woman's, and lighted by a pair of clear, dark, golden eyes. . . . Terrible mad eyes that I have never forgotten. . . .

comes in and falls to talking of the greatness of the Ormond-Butlers; Sir John is there, and Colonel John Butler, broad and squat; Daniel Claus of the Dynasty; Guy Johnson and McDonnell, and with them Clare Putnam, Sir John's former mistress (his wife is in New York), Magdalen Brant, and all the lovely Loyalist ladies. Walter Butler "with amazing vanity offers a toast to the Ormonds and the Earls of Arran," and later with Daniel Claus humming "Pibroch o' Hirokoue" he drinks "to our Red Allies," and draws a blood-red cross with wine on the tablecloth. The meeting is secret, for Schuyler's riders are in the vicinity. It is interesting that the author has not seen fit to have the Mrs. Butler, Walter's mother, present at such loose revelry.

Ormond, the hero, protests against the dread idea of loosing the Iroquois, while Walter Butler dominates the board with his fierce self-confidence and his plans for his red allies, until they go drunkenly out into the divine valley dawn singing an old Jacobite lay, and shouting "The Army! Sons of the Army!" with the same savage madness the Highlanders showed for the young Chevalier outside Holyrood halls in '45.

It is unquestionably history. It is unquestionably the perfect reproduction of old ideas, old ways, that animated the New York Loyalists to a point where they could no longer realize men were fighting for other things, new loyalties beyond kings and clans.

There is a dire story of the capture of Beacraft with his horrible scalp map, and the Continental Scout who looks down on the terrific rites of the False Faces till even Morgan's Riflemen can stand no more, though Magdalen Brant and Lyn Montour, the "Cherry-Maid," dance naked before the warriors. A dispatch from Marinus Willett tells of a scout under Walter Butler, sixteen Tories and two Mohawks, that have slain three young girls, picking berries, and a Continental scout, coming out of the woods, that see "the new flag" break out over Stanwix. Oriskany is superbly told; the news comes in from Bennington; they capture Ormond, and the Mohawks clamor to kill him. "Would you murder him and lose Walter Butler forever," a Loyalist officer asks. "Give the prisoner to us! What do we care for your Walter Butler," the savages answer, as they might have answered Ross four years later in the snowy woods past Johnstown.

The Hidden Children tells of Sullivan's Campaign, and of the march from Tioga to the smoke of Catharinestown and the destruction of the Dark Empire where the Eries, the Cat Nation, had its bloody altar. Boyd, whose scout was captured at the Genesee Castle, accompanies the hero through the book. They are on their way to Otsego Lake where James Clinton is massing; they pass Cherry Valley

where, through the wintry dawn, young Walter Butler damned his soul for all eternity while men, women and children, old and young, died horribly amid the dripping knives and bayonets of his painted fiends, or fell under the butchering hatchets of his Senecas.

The details of this muster at Otsego Lake of the New York

brigade are available to all, but only a painter, such as Chambers is, could reproduce the life and movement of those days on a printed page.

The artillery jolted and clinked away down the rutty road which their wheels and horses cut into new and deeper furrows; a veil of violet dust hung in their wake, through which harness, cannon, and drawn cutlass glittered and shimmered like sunlit ripples through a mist. Then came our riflemen, the green thrums rippling and flying from sleeve and leggin' and open double-cape, and the racoon-tails all a-bobbing behind their caps like the tails that April lambkins wriggle.

A woman tells of seeing Walter Butler's mother in Albany, a sad and pitiable woman. "Every furtive glance cast after her seemed to shout aloud the infamy of her son, the murderer of Cherry Valley." Even Joseph Brant, she says, has spurned him, since Cherry Valley. She goes on

I try to think of Walter as a murderer of little children, and it is not possible. Why, it seems but yesterday that I stood plaguing him on the stone doorstep at Guy Park — calling him Walter Ninny and Walter Noodle to vex him. You remember his full name is Walter N. Butler, and that he would never tell us what the N. stands for, but we guessed it stood for Nellis, in honour of Nellis Fonda.

A scout goes out to the Susquehanna and sees the Niagara army pass in the night coming down to Chemung," young Walter Butler in his funereal cloak, white as a corpse under the black disorder of his hair, and staring at nothing like a damned man"; old John Butler passes "balancing on his saddle with the grace of a chopping block," and "quite alone, stalked an Indian swathed in a scarlet blanket edged with gold, on which a silver gorget glittered" — Brant; and then the flower of the warriors of the Long House — the Mohawks "in the barbaric magnificence of paint and feathers and shining steel, a hundred lithe-stepping warriors, rifles swinging a-trail, and gorgeous beaded sporrans tossing at every stride."

The Reckoning is the tale of Carus Renault, one of Washington's spies in New York City, during the summer of 1781. He falls in love with a fair visitor from Canada, Elsin Grey, and, while he woos her, Walter Butler arrives from Canada in a packet — it could well have been. Elsin Grey says that Butler danced with her at Niagara, where "he had not spared her hints of that impetuous flame that burned for all pure women deep in the blackened pit of his own damned soul." There is a rumor that he is married and that he denies it — "at his Mohawk Valley tricks again."

And then Butler comes into the room in his "strange regimentals, the silver buttons stamped with a motto in relief, the curious sword knot of twisted buckthong heavily embroidered in silver and scarlet wampum." He tells of the purpose of his visit.

Had I my way this port should be burned from river to river, fort, shipping, dock, all, even to the farms outlying on the hills — and the enervated garrison marched out to take the field. I should fling every man and gun pell-mell on that rebels' ratnest called West Point, and uproot and tear it from the mountain flank! I should hurl these rotting regiments into Albany and leave it a smoking ember and I should tread the embers into the red-wet earth! That is the way to make war!

It is certainly Walter Butler speaking and if it had been done it might have won the war. The rotting regiments were 16,000 strong and there were 2,500 men in the rat nest at West Point.

The story tells of Lyn Montour, his Indian paramour "with hair like midnight and two black stars for eyes"; and Butler curses, as he would have, the "tinseled hierarchy" around Sir Henry Clinton; and then again, as the men are waiting to go in to dinner, Walter Butler comes in, greets them all with his "pretty, genteel" manner, though Sir Henry Clinton ignores him.

There is music and he says thoughtfully,

I love music too, but have heard little for a year save the bellow of conchhorns from the rebel riflemen. O'Neil sat down at the piano and played "The World Turned Upside Down" all drifting into the singing, voice after voice, and the beauty of Walter Butler's voice struck all, so that presently one by one we fell silent, and he alone carried the quaint old melody to its end.

They bring a guitar and "without false modesty or wearying protestation" he sang: "Ninon! Ninon! Que fais-tu de la vie?" "Sad and sweet the song faded, as the deep concord of the strings died out. All were moved. We pressed him to sing more and he sang what we desired in perfect taste and with a simplicity that fascinated us all."

Renault, the spy, escapes and goes north to join Willett near Johnstown. It is October, 1781. He goes to Butlersbury seeking confirmation of Walter Butler's marriage to Lyn Montour, the "Cherry-Maid." There "the year had already begun to die; in the clear air a faint whiff of decay from the rotting leaves — decay, ruin and the taint of death; and, in the sad autumn stillness, something ominous, something secret and sly, something of malice." It is there, this weird miasma, today.

There is the marvelous scene at the council fire at Thendara, the muster to meet Ross at Johnstown, with Butler mad with blood-lust at the end, as he drew his tin cup from his belt and saw reflected there what Christ alone knows. He is shot and scalped.

As I gazed down at him the roar of the fusillade died away in my ears. I remembered him as I had seen him there at New York in our house, his slim fingers wandering over the strings of the guitar, his dark eyes drowned in melancholy. I remembered his voice, and the song he sang, haunting us all with its lingering sadness — the hopeless words, the sad air, redolent of dead flowers — doom, death, decay.

In all these books there is a superbly accurate drawing of the Iroquois and their way of war. They are written by a great scholar. The romance is glorious, and men, as in Housman's poem, are "drunk forever with liquor, love, or fights." The point of view is essentially that of the Revolutionists. The teller of each tale is a well-bred, intelligent Continental officer, horrified that there should be war except against men in arms, deeply moved at the plight of the valley folk, who were raising grain for the army, in fear of their lives from invasion or a shot in the back from an old neighbor of a "friendly" Indian.

They are tales of the wildest, most dangerous frontier of the time, and of the brave men and women who were exhorted by Governor Clinton and the Continental High Command to stick there, at harrow, plow and scythe, lest the army starve.

Chapter XII

THE END AT NIAGARA

The judgment against Walter Butler has so definitely to
with the use of Indians and the conduct of Tories that '
must again struggle with the strings of that bloody knot. T
British use of Indians was an evil business, but, as we ha
seen, there was little alternative. The American position tł
the aborigines would have remained for eight years in str
neutrality is untenable. We have dealt, it is true, with thc
issues in the third chapter, but the primary evidence sir
presented is both so varied and so vital that we must, at t
risk of repetition, review and sum it up before we come to t
end at Niagara.

The land was cursed by the Indian presence, yet unquestic
ably it was their land, and, unless Whig and Tory had deferr
their war until the Indian was exterminated, it is hard to s
how he was to be excluded from it. Probably every wh:
man in North America at the time wanted the Indians shov
west of the Mississippi and back and back till he was no moɪ
He must go as he had gone out of Massachusetts and low
New York and New Jersey and the whole seaboard. T
Iroquois warrior was a merciless foe, but doubtless ev
the bloodiest and most ignorant of them were stirred
some deep race tension, as year after year the old men to
them how the white man was sweeping away their hom
their council fires, their laws, their ways, and their gods. E
fore the Revolution their dead line was at Stanwix, and S
William Johnson, though he tried to protect them in thɛ
died as Dunmore's men were violating even that conventic

It was an unescapable tragedy. In a general way the Indi:
Superintendencies preserved law and order in the red lan
before the Revolution. The Superintendencies were the usu

machinery which a conservative government sets up to deal with such a problem, giving a semblance of security while time and change works out the necessary compromise. But the government of the Continental Congress was a most radical government that wanted all the lands for its own people, and its own people regarded Indian rights and lives less highly than those of the buffaloes who gave them furs and meat. Forests, Indians, wild life, were all to go before this consuming white conquest. The Superintendencies regarded North America as a colony whose great natural resources were to benefit England, and the Indian problem as simply an annoying phase of the exploitation, to be handled as seemed best. The whole mental attitude of the frontiersmen and their financial backers was at the other pole. Out, the Indians!

Given the situation there seems to have been no alternative to the employment of Indians, yet the condemnation of the British government for using them is universal from both Englishmen and Americans. The deepest cause of this is that apparently hundreds of Tories mingled with the Indian bands, dressed and painted like Indians, committing the same foul murders which the Indian's conscience permitted him.

In the past the explanation of this horrible and almost incomprehensible conduct has been the easy assumption that all patriots were good men and all supporters of the King evil men. But there is mounting evidence that the Loyalist ranks were full of well-educated, well-to-do men of principles as well as property. There were one hundred Harvard graduates in the various Loyalist corps, and of course the roster of Loyalists is imposing in its distinguished names, including not a few sons of King's College and Yale.

The answer to this has been that people of wealth are indifferent to the woes of the unfortunate, that it was nothing to a well-bred gentleman, fighting for his king, that wandering bands of Tories stormed lonely farmhouses, killed women and children, and behaved with revolting savagery against anyone less able to take care of himself than the Continentals.

In the case of the Tryon frontier, there were deep and ancient hatreds, rising from the clash of Dutch Palatine blood with Irish, Scotch, and English. If Tory atrocities were limited to Tryon this might be the whole answer, but, if not in number, certainly in ferocity, they are duplicated from Champlain to Georgia.

The philosophy of history indicates that established governments, in dealing with rebellion, sanction methods of suppression that they would not use against another state at war with them, and it is not claimed that British officers were ever known to punish Tory murderers for acts that British officers might themselves regard with horror.

Still this level of conduct is not satisfactorily explained, but an important part of the answer appears to the present author to lie along this line: the thirteen colonies must have had, like all new places, a great riff-raff of ne'er-do-wells and criminals. The war offered an opportunity for murder and plunder to these men which they eagerly embraced. No army in wartime inquires very closely into the past morals of its recruits or its allies. The breakdown of civil law unbridles such men. The desperadoes, deserters, and ruffians who operated between the lines in Westchester lacked only scope and Indians to duplicate the atrocities of Tryon. Reference has been made to Governor Clinton's concern over wandering criminals terrorizing the state.

This does not mean to say that a heavy judgment does not lie against the Tories, but that it is incredible, that the Tories, even of Tryon, were universally a wholly different class morally from other men. They had farms and homes, wives and children, hopes, plans, ambitions, and, with all these things, they could not all have suddenly become monsters, guilty of murdering little children and women in childbed, and even, as some say, of cannibalism — only to become, with the peace, perhaps, the finest stock in Canada. Even in Butler's Rangers must there not have been simple men, like the good soldier, Pinsil, who wanted to go to the wars but wanted his old mother looked out for first — or the unknown man they shot on the Albany road after he had said he had given no more to his king because he had no more to give?

But the brief fact is that in war no side has ever inquired very deeply into the credentials of those who injure that side's enemy. Much of the Indian-Tory murder may have been the work of public enemies to whom no king or country mattered. Unquestionably there was a British policy of terrorism aimed at all the back settlements. It was a horrible business. Ross and Walter Butler burned seven miles of the Valley in '81 and appeared not to be accused of killing women and children; this terrible deed is not held against them as a war crime, yet deaths and griefs must have arisen from it perhaps more numerous than in Doxstader's fight the week before, near Schoharie, where the eight prisoners were butchered.

The whole Tryon war is like some bloody kinetoscope, but the history of wars and men indicates that not all virtues could have lain with us. Only a few years later the conduct of John Sevier, a man of education, a member of the Society of the Cincinnati, and a follower of Washington, toward Indians under his protection was so horrible that the frontiersmen of the Cumberland were themselves aghast.

We are faced with the question of Walter Butler's personal responsibility. Without doubt he did share it along with his father, the Johnsons, Haldimand — who as early as 1760 had been commander at Fort Ontario, near Oswego, and knew the Indians as well as any man — Hamilton, De Peyster, Bolton, and the whole high command. But they had used Indians in all the wars this continent had known.

It is plain from the Claus letter of condemnation that both Butlers tried, against the wishes of the Johnsons, to keep the Indians from the conflict until St. Leger came down the river in '77. There is repeated evidence, particularly in his desire to go into an "established regiment," that he would be glad of other service. Stone and Cruikshank, have pointed out that, while we know what his enemies thought of him, "what he seemed to his friends and comrades has never been told."

To his enemies he is the bloody and infamous monster rejoicing in the death of babies at Cherry Valley, gloating in the tortures of Boyd, treacherous, cowardly (in one authority he is killed hiding behind a tree), and revengeful. Brant shrinks, according to Campbell, from him, but prevents his slaying an unborn child, and Butler seems little more than a degenerate. Yet the process by which such legends can be developed is well known. Roosevelt says of the frontiersmen of both sides:

Their deeds were not put into books while the men themselves lived; they were handed down by tradition and grew dim and vague in the recital. What one fierce partisan leader had done might dwindle or might grow in the telling or might finally be ascribed to some other; or else the same feat was twisted into such varying shapes that it became impossible to recognize which was nearest the truth or what man had performed it.

The documents of this book do not confirm the orthodox legend. Walter Butler's first letter is an offer to defend a poor man in jail for debt apparently without expectation of reward. His letter, on the eve of Lexington, has to do with a case of Cuppernal vs. Garrison that sounds as dull and musty as Jarndyce vs. Jarndyce in *Bleak House*. He is in the early fighting at the Cedars, at Montreal, and at Oriskany, and then is captured and condemned to be hung, after being taken in the German Flats. His former schoolmates, then officers of the New York line, protest to Arnold, who sets aside the verdict and Butler goes down to Albany, a prisoner, along with Ten Broeck, an officer of the Rangers and a scion of one of the great Dutch families, divided against itself. In prison General Schuyler himself intervenes for him, and he is transferred to a private home. So far the best of the Albany patriots, Schuyler and the regimental officers, have been his friends, and Peter Van Schaack, a dry, musty, old fellow, but a gentleman of recognized nobility, has been his correspondent.

He escapes dramatically and goes to Niagara, and that fall there is Cherry Valley. It is said that he went there knowing fully what the Indians would do, and, in fact, taking them there to do it. At the time his mother and sister, Deborah, were hostages in Albany and he seems deeply devoted to them. Against this interpretation of his intention we have his own word — and must presumably disregard it as biased evidence, but we have also the contemporary letter from the Ranger Loyalist to a friend, to whom there was no use in lying, which says that he detached men from his command to protect the people as soon as he saw the Indians were out of hand and that he would never again serve in a command where Indians were in the majority — nor did he. Also in his favor is the failure to connect him with any other butchery, and the proper conduct of Ross's troops under him in 1781.

The issue of guilt at Cherry Valley revolves partially around Brant. One side says that Butler instigated the murders for revenge, but after all they were Brant's Indians and it appears absurd to hold Brant, the Indian leader, up as a sort of Saladin and relieve him of all responsibility for his men's behavior. The secondary sources say that Brant pointed to his conduct when not with Butler in proof of Butler's guilt. But the fact is that his men at Andrustown, the German Flats, Minisink, and elsewhere behaved atrociously quite as they did at Cherry Valley. After Cherry Valley it is impossible to place Walter Butler in the Mohawk Valley or the Schoharie hills until the twenty-fourth of October, 1781, when he was there with Ross's column. All the atrocities of those thirty-six months, at any rate, were not his. This is one of the great facts about him that has been overlooked. It would certainly be reasonable to expect at least one of his letters to gloat in the killings, if they had really brought him pleasure or appeased this thirst for revenge that is said to have animated him; but none betrays this feeling. Caldwell and Chrysler certainly mention what they did and their journals correspond with their foes' accusations.

If Walter Butler was the blood-thirsty degenerate he is described as being, then his whole short life was recorded by him in his letters with masterly deception. The writer of the letters is a restless, proud young man, writing and spelling

far above the level of his times, who is animated through
the war years with the great desire to get his mother and sister
out of his enemy's hands, who persistently volunteers for the
most daring and arduous tasks, and who is finally killed, after
he has successfully covered the retreat of his commander and
his forces. In his brief Journal, too, he speaks of the sky
and water and land and the mist of the Falls of Niagara as
criminals are not accustomed to do. His character is not now
to be vindicated or established by argument, but it is reasonable to conclude that he was always ready to die for his cause,
that he appears to have cared for his men and their little
troubles like a good officer, and that, except for Cherry Valley,
he is placed by no one at the many massacres.

There is much that we do not know about him, and it is a
tragic irony that the date of his birth and the place of his burial
should neither be known. It is probable that the hardships
of his confinement in the Albany jail actually undermined
his health, as is claimed, and his absence from Wyoming
may likely have been due to that. He mentions later in his
letters to Mathews, that the ague has come back, and the bearskins, ordered in August, even for northern New York, seem
to indicate a necessary thought for his health.

Looking back on his life, perhaps the first important thing
of which we should like to know more is the scene at Butlersbury when his father and he said good-by to Mrs. Butler
and slipped away in the June night to Canada; and then the
scene at St. Leger's camp in the sultry August heat when
he left with the flag for Shoemaker's. Who suggested that he
go, did his father offer to have him, did he think of it himself,
did he think he would ever come back?

And that winter in the Albany jail — apparently trying
to goad Ten Broeck to escape with him? And the long winter
nights at Niagara? With whom was he in love? Somewhere
in Canada are there letters of his written to some long-dead
maiden, who never married after word came through that he
was left lying by the creek in Tryon? Or are the legends true,
and were the slim Indian girls at Niagara all his concubines,

and Mrs. Robinson his mistress, and did blond Palatine girls forgive him great crimes for love's sake? Perhaps further search will reveal something of that other side of his life, in Detroit, where years before a love-sick girl waited in vain for the great Sir William to come back, or in wintry Montreal, as he went up the steep streets to some warm room, wrapped in his long black cloak, with his boots crunching the snow.

On October 25, 1781, when he crossed the Mohawk going north, the old road to Johnstown went over the hill past Butlersbury. It was down that road he was led, as a child, to see Sir William Johnson, the greatest man in North America, come riding home from the wars with his red warriors beside him. What wonder that Walter Butler found the Iroquois his natural allies? The tired column halted where the road comes in from Butlersbury a quarter of a mile away, and he went up to the lonely looted house his grandfather had built. He must have passed it in that forlorn sundown, and he probably had not seen it since June in '75 when he rode away after news of Bunker Hill reached the Valley.

What he might have done, had he lived on after the war, is hard to say. Simcoe, a great Loyalist partisan leader, was to be the greatest man in Canada, but it is hard to think of Walter Butler at the slow business of statecraft. Possibly in some "established regiment" he would have gone out to India with Lord Cornwallis, who succeeded Warren Hastings as Governor General, there to come to great estate, or perhaps to found the Guides for the defense of that other perilous Northwestern Frontier in India, fifty years before Harry Lumsden did. There is little way of knowing what he wanted from life, but by 1781 he must have been haggard and worn with the terrible hardships of the Upper Posts, from which others were constantly seeking transfer. Probably a little peace was all, and a sight of England which he yearned to see.

It would be of vast interest to know whether he had read Horace Walpole's *The Castle of Otranto* which appeared in 1764 and was widely read both sides of the Atlantic. Sir John might have brought it home from London in '68 for his father's library, certainly not for himself, and Walter Butler found it there. In many ways his manners suggest that he may have been influenced by the romantic melancholy of those haunted pages. The hills along the lake looked to him like a "romantic wild ruinn," when he is banished from his own. Haldimand and De Peyster both comment on his gentle aristocratic manners which seem to be in contrast to the men around him. He is said to have been very insistent on his descent from the great Ormond-Butlers; he is somewhat given to being persecuted or misunderstood by people like De Lancey or Ten Broeck or McLean, all of which provides a rough but very interesting parallel to Walpole's Theodore Falconara, with his birth mark of a "bloody arrow" and the other dark heroes of such books — young men of pale aristocratic melancholy, banished from their own, persecuted but valorous. It would not be the first time that a single book influenced enormously the early life of a young man.

The mysterious legend of his burial under old St. George's Church in Schenectady might almost be in the Otranto tradition. The published *History of St. George's Parish* does not mention it, and the historian, Mr. Willis T. Hanson, Jr., who had access to all papers and records available, does not credit it. It will be recalled that it was said that Colonel Butler offered a large sum for the recovery of his son's body, but that it was abandoned to the wild beasts of Tryon. Lossing observes that the mound that marked the grave has long ago been washed away. This is apparently an after-thought of his, as there is no evidence even of the burial.

There has been, however, the persistent tradition of his secret burial at St. George's, and an early rector is credited with the following doggerel:

> Beneath the pew in which you sit
> They say that Walter Butler's buried.
> In such a fix, across the Styx
> I wonder who his soul has ferried.

And so the ages yet unborn
Shall sing your fame in song and story
How ages gone you sat upon
A Revolutionary Tory.

During the Revolution the church was closed because of the Tory sympathies of the rector.

It is claimed that, after Walter Butler was killed, Tory sympathizers, or friends of his father, secretly brought his body down the river by night to bury it in hallowed ground. The north shore of the Mohawk River was much more Loyalist in its sympathies than the Schoharie side, and by Indian trails on the north shore, with pauses in Tory homes, or refuge in outbuildings, this secret funeral is said to have come. It is hinted that Masonic brothers of his father were ready to help provide decent burial; it does not seem to be a fact that Walter Butler was himself a Mason. It is said that interment in the church was provided for at that time, at a fixed expense, and that in the church before the restoration there was much more space between the altar and the pews than now. To the late Dr. Taylor, rector of St. George's, is accredited the statement that Walter Butler lies under the third pew from the front, in the right aisle; and it is said that even recently, when an old woman in the Valley heard of it, she endeavored to start a movement to dig up the body and crucify it.

As to the facts, it was snowing at Canada Creek and unquestionably wolves were closing in on the army. It is hard to see how his body could have been recovered and brought back through a countryside enflamed against him. Yet the scene of fighting can be desolate and lonely in a few hours after the troops have gone, and resolute men could have done it. There are other Butler children buried at St. George's.

A romantic, mysterious figure, of whom less is known than probably anyone of equal importance in the Revolution, and, beyond all possible question, it is plain that, laying aside the question of war guilt, he was a far different type from most of those around him — far different from the Butlers of the sec-

ondary sources. Certainly there is nothing valid in the legend
of any friendship between him and the Johnson Dynasty.
They were enemies. Bolton seems to have regarded him usually
with surprise, Haldimand with good-will but caution lest he
try to go too fast, the Rangers themselves appear to have
liked him — it would be in the Otranto tradition to look out
for your inferiors — and they all seemed sure that he would
not shirk toil or danger.

Willett, his Nemesis, who was judge advocate at the court-
martial and in at his death, was a good fighter, though from
his narrative it is apparent he was one of the types most abom-
inated at the front, a collector of souvenirs, Walter Butler's
commission among them. It is easy to think of him as a spot-
less patriot, but when another man was to be promoted over
him he wrote [1] Clinton that if it was confirmed it was his
intention "to retire to some business." This was in mid-war.

Gansevoort, in the high warrior manner, was a courageous
and intelligent officer, the savior of the Valley at Stanwix, and
the writer of some of the most superb invective the British
army can ever have received. George Clinton, Governor of
New York, unceasingly appears one of the finest of men, a
superb patriot, and Washington's great supporter. Haldimand
is an earnest, cautious man trying to win the war by making
diversions to help Sir Henry Clinton who will take no action.
The war to Haldimand was one long worry over money and
how to feed that long upper arm. The Johnsons are whis-
perers; De Peyster an alarmist; Bolton an old-school officer
writing reports all day. John Butler was a different man from
any of these. In all the years of the war there is no word of
personal complaint from him, or from Walter Butler, nor
is there any complaint of mutiny or lack of fighting qualities
in their Rangers.

Washington wrote to Governor Clinton, November 5, 1780,

I am sorry that the troops from your State should look upon it as a
hardship to do the garrison duty at Fort Schuyler. I had always allotted

[1] *Papers of George Clinton*, Vol. IV, p. 656.

it to them as thinking it would be agreeable to both officers and men to guard their own frontiers. Pennsylvania and Virginia have not been relieved in two years

nor were the Rangers at Niagara, Detroit, or before Fort Pitt, ever relieved. They stuck to it for the duration of the war. But the frontier over which the New Yorkers contended was different. "The long nights," it is said, "would be turned into a recital of their sufferings during the flight into Canada from Johnstown. . . . Many of the women, through the wilderness, carried their children on their backs." They were years of unalleviated burdens and sorrows to the Butlers. They were not alien invaders who, if they lost the war, could go back to homes across the seas. They were of this country, like the other Loyalists. Beverly Robinson, of Sir Henry Clinton's staff, wrote Ethan Allen during the conspiracy, "I am an American myself, feel much for the distressed situation my poor country is in, and am anxious to be serviceable toward restoring it to peace."

Draper, travelling to Niagara in 1863, had an interview with William Caldwell, the son of one of Butler's captains, who told him "Colonel Butler could never get reconciled to the death of his son Walter" [2] Surely the old man must have felt that he had tried to serve his king faithfully for forty years, only to lose everything at the end — including his eldest son. He wrote February 24, 1788, from Niagara to Colonel Vrooman at Schoharie, on some business matters, and ended the letter:

I am with my best respects to you and the rest of my old friends, if they will accept of them, which I imagine they will if they consider me as an honest man who does his duty when ordered, however disagreeable to himself.[3]

He was growing old and ill and lonely at Niagara where he was now Superintendent of Indian Affairs. It had been thirty years since the July day when it capitulated to Sir William Johnson, and he had been in the company. There was great

[2] Draper Collection, 17S, p. 237.   [3] Ibid., 3F, p. 16.

terror and bloodshed still over the western lands, but slowly the frontiersmen were driving back the Indians and the tenacious upper posts of the British. The Indians were soon fighting in Ohio with a desperate last-stand ferocity beyond anything Tryon had ever seen. Burr and Wilkinson and dozens of other Continental officers were on the Mississippi. Timothy Pickering, later to be American Secretary of State, now settled in the Wyoming Valley, was appointed a delegate to meet Butler, whom he had called a bandit, at a council at the Painted Post.

That year it became necessary for Colonel Butler to appeal to the Government for aid — not for knighthood as some books have said. The backwash of the vast confiscation of Loyalist property was just being felt. Sir William Pepperell's Maine holdings, extending thirty miles along the coast; the Philipse heritage in New York, embracing three hundred square miles; the property of the Penns; and the Fairfax estate, "stretching out in Virginia like a Province," as Beard has said, were but a few of those that were lost. The appeal [4] reads:

Your memorialist's person is attainted and his estate real and personal forfeited . . . being worn out with fatigue, he and his family are reduced to a situation which compels him to solicit the aid, and threw himself upon the beneficence of government.

There is no mention of the loss of his son. The memorial goes on:

He was settled on his own estate . . . early in 1775 he was written to by Mr. Duane, a member of Congress, to take part with them, which he refused. . . . His slaves were sold by the Americans. Two of them ran away from their masters and came to him in Canada. One died soon after, and the other is now his hired servant.

It is incredible that this man should have been a monster of cruelty. What unbelievable difficulties must have been in the way of those slaves finding their master.

He was compelled to leave his possessions and family as early as May,

[4] Loyalist Papers, Vol. XXXXIII, p. 636 et seq., N. Y. P. L.

1775, that in the autumn of that year he was sent by General Carleton to Niagara entrusted with the direction of the Indian Nations which he conducted tho' in the most difficult and precarious situation to the entire satisfaction of His Excellency who was afterwards pleased to allow your memoriallist to raise a corps of Rangers, first of eight companies with the rank of Major, afterwards of ten companies with the rank of Lieutenant Colonel, which he did compleatly and with whom he has often fought the enemy upon their own terms.

There were affidavits with the memorial. Sir Guy Carleton said, "When there was danger and difficulty he carried through the business with ability, valor and success . . . he is very modest and shy." Sir Frederick Haldimand wrote "His services as well in the field, as in the management of Indian Affairs having been uniformly zealous, brave and judicious, have deservedly obtained my fullest testimonies of approbation." The Dynasty testified to the extent of his lands and his cattle.

With what letters there are from Walter Butler in the British Museum, there is one curiously misfiled, evidently of a much earlier date, though it bears neither date or place but is addressed to the low countries, and signed, "Your most affectionate Brother, Walter Butler." Possibly it was written to the great Duke of Ormonde, but it applies, like Stirling's despatch, to the old warrior at Niagara. "Your present post," it says, "renders you serviceable to your King; if you be the man I always took you for you will hazard all that is dear to you and serve him."

Niagara was meanwhile become a town with farms around it, and, with the assistance of Colonel John Butler, a parish church was built and the Reverend Dr. Addison was sent out by the Society for the Propagation of the Gospel.

Toward the end of the eighties Patrick Campbell, who wrote *Travels in North America* (published in Edinburgh in 1793), came out with a letter of introduction to Colonel John Butler at Niagara. He travelled widely, observed carefully, and met many men in America. He speaks of the Rangers "led on by a son of Colonel Butler, a gallant young officer who was killed in the war. This chosen corps — this band of brothers, was rarely known to be worsted in any skirmish or action." All travellers of consequence going through Niagara saw Colonel Butler there. Ezra Stiles, who played the part of John Butler in the Wyoming Pageant at Yale, says in his diary that "Colonel Butler of Niagara told Dr. Eliot in 1790 that Missasauga Indians N. and N. W. of Lake Ontario once a year sacrificed a dog." But travellers found Colonel Butler growing old. The old times were over. Washington was now President of a federal government soundly organized; the young Republican armies of France were overrunning Europe.

On November 3, 1792, there was a council of the Six Nations held at Buffalo Creek. Colonel Butler was there, and young Walter Butler Sheehan, his nephew, who as a boy had been a hostage in Albany, was there as an interpreter. On January 6, 1793, the first baptism was held in St. Mark's Parish at Niagara. There is a pathetic charm in the fact that the infant was "Jane, a daughter of Martin, Colonel Butler's negro," one of the slaves who long ago had run away to join him. That spring an infant of Thomas Butler's, named Walter Butler, died there and was buried, and again the next year, another infant of that name, as with each new boy they tried to carry on the name of the eldest son.

John Butler was now sixty-eight. On May 29, 1793, Catharine Butler his wife, died "and left the world," they said, "as a weary traveller leaves." What a world of woe had been hers since the day she had come to Butlersbury as a girl of sixteen to be the wife and mother of the "notorious" leaders of the Rangers.

A month later, June 23, the worn-out old man was ordered to go with Alexander McKee to a meeting on the lower Sandusky in Ohio, between the United States of America and the Indian American Nations. Strange how this Indian business was never to be thrown off. An Indian at the last took his son's scalp. Haldimand's instructions as to dealing with the Indians for their lack of support of Ross accompanied his condolence on Walter Butler's death. In the still fresh grief for his wife he is ordered away on their endless wearying business. If he had sinned greatly in having them as allies he was never allowed to forget it. No change nor rest for him. Simcoe himself said of the Indians that year, that the British "Connexion and Command rest upon the personal tenure of the frail lives of Butler or McKee." His health was broken by years of hardship and unhappiness. That winter, though, his third son, William Johnson Butler, named for the great Sir William, married Eve, daughter of Colonel Christopher Yates, of the powerful patriot family, and of the Committee for Detecting Conspiracies. It had been nineteen years since this lad, with his mother and sister, was a hostage in Albany, and it must have been in the childhood play of those five long years that he knew Eve. It was Abraham Yates, a brother, who reported, that April night in '78, that Walter Butler had gotten away and there was small chance of bringing him back. It is said that Colonel Yates was later executor of John Butler's will, and it is of interest, and possibly of significance, that he was a parishioner at St. George's in Schenectady.

All hope that the "less luck" would turn was gone forever. Strange that even a last plea for recognition, fourteen years after his death, should fail like all the others:

Heirs of the late Captain Walter Butler: Petition stating the petitioners never to have had the lands due to the said Walter Butler and now pray for such lands due as he was entitled. Rejected.[5]

"Rejected." So read the answer of Simcoe and the Executive Council, August 5, 1795.

On January 22, 1796, William Johnson Chew wrote [6] from Niagara to his brother at Detroit, "John Butler has lost the use of his legs at Niagara and is worried about his old accounts." No peace at the last. All winter he was paralyzed and on into May. The fourteenth of May he died. There is a tablet now to him in St. Mark's Church, Niagara-on-the-Lake:

[5] *Ontario Archives for 1929*, p. 124.
[6] Hist. Coll. Mich. Haldimand Papers, Vol. X, p. 20.

Fear God
Honour the King

In Memory of Colonel John Butler

A sincere Christian as well as a brave soldier, he was
one of the founders and the first patron of this parish.

There is brief mention of him in Mrs. Simcoe's Diary:

Monday — 9th — a wet cold day.
Thursday — 12th — Received a cap from Miss Bond from Philadelphia.
Sunday — 15th — Whitsunday. Coll. Butler buried (His Majesty's
Commissioner for Indian Affairs).

No word even of a bugler in a green coat by the lonely
grave, blowing the Last Post from a curly bugle-horn through
the cold rain from the Falls.

BIBLIOGRAPHY

In preparing a bibliography for a work of this sort, an author faces a dilemma. Shall he cite all the books he has used? By so doing, does he implicitly approve their validity? Shall he give no bibliography, like Trevelyan, or dazzle the reader with his erudition, like Buckle? He certainly has a twofold obligation: to make as many sources as possible available to other scholars working in the field, and to supply the general reader with the main literature readily available on the subject. The second list should include books whose conclusions are at variance with his own. Therefore I have divided my bibliography into those unpublished and published sources which I believe essential to a study in this field, and have added a third list of books which the general reader may desire to consult.

UNPUBLISHED

Individual original letters in the following collections:

Library of Congress, Washington, D. C.

British Museum, London.

Chicago Historical Society, Chicago.

Public Records Office, London.

Manuscript Room, New York Public Library, New York City.

Reference is made to such letters in the text. Other sources are:

British Head-Quarters Papers, in possession of Mr. John D. Rockefeller, Jr.

Claus, Daniel, Papers, Canadian Archives, Ottawa.

Clements Collection, Ann Arbor, Michigan.

    Sir Henry Clinton Papers.

    Lord George Germaine Papers.

    An Historical Detail of Seven Years Campaigns in North America, 1775-1782.

Draper, Lyman C., Manuscripts, Wisconsin Historical Society, 25 vols., Brant Manuscripts.

Fonda, Jelles, Journal of, New York Historical Society.

Gates, Horatio, Papers, New York Historical Society.

Haldimand Papers, Canadian Archives.

Loyalist Papers, 60 vols., transcripts from the Public Records Office, London, New York Public Library.

Orderly Book of the Northern Army, August 21-December 31, 1777, New York Historical Society.

Schuyler, Philip, Papers of, New York Public Library.

Schuyler, Philip, Calendar, New York Public Library.

Tryon County, New York, The Minute Book of the Committee of Safety, Emmet Collection, New York Public Library.

Willett, Marinus, Narrative of the Military Actions of, Emmet Collection, New York Public Library.

Willett Papers, New York Public Library.

PUBLISHED

Adams, Randolph G., Sir Henry Clinton Maps, Ann Arbor, 1928.

Alvord, C. W., Mississippi Valley in British Politics, 2 vols., Cleveland, 1917.

American Archives, 4th and 5th Series, Washington, 1837.

American Historical Association, Annual Report, Vol. II, Washington, 1907.

Bancroft, George, History of the United States of America, 6 vols., New York, 1888.

Barber, J. W., and H. Howe, Historical Collections of the State of New York, New York, 1842.

Beard, Charles and Mary R., The Rise of American Civilization, 2 vols., New York, 1927.

Benton, Nathaniel S., History of Herkimer County, Albany, 1856.

Boudinot, Elias, Journal of American Events during Revolutionary War (reprint), Philadelphia, 1894.

Boyd, Thomas, Simon Girty, New York, 1928.

Browne, Douglas G., "Butlers of Butlersbury," *Cornhill Magazine*, London, November 19, 1921.

Burgoyne, Lieutenant General [John], A State of the Expedition from Canada, London, 1780.

Burr, Aaron, Memoirs of, 2 vols., New York, 1836.

Butterfield, C. W., History of the Girtys, Cincinnati, 1890.

Butler, Walter, Journal of, An Expedition along the North Shore of Lake Ontario, 1779, ed. by James F. Kenney, *Canadian Historical Review*, December, 1920, Toronto.

Campbell, Patrick, Travels in North America, Edinburgh, 1793.

Campbell, William W., Annals of Tryon County, 2d ed., New York, 1924.

Cartwright, Richard, Life and Letters, Toronto, 1876.

Caulkins, Frances M., History of New London, New London, 1860.

Chambers, Robert W., Cardigan, New York, 1901.

—— The Maid at Arms, New York, 1902.

—— The Reckoning, New York, 1907.

—— The Hidden Children, New York, 1914.

—— The Little Red Foot, New York, 1921.

Clark, George Rogers, Papers of, 1771-1781, ed. by J. A. James, Chicago, 1912.

Claus, Daniel, Narrative, Society of Colonial Wars, State of New York, June, 1904.

Clinton, George, Public Papers of, 10 vols., Albany, 1899.

Cruikshank, Ernest A., The Story of Butler's Rangers, Welland, Ontario, 1893.

Day, Richard E., Calendar of Sir William Johnson Manuscripts, Albany, 1909.

De Veaux, Samuel, The Falls of Niagara, or Tourists' Guide, Buffalo, 1839.

Dictionary of American Biography, ed. by Allen Johnson and Dumas Malone, New York, 1928.

Draper, Lyman C., Kings Mountain and Its Heroes, new ed., New York, 1929.

Dwight, Timothy, Travels in New England and New York, 4 vols., New Haven, 1821.

Flick, A. C., Loyalism in New York during the American Revolution, New York, 1901.

—— "New Sources on the Sullivan-Clinton Campaign," *Quarterly Journal of the New York State Historical Association*, Vol. X (1929), 185-224, 265-317.

—— [chairman], The Sullivan-Clinton Campaign in 1779, Albany, 1929.

Fortescue, Sir John, History of the British Army, 11 vols., New York, 1915.

Frederic, Harold, In the Valley, New York, 1890.

Gage, General Thomas, The Correspondence of, with the Secretary of State, 1763-1775, ed. by C. E. Carter, New Haven, 1931.

Gilbert, The Captivity and Sufferings of Benjamin (reprint), Cleveland, 1904.

Greene, Evarts B. and Richard B. Morris, A Guide to the Principal Sources for Early American History, 1600-1800, in the City of New York, New York, 1929.

Greene, F. V., The Revolutionary War and the Military Policy of the United States, New York, 1911.

Greene, Nelson, ed., History of the Mohawk Valley, 4 vols., Chicago, 1925.

Haldimand Papers, Historical Collections of the State of Michigan.

Hough, J. B., The Northern Invasion of 1780, New York, 1893.

Infantry Drill Regulations, Washington, 1917.

James, J. A., The Life of George Rogers Clark, Chicago, 1928.

——— To What Extent Was George Rogers Clark in Military Control of the Northwest at the Close of the American Revolution, Washtington, 1920.

Johnson, Sir John, Orderly Book of, 1776-1777, Albany, 1882.

Johnson, Sir William, Papers of, 7 vols., Albany, 1921-1931.

Johnston, Henry P., The Storming of Stony Point, New York, 1900.

——— Nathan Hale, 1776, New Haven, 1914.

Jones, Pomroy, Annals of Oneida County, Rome, N. Y., 1851.

Jones, Thomas, History of New York during the Revolutionary War, ed. by E. F. De Lancey, New York, 1879.

Journals of Continental Congress, 27 vols., Washington, 1904-.

Ketchum, William M., History of Buffalo, Buffalo, 1864.

Kirby, William, Annals of Niagara, Toronto, 1896.

Lee, Charles, Papers of, 2 vols., New York Historical Society, Publications, New York, 1871.

Lefferts, Charles M., Uniforms in the War of the American Revolution, New York, 1926.

Little, Mrs. William S., The Story of the Massacre at Cherry Valley, Rochester Historical Society, New York, 1890.

Lossing, Benson J., Life and Times of Philip Schuyler, New York, 1872.

——— Pictorial Field-Book of the Revolution, 2 vols., New York, 1860.

Madison, James, Papers of, New York, 1841.

Maclay, William, Journal of, New York, 1890.

Marshall, John, Life of Washington, new ed. 2 vols., New York, 1930.

McLean, J. P., An Historical Account of the Settlements of Scotch Highlanders, 2d ed., Cleveland, 1900.

Massachusetts Historical Society, Publications of, 2d series, 1885-86.

Life and Adventures of Timothy Murphy, in *Middleburgh* (N. Y.), *Gazette*, August 1, 1912.

Miner, Charles, History of Wyoming, Pa., Philadelphia, 1845.

Morris, Richard B., *see* Greene, Evarts B.

New York, Calendar of Historical Manuscripts, State of, Albany, 1868.

——— Documents Relative to Colonial History of the State of, 11 vols. (*see* General Index), Albany, 1856-1861.

——— Journal of the Legislative Council of, 1743-1775, Albany, 1861.

——— Marriage Licenses of, Prior to 1784, New York, 1860.

——— Third Annual Report of the State Historian, Albany, 1899.

New York Journal and the General Advertiser, November 19, 1781 (file New York Historical Society).

New York Packet and American Advertiser, November 8, 1781 (file New York Historical Society).

Niagara, Contributions toward a Bibliography of the Region of, Buffalo Historical Society Publications, Vol. VI, 1903-4, Vol. IX, 1906.

Parkman, Francis, Conspiracy of Pontiac, Boston, 1879.

Peck, George, History of Wyoming, New York, 1868.

Riddell, W. R., Life of John Graves Simcoe, Toronto, 1926.

Roosevelt, Theodore, The Winning of the West, 4 vols., New York, 1894.

Ryerson, Egerton, Loyalists of America, Toronto, 1880.

Sabine, Lorenzo, Loyalists of the American Revolution, 2 vols., Boston, 1864.

Schuyler, Philip, Trial of, Revolutionary Papers, 2 vols., New York Historical Society Collections, 1879.

Seaver, James Everett, A Narrative of the Life of Mary Jemison, new ed., Philadelphia, 1932.

Severance, F. H., Old Trails of Niagara Frontier, Buffalo, 1899.

Siebert, W. H., The Loyalists and Six Nation Indians in the Niagara Peninsula, Ottawa, 1915.

Simcoe, John Graves, Military Journal of, New York, 1844.

Simcoe, Mrs. John Graves, Diary of, Toronto, 1922.

Simms, Jeptha R., Frontiersmen of New York, 2 vols., Albany, 1882.

——— Schoharie County and Border Wars of New York, Albany, 1845.

Simms, Jeptha R., Trappers of New York, Albany, 1851.

Steele, Joel Dorman, School History of the United States, New York, 1919.

Stiles, Ezra, D.D., LL.D., Extract from the Itineraries and Other Miscellanies of, new ed., New Haven, 1916.

Stone, William L., Border Wars of the Revolution, new ed., 2 vols., New York, 1900.

—— Life of Joseph Brant, 2 vols., New York, 1838.

Sullivan, General John, Indian Expedition of, Albany, 1879.

—— Letters and Papers of, 2 vols., Concord, N. H., 1930.

Tarr, Ralph S., Physical Geography of New York State, New York, 1902.

Thwaites, Reuben Gold, Wisconsin Historical Collections, Madison, 1908.

Trevelyan, Sir George Otto, The American Revolution, 4 vols., New York, 1928.

Upton, Emery, Military Policy of the United States Government, Washington, 1917.

Van Deusen, A. H., Roster of Butler's Rangers, *New York Genealogical and Biographical Record*, New York, 1900.

Van Schaack, Henry C., Life of Peter Van Schaack, New York, 1842.

Van Tyne, C. H., The Loyalists in the American Revolution, 2d ed., New York, 1929.

—— The War of Independence, Boston, 1929.

Washington, George, Writings, ed. W. C. Ford, 14 vols., New York.

Whitlock, Brand, Life of Lafayette, 2 vols., New York, 1929.

Wilkinson, J. B., Annals of Binghamton, Binghamton, 1840.

OTHER BOOKS ON THE SUBJECT

Abbott, William C., New York in the American Revolution, New York, 1929.

—— Conflicts with Oblivion, New Haven, 1924.

Bradley, A. G., Colonial Americans in Exile, New York, 1932.

Canniff, William, The History of the Settlement of Upper Canada, Toronto, 1869.

Frothingham, Thomas, G. Washington, Commander-in-Chief, New York, 1930.

Halsey, Francis Whiting, The Old New York Frontier, New York, 1901.

Hough, J. B., Independence, A Story of the Revolution, New York, 1893.

Hudleston, F. J., Gentleman Johnny Burgoyne, New York, 1927.

Hughes, Rupert, George Washington, Vol. III, New York, 1930.

Pound, Arthur, Johnson of the Mohawks, New York, 1930.

Reid, W. M., The Mohawk Valley, New York, 1901.

———— The Story of Old Fort Johnson, New York, 1906.

Seymour, Flora Warren, Lords of the Valley, New York, 1930.

Williams, Sherman, New York's Part in History, New York, 1915.

INDEX

The index is the work of Miss Suzanne Baron and of Mr. Cornelius D. Allen of the School of Commerce staff of New York University, for whose skill and patience I am most grateful.

Herkimer, Lieutenant George, 67, 86
Herkimer, Brigadier General Honikol, 80, 85, 86
Herkimer, Johan Jost, 163
Hite, Isaac, 186
Howe, Sir William, 79-82
Hubbard family, losses at Cherry Valley, 155
Huron, 63

Indians: need for friendship of, 9, 12, 18, 271; Fort Stanwix boundary treaty with, 21, 34; selling of rum to, 22, 129; cost of maintenance, 17, 23, 43, 44, 48, 66, 69, 70, 103, 117, 236; use of, by British, 43-45, 48, 64, 271, 272; scalping atrocities of, 43, 45-47, 274, 276; use of, by Americans, 44, 45, 48; military worthlessness of, 44, 48, 64, 97, 198, 244; "blue-eyed," 53; John Butler urges neutrality of, 65, 66, 69, 104; council at Oswego, 63; killing of prisoners by, 72; armed strength of, losses at Oriskany, 98; at Wyoming, 130, 135; William Butler (Am.) raids, at Unadilla, 143; at Cherry Valley, 144, 153, 165; Washington attempts to induce Indians to deliver Walter Butler, 178, 189; colonists' desire for Indian lands, 8, 21, 45, 271, 272; fur trade, 9, 175; at Chemung, 198; effects of Sullivan campaign, 204, 216; being driven from their lands, 271; became uncontrollable, 276; fighting in Ohio, 283

Jefferson, Thomas, 216
Johnson, Guy (son-in-law of Sir William): marriage, 18; Guy Park, 19; colonel of militia, 21; becomes superintendent for Indian Affairs, 35; goes to Oswego, 62, 63; goes to Montreal, 64; goes on leave to England, 65, 150; intrigue with Claus against the Butlers, 65, 104; writes to Lord Germaine, 70, 114; wishes the Indians let loose, 104; Johnson-Butler feud, 120, 121; jealousy over the Rangers, 197; attainted, 202; letter from Claus regarding Butler's expenses, 224; letter to Germaine concerning Indian expenses, 236;

fails to support Ross expedition, 239
Johnson, Sir John (son of Sir William): resides at Fort Johnson, 17; trip to London, 20; marriage, 29, 31; becomes commandant of militia, 35; as a Loyalist, 52; stays at Johnson Hall, 62; fortifies Johnson Hall, 67, 68; gives parole and then breaks it, 68; not at Oriskany, 85; letter from Claus about Walter Butler, 117; letters to Claus criticizing John Butler, 134, 174; attainted 202; invades Mohawk Valley, 213, 214; retreats from Mayfield, 215; second invasion of Mohawk Valley, 221; fails to join the Ross invasion, 240
Johnson, Lady Mary, 70, 75
Johnson, Mary (wife of Guy), 18
Johnson, Nancy (wife of Daniel Claus), 16
Johnson, Peter (son of Sir William). See Loyalist officers
Johnson, Sir William (father of Sir John): position and character, 8; leads expedition against Fort Niagara, 13; at Detroit, 16; Pontiac submits to, 20; last will, 32; death of, 35; erroneously mentioned with St. Leger by Burgoyne, 83
Johnson Dynasty, intrigue against the Butlers, 32, 65, 103-5, 117, 121, 134
Johnson Hall, 17, 28, 62, 67, 68, 72-73
Johnstown, 240
Jones, Robert, 137

Kaskaskia: 123; fall reported to Lieut. Governor Hamilton, 140
Kenton, Simon, 6
King's College, 33, 272
Kingston, burned by Sir Henry Clinton, 102
Kirkland, Samuel, 69, 71
Klepsattle, Captain Adam, 62
Klock, Colonel Jacob. See Tryon County militia officers
Knox, William (Secretary in the War Office in London), receives letter from Claus concerning alleged mismanagement of supplies by John Butler, 103, 104
Knyphausen, Lieut. General: in command at New York, 204; letter from

MILITARY AND COLONIAL HISTORY CLASSICS
Reprinted by

The Scholar's Bookshelf

THE AMERICAN REVOLUTION

THE AMERICAN REVOLUTION AND THE BRITISH EMPIRE, *R. Coupland*
This 1930 work presented pioneering studies of the impact on the British Empire and the roots of British imperialism of the defeat suffered in the American Revolution. The author discusses, in a series of studies, how the British leaders and George III analyzed and faced up to the consequences of the loss of the American colonies, the subsequent loss to France of several Caribbean possessions, the reawakening of Irish revolutionary restlessness, and the necessity for new directions in mercantilist and imperialist policy, the new importance of Canada, and the emergence of the idea of Commonwealth. 2005: 331 pages, softcover. ISBN: 0-945726-71-6.

DEFENCES OF PHILADELPHIA IN 1777, *Worthington Chauncey Ford, Editor*
An essential documentary history of the defense of Philadelphia as organized and carried out by Washington and his generals. The work consists of more than 220 letters to and from all involved during the year, all recording in detail how Washington, Greene, Wayne, and many others assessed the situation, preparing for a British naval invasion and evaluating how the city might be fortified. Reprint of the 1897 publication. 2005: 300 pages, softcover. ISBN: 0-945726-56-2.

THE DELAWARE CONTINENTALS, 1776-1783, *Christopher Ward*
The landmark study in the military history of the American Revolution written by the author of "The War of the Revolution." The work is an exhaustive study of the organization of this regiment and its action throughout the war, especially at Long Island, Brooklyn, Trenton, Princeton, and the middle Atlantic states and its later service at Camden, King's Mountain, Guilford Court House, and Yorktown. Unabridged reprint of the original 1941 edition. 2005: 620 pages, illustrated. Softcover. ISBN: 0-945726-65-1.

THE LIFE OF ARTEMAS WARD; The First Commander-in-Chief of the American Revolution, *Charles Martyn*
The basic biographical study of the man who commanded the Americans at the Battle of Bunker Hill and later figured in military operations around Boston, eventually becoming the commander of the Eastern Department. The work presents a highly detailed account of the war in Boston from 1775 to 1777, and also covers Ward's post war career as a Federalist Congressman. 2005: 334 pages, illustrated. Softcover. ISBN: 0-945726-52-X.

THE LIFE OF BENEDICT ARNOLD; His Patriotism and Treason, *Isaac N. Arnold*
The author, not a relative of the Revolutionary War general and traitor, published this book in 1879 in an attempt to "ask a fair hearing and justice," though not a defense for Arnold's treason. The book was the first substantial study of Arnold's services in the war at Ticonderoga, in Canada, at Saratoga, Valcour Island, and in other Hudson Valley campaigns, detailing his services to the Revolutionary cause, his wounding, good relations with Washington, and then his downfall, with chapters on his wife, Major Andre, his trail, and his later services with the British army. Remains the most complete study of Arnold's career. 2005: 444 pages. Softcover. ISBN: 0-945726-55-4.

ARNOLD'S EXPEDITION TO QUEBEC, *John Codman*
The first and still the most thorough study of Arnold's 1775 attempt to capture Quebec, with a full account of its planning and execution, the tremendous difficulties imposed by the terrain and the weather, the assault, the death of Montgomery, and the ultimate failure of the expedition. Includes the 2 original oversize foldout maps, 14 1/2" x 5 1/2" and 11" x 14". 2005: 340 pages, illustrated. Softcover. ISBN: 0-945726-61-9.

MAJOR-GENERAL ANTHONY WAYNE AND THE PENNSYLVANIA LINE IN THE CONTINENTAL ARMY, *Charles J. Still*

First published in 1893, this was the first full-length study of Wayne and his role in Washington's army at Valley Forge, the campaigns in New York, New Jersey, and Pennsylvania, the role of the Pennsylvania Line at the time of Arnold's treason, the closing battles in Virginia and Georgia, and Wayne's service after the war. Exhaustive in detail and filled with documentary material, the book remains essential for studies of Wayne and how the Continental Army was formed and operated. 2005: 441 pages, many illustrations. Softcover. ISBN: 0-945726-46-5.

OUR STRUGGLE FOR THE FOURTEENTH COLONY; Canada and the American Revolution, *Justin H. Smith*

The still-definitive study of the effort of the thirteen colonies to bring Canada into the American Revolution from the earliest efforts of the Boston Committee of Correspondence on through the carrying of military operations up through the Hudson Valley and on to Quebec, Canadian defenses under Carleton, and concluding with the failure of Arnold's expedition and the ultimate abandonment of the efforts of the American revolutionaries. Unabridged reprint of the New York: 1907 edition. 2005: 638 + 635 pages. Softcover. Set of 2 Volumes. ISBN: 0-945726-68-6.

THE STRUGGLE FOR AMERICAN INDEPENDENCE, *Sydney George Fisher*

Reprint edition of Fisher's massive history of the American Revolution, a major history which debated many points with the earlier works of Fiske and Trevelyan, pioneered the study of many aspects of the military history of the war, including its political background and the actions of important British generals and politicians, and presented what remains one of the most comprehensive histories of the war. 2005: 574 + 585 pages, illustrated. Softcover. Set of 2 Volumes. ISBN: 0-945726-54-6.

THE VIRGINIA CAMPAIGN AND THE BLOCKADE AND SIEGE OF YORKTOWN 1781, *Col. H.L. Landers*

An invaluable, highly detailed history of the closing campaign of the American Revolution, with extensive material on the French-American alliance and the roles played both in the diplomatic background and the military history of the campaign by Louis XVI, Franklin, Vergennes, D'Estaing, Rochambeau, and Lafayette. The work includes special chapters on Clinton and Cornwallis, the sea battle off the capes of Virginia, and the siege and surrender of the British. Includes seven specially prepared maps and views. Originally published in 1931 by the U.S. Government Printing Office to commemorate the 150th anniversary of the events. 2005:219 pages, illustrated. Softcover. ISBN: 0-945726-43-0.

WAR OUT OF NIAGARA; Walter Butler and the Tory Rangers, *Howard Swiggett*

The only full-length study of the American Revolution in northern New York presents a full account of the Loyalist issues of the area, the role of the Mohawk Indians, battle actions in 1778-1780 involving many diverse issues and forces, and the controversial role of Walter Butler's Rangers and the battle at Cherry Valley. Reprint edition. 2005: 309 pages, illustrated. Softcover. ISBN: 0-945726-53-8.

THE BRITISH NAVY IN ADVERSITY; A Study of the War of American Independence, W.M. James

A remarkably comprehensive and well informed study originally published in 1926 and written by a Royal Navy captain who focused on the challenge presented to British seapower by the American Revolution with its issues of international maritime warfare, challenges to the Admiralty which had let the Royal Navy fall behind its rivals, neutrality, commerce, and other questions. The author presents a narrative history of British naval operations around the world during this time, the military and civilian leaders, strategies, and overall results. Extensive documentary material includes lists of commissioned ships. Many illustrations and maps. 2005: 459 pages, softcover. ISBN: 0-945726-10-4.

FRANCE IN THE AMERICAN REVOLUTION, James Breck Perkins
The still indispensable, most fully documented study of the pivotal role of France in the world politics of the American Revolution, tracing France's new world situation as the Revolution neared, American diplomatic efforts to ally with an enemy of Britain, the role of such individuals as Silas Deane, Benjamin Franklin, Lafayette, and Rochambeau, and the decisive French military intervention at the end of the war. Reprint of the original 1911 Houghton Mifflin publication. 2005: 544 pages. Softcover. ISBN: 0-945726-18-X.

GENERAL WASHINGTON'S SPIES ON LONG ISLAND AND IN NEW YORK, Morton Pennypacker
One of the very few works on Washington's secret service, this book remains the central study of espionage activities centering around New York during the American Revolution, identifying some twenty prominent families and family members under the leadership of Robert Townsend of Oyster Bay and Abraham Woodhull of Setauket, and including Anna Strong, William Floyd, Caleb Brewster, and others. The book includes the first major studies of Nathan Hale and the Benedict Arnold treason. Reprint of the original 1939 publication of the Long Island Historical Society. 2005: 302 pages, illustrated. Softcover. ISBN: 0-945726-18-X.

THE MAJOR OPERATIONS OF THE NAVIES IN THE WAR OF AMERICAN INDEPENDENCE, Alfred Thayer Mahan
Mahan's uniquely informed perspectives pioneered the study of the naval aspects of the American Revolution, and presented detailed and carefully organized chapters on the naval campaigns on Lake Champlain, Boston, Charleston, Narragansett Bay, the reaction to British invasions in New York, Philadelphia, and the Hudson Valley, the repercussions of naval wars abroad, the operations at Yorktown, and subsequent battles in the West Indies. Reprint of the original London: 1913 edition. 2005: 280 pages, illustrated. Softcover. ISBN: 0-945726-14-7.

THE NINETEENTH OF APRIL, 1775, *Harold Murdock*
First published in the early 1920s, this study by a professional historian was the first to present a complete reconstruction of the day which saw the beginning of the American Revolution, and remains unparalleled for its record of the events, large and small, that took place. The work drew on both British and American sources and offered some favorable reflections on the British conduct of the encounter as well as the retreat to Charlestown. Includes several period illustrations and maps. 2005: 134 pages, softcover. ISBN: 0-945726-15-5.

THE CAMPAIGN OF 1776 AROUND NEW YORK AND BROOKLYN, Henry P. *Johnston*
This work, from which all other military historians of the American Revolution have drawn, presents an exhaustive account of the American Revolution battles of Brooklyn, Long Island, Kip's Bay, Harlem Heights, and on to Trenton and Princeton and the closing of the 1776 campaign. The work is supplemented by more than 60 letters and reports describing the events by participants. Reprint of the original 1878 publication of the Long Island Historical Society. Includes the original 36 x 15 3/4 foldout map. "Indispensable." David McCullough. 2005: 509 pages. Softcover. ISBN: 0-945726-12-0.

THE COMMAND OF THE HOWE BROTHERS DURING THE AMERICAN REVOLUTION, Troyer Steele Anderson
A classic study which offers essential perspectives on nearly every aspect of the American Revolution during the first two years, with a great deal of valuable material on the British estimate of the crisis, preparations, the battles at Boston Long Island, New Jersey, and Pennsylvania, all focused on the roles of Richard and William Howe. "In no book has Sir William Howe been more fairly treated and, by consequence, in none has his inadequacy been more completely laid bare." American Historical Review. Reprint of the original 1936 Oxford University Press edition. 2005: 368 pages. Softcover. ISBN: 0-945726-02-3.

GENERAL GAGE'S INFORMERS; New Material Upon Lexington and Concord: Benjamin Thompson as Loyalist and the Treachery of Benjamin Church, Jr., *Allen French*
Reprint edition of this 1932 work by the most important historian of the events of April, 1775, the first work to draw on the Gage MSS. The work showed how Gage kept informed about American sentiments and plans and gathered sixteen basic documents and accounts detailing the events of the day as well as a chapter on the story of Benjamin Thompson, later Count Rumford. The author also presented evidence that the Americans fired first at Lexington. 2005: 207 pages, illustrated. Softcover. ISBN: 0-945726-07-4.

HISTORY OF THE SIEGE OF BOSTON AND THE BATTLES OF LEXINGTON, CONCORD, AND BUNKER HILL, *Richard Frothingham*
Originally published in 1849, this was both a celebration of American independence as represented in the creation of the Bunker Hill Monument, and a surprisingly comprehensive history of the 1775 military operations that started the American Revolution and the siege of Boston that followed the Battle of Bunker Hill, with detailed accounts of British rule of the city, their evacuation of the city, many original documents, and the celebration of the victory. This is a reprint of the 4th, 1873 edition which included many revisions, additions, additional documents and illustrations. Includes the two original oversize foldout maps. Map sizes 12 x 18 and 17 x 19 3/4. 2005: 422 pages, illus. Softcover. ISBN: 0-945726-09-0.

A NAVAL HISTORY OF THE AMERICAN REVOLUTION, *Gardner W. Allen*
Still in many ways the most comprehensive work of its kind, this massive study presented highly detailed accounts of battles at Lake Champlain, off Boston and Maine, Charleston, Delaware Bay, and year-by-year histories of all other significant engagements both along the American coast and at sea. The work also presents extensive coverage of the ships of the revolutionary navy, its commanders, foreign alliances, diplomacy, prisoners, and naval conditions during this era. Reprint of the original 1913 edition. 2005: 752 pages, 2 Vols in 1. Softcover. ISBN: 0-945726-00-7.

THE ORGANIZATION OF THE BRITISH ARMY IN THE AMERICAN REVOLUTION, Edward E. Curtis
A fully detailed study of the British Army focused on its operations in the American Revolution, with separate chapters on its administrative machinery, recruiting, provisioning, and transportation. The book remains unique for its gathering of contemporary documents illuminating aspects of these topics. Reprint of the original 1926 Yale University Press edition. 2005: 223 pages. Softcover. ISBN: 0-945726-06-6.

OUR FRENCH ALLIES; Rochambeau and His Army, Lafayette and His Devotion, D'Estaing, DeTernay, Barras, DeGrasse, and Their Fleets in the Great War of the American Revolution from 1778 to 1782, *Edwin Martin Stone*
An exhaustive account of virtually every aspect of the role of the French in the American Revolution, covering not only the actions of the French but also of the American forces as they engaged in various campaigns with French support. The work identifies hundreds of military and naval figures on both sides, reprints many of their first-hand accounts of events, and details the ways in which figures on both sides contributed to the cause and welcomed each other. First published in Providence, Rhode Island in 1884, the work also includes a great deal of unique material on military operations there. Includes much unique documentation of individual units and leaders as well as many contemporary illustrations. Also includes the original 22" x 17" foldout map. 2005: 632 pages. Softcover. ISBN: 0-945726-19-8.

THE PRIVATE SOLDIER UNDER WASHINGTON, *Charles Knowles Bolton*
Still the standard work on how Washington's army was formed and maintained; the varieties and sources of food and equipment; relations between officers and the ranks; camp duties and diversions; hospitals and prison ships; army maneuvers; and the attitudes of the ordinary foot soldier as expressed in diaries, letters, journals, and other writings. Reprint of the original 1902 Scribner's publication. Illustrated. 2005: 258 pages, softcover. ISBN: 0-945726-05-8.

THE TAKING OF TICONDEROGA IN 1775; The British Story, *Allen French*
The author used several first-hand accounts by British officers and soldiers to provide an excellent chronological history of British planning and operations in the Hudson Valley campaigns and also established in this book for the first time the roles of Benedict Arnold and Ethan Allen in the American defense. Reprint of the original 1928 Harvard University Press edition. 2005: 89 pages, softcover. ISBN: 0-945726-07-4.

THE TURNING POINT OF THE REVOLUTION; Or, Burgoyne in America, *Hoffman Nickerson*
Still the standard and unmatched study of Burgoyne's campaigns intended to split the American colonies. Shows how the strategy was worked out and prepared, how Burgoyne was selected, and how the battles at Bennington, Ticonderoga, Stanwix, and the Highlands went against the British, brought about their retreat and surrender, and opened the way for the French alliance. Reprint of the original 1928 edition. 2005: 500 pages, illustrated. 2 Vols in 1. Softcover. ISBN: 0-945726-16-3.

NAVAL AND OTHER MILITARY HISTORY

COMMODORE JOHN BARRY; Father of the American Navy, *Joseph Gurn*
The first full-length biographical study of Barry remains fundamental not only to the study of his career but also the foundation of the American navy. The work presents unmatched, detailed accounts of his career spanning the era from the American Revolution to the first diplomatic and military challenges posed by France to the Adams administration, tracing in detail his rise to high rank, his and George Washington's cooperation and military thought, the construction of early naval ships, including the *Constitution*, and his legacy for American naval history. Reprint of the 1933 edition. 2005: 318 pages, softcover. ISBN: 0-945726-72-4.

A HISTORY OF AMERICAN PRIVATEERS, *Edgar Stanton Maclay*
A still unreplaced work in American naval history, this 1899 study (dedicated to Theodore Roosevelt, "Pioneer of the Modern School of Naval Writers") remains the most comprehensive study of the role of the early privateers in the establishment of the American navy and their support of naval operations against Britain. The work traces the history of colonial privateering, its special dangers, and the roles of such figures as Truxtun, Porter, Biddle, Decatur, Perry, as well as such leading privateers as Silas Talbot, Jonathan Haraden, Solon Drowne, Thomas Boyle, and many others in early national privateering and navy building. Reprint edition. 2005: 519 pages, illustrated. Softcover. ISBN: 0-945726-63-5.

OUR NAVAL WAR WITH FRANCE, *Gardner W. Allen*
The basic study of the spoliation of American commerce by the French in the years 1799-1801, describing the events, their economic costs to the new nation, and how the United States faced up to its first international crisis through diplomatic efforts and through laying the foundations for a navy. 2005: 323 pages, illustrated. Softcover. ISBN: 0-945726-58-9.

OUR NAVY AND THE BARBARY CORSAIRS, *Gardner W. Allen*
The first full study of the events of a forty-year period from 1778 to 1818, showing how the United States managed to build a navy with such ships as the *George Washington, Philadelphia, Constellation, Constitution,* and others, and eventually defeat the depredations of the Barbary pirates in battles at Tripoli and Algiers under Bainbridge, Prebel, Porter and Decatur. Reprint of the original 1905 Houghton Mifflin edition. 2005: 354 pages, illustrated. Softcover. ISBN: 0-945726-01-5.

JACKSON AND NEW ORLEANS; An Authentic Narrative of the Achievements of the American Army under Andrew Jackson Before New Orleans, *Alexander Walker*
An exhaustively detailed, chronological account of Jackson's defense of New Orleans, originally published in 1856, vividly written, and exploring, among many other things, Jackson's strategies and tactics, the roles of Packenham and Lafitte, and how the opposing forces planned, organized, and executed their offensive and defensive moves, all the actions along the way, and the reasons for the ultimate American victory. 2005: 411 pages, softcover. ISBN: 0-945726-70-8.

THE WAR OF 1812 ON THE NIAGARA FRONTIER, *Louis L. Babcock*
Still the most detailed account of the campaigns and battles on the Niagara, with detailed
accounts of the skirmishes and battles at Queenston Heights, York, Fort George, Lundy's Lane,
Izard's campaign down the Niagara, and all the intervening events. The book includes valuable
documentary data on war losses as well as many maps. Reprint of the original 1927 edition.
Includes all the original oversize foldout maps. 2005: 385 pages, illus. Map size 14x7 1/2.
Softcover. ISBN: 0-945726-04-X.

THE FALL OF CANADA; A Chapter in the History of The Seven Years' War, *George M. Wrong*
Still the definitive study of the events of 1759-1760 surrounding the British campaign under
Amherst to take Montreal and Quebec, with detailed studies of the strategies and tactics involved,
the French defense, and the worldwide implications of the fall of New France. Reprint of the
original 1914 Oxford University Press edition, complete with the original oversize foldout map.
2005: 272 pages. Map size: 21 x 13 1/2. Softcover. ISBN: 0-945726-21-X.

DRAKE AND THE TUDOR NAVY; With a History of the Rise of England as a Maritime Power, *Julian S. Corbett*
Reprint of the second edition (1899) of this classic study of a critical period in the evolution of
the British Navy focusing on Hawkins, Drake, the struggles in the Spanish Main, Drake's
circumnavigation, the defense against the Armada, and Drake's subsequent expeditions and
eventual disgrace. Exhaustive in content, the work presents unique information about Drake and
his contemporaries, their pioneering discoveries, the evolution of the British Navy, its political
background, and the international conflicts of the Elizabethan world. 2005: 415 + 461 pages,
fold-out maps. Softcover. Set of 2 Volumes. ISBN: 0-945726-67-8.

THE EVOLUTION OF NAVAL ARMAMENT, *Frederick Leslie Robertson*
Written by an Engineer Commander in the Royal Navy, this work traces the evolution of the
smooth-bore gun, carronade, truck carriage, shell gun, rifle gun, and their propelling machinery
during the age of fighting sail and up to the coming of the ironclad. The work is highly detailed
and includes expert appraisals of various developments over the decades in an accessible writing
style. 2005: 307 pages, illustrated. Softcover. ISBN: 0-945726-64-3.

A HISTORY OF THE ROYAL NAVY FROM THE EARLIEST TIMES TO THE WARS OF THE FRENCH REVOLUTION, *Nicholas Harris Nicolas*
First published at London in 1847, this remarkable and irreplaceable work was intended to fill
the lack, at that time, of an adequate History of the foundation, rise, and establishment of "that
mighty Navy to which [England] owes alike her security and her pre-eminence among Nations."
The two volumes reprinted here chronicle both the civil and military history of the British navy
from ancient Roman Britain to the age of Henry V, with very detailed coverage of causes,
developments, royal and military leaders, the evolution of ships, significant engagements, and
the contributions and mistakes of kings, admirals, and ordinary seamen. Includes many
documentary appendixes. Reprint edition. 2005: 469 + 534 pages. Softcover. Set of 2 Volumes.
ISBN: 0-945726-66-X.

THE CRIMEA IN 1854 AND 1894, *Gen. Sir Evelyn Wood*
A participant's highly detailed first-hand account of the Crimean War and the battles of the Alma,
Sevastopol, Balaklava, Inkerman, and the conclusion of the war and death of Lord Raglan. The
book was first published in 1895 and was occasioned by the author's return to the areas in which
he fought, and he expresses severe criticism of the British government's mismanagement of the
war. 2005: 400 pages, illustrated. Softcover. ISBN: 0-945726-51-1.

FIGHTING INSTRUCTIONS, 1530-1816, *Julian S. Corbett, Editor*
This 1905 publication pioneered the study of British naval tactics by making available a
substantial group of chronologically arranged writings which document the process of thought
and lines of argument by which the classic tacticians arrived at their theories and
recommendations about tactics, weapons, movement, the management of ships and men, and
managing the challenges of evolving naval technology both in England and abroad. The writers
include Lord Lisle, Sir Walter Ralegh, Lord Wimbledon, the Duke of York, Prince Rupert, Lord
Anson, Sir Alexander Cochrane, and many others. 2005: 366 pages. Softcover. ISBN: 0-945726-60-0.

A TREATISE OF ARTILLERY, *John Muller*
Facsimile reprint of the third, London: 1780 edition of this eighteenth-century British treatise on the construction of guns, their measurements and capabilities, movement, ammunition, stores, and use aboard ships. This edition included special material on the use of gunpowder. Includes all the original detailed illustrations and reference material. 2005: 216 pages, softcover. ISBN: 0-945726-47-3.

GENERAL WOLFE'S INSTRUCTIONS TO YOUNG OFFICERS, *James Wolfe*
Facsimile reprint of Wolfe of Quebec's 1780 publication, a basic text for the military man of his time, covering with great logic and actual event illustrations such topics as drill, clean living, the deployment of troops, transport, and materiel, and the role of adjutants and quartermasters. Includes the texts of many of his orders intended to properly organize and command an army. 2005: 106 pages, softcover. ISBN: 0-945726-49-X.

AMERICAN COLONIAL HISTORY

THE AMERICAN COLONIES IN THE SEVENTEENTH CENTURY, *Herbert L. Osgood*
Complete reprint edition of Osgood's pioneering, still-indispensable, and exhaustive history of the American colonies, and virtually every aspect of their establishment, evolution of governmental and financial systems, and the problems of imperial control, especially during the interregnum. Substantial chapters on each colony from Massachusetts Bay to the Carolinas constitute the starting point for the study of the American colonies. Unabridged reprint of the original London: 1904-1907 edition. 2005: 1619 pages, softcover. Set of 3 Volumes. ISBN: 0-945726-76-7.
Vol I. The Chartered Colonies. Beginnings of Self Governmment, 2005: 578 pages. ISBN: 0-945726-76-7
Vol II. The Chartered Colonies. Beginnings of Self Governmment, 2005: 490 pages. ISBN: 0-945726-74-0.
Vol III. Imperial Control. Beginnings of the System of Royal Provinces, 2005: 551 pages. ISBN: 0-945726-75-9.

HISTORY OF THE CITY OF NEW YORK IN THE SEVENTEENTH CENTURY, *Mrs. Schuyler van Rensselaer*
Exceptional for its comprehensive coverage of the discovery, settlement, and political, social, cultural, and economic life of New York City under the Dutch and the Stuarts, this work remains the foundation stone for historical studies of the city and also early colonial America. The author also treats in detail relations with the Indians, the administrations of the various Dutch and English governors, discontents and rebellions, the evolution of political organization. The work closes with a full account of the Jacob Leisler episode. Unabridged reprint of the original New York: 1909 edition. 2005: 533 + 640 pages. Softcover. Set of 2 Volumes. ISBN: 0-945726-48-1.

KING PHILIP'S WAR, *George W. Ellis and John E. Morris*
First published in 1906, this work remains the central, indispensable, and most comprehensive study of New England in the years 1675 and 1676 and how the new colonists were forced into cooperative union in the face of the challenges of the Indians. The book was the first to draw on contemporary correspondence between the governors and military, religious, and other leaders of the time in order to identify the principal participants, especially the Indian leaders, and present a chronological history of the events and their outcome. 2005: 326 pages, softcover. ISBN: 0-945726-69-4.

NARRATIVES OF THE INSURRECTIONS, 1675-1690, *Charles M. Andrews, Editor*
The basic documentary source for the significant insurrections and rebellions in the American colonies, including Bacon's, the Carolina proprietors of 1680, the events of 1689-1691, and other events of the 1690s. Reprint of this volume from the "Original Narratives of Early American History" originally published in 1915 by Scribner's. 2005: 414 pages, softcover. ISBN: 0-945726-03-1.

NARRATIVES OF THE INDIAN WARS, 1675-1699, *Charles H. Lincoln, Editor*
A basic source for the New England Indian Wars of the late 1600s, documenting the wars of 1675, the captivity of Mary Rowlandson, and the Decennium Luctuosum of Cotton Mather (1699), an account of the 10-year struggle with the Indians in the last decade of the 17th century. Much of the material reflects the international aspects of these struggles in the light of events abroad. Reprint of this volume from the Original Narratives of Early American History of the 1913 edition. Includes the original 14 x 12 map. 2005: 316 pages. Softcover. ISBN: 0-945726-12-0.

WORLD WAR I

AS THEY SAW US; Foch, Ludendorff, and Other Leaders Write Our War History, *George Sylvester Viereck*
Viereck's 1928 publication gathered texts such as "The American Soldier in the World War as Seen by a Friend," by Marshal Ferdinand Foch, "The American Soldier in the World War as Seen by a Foe," by General Erich Ludendorff, and seven other essays on the A.E.F. and its operations at the Aisne-Marne Triangle, St. Mihiel, and the Meuse-Argonne in the Fall of 1918, all written by German or French officers. The book provides not only unique material on the military history of the war but also on how the opponents viewed each other a decade later and what the prospects were at that time for "universal brotherhood." 2005: 379 pages. Softcover. ISBN: 0-945726-20-1.

A.E.F.; Ten Years Ago in France, *Major General Hunter Liggett*
One of the first reliable and comprehensive histories of the American participation in WWI. First published in 1927, the seven chapters by the Commander of the First Army of the A.E.F. presented separate studies of the background of U.S. entry, and detailed descriptions of the campaigns at Chateau-Thierry, Belleau Wood, the Marne, St. Mihiel, and the Meuse-Argonne. Includes documentary records of the staffs of the Third Army and other units. 2005: 335 pages, softcover, illustrated. ISBN: 0-945726-13-9.